This page has been intentio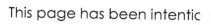

POOR MAN'S AIR FORCE

A guide to how small drones might be used in domestic unrest or low intensity conflicts

Researched and written by:

Don Shift

Disclaimer, definitions, and preface

This work presumes that the reader has basic familiarity with small drones, in particular quadcopters, and understands the basic principles of flight. This is not a "how to fly a drone" manual and the basics of piloting are not covered. This work is a theoretical discussion of the application of small unmanned aircraft systems (sUAS) in small-scale domestic paramilitary conflicts and civil unrest where the rule of law is absent.

A major presumption here is that for reasons of political or domestic instability it is necessary for citizen defenders to use drones to augment their personal self-defense. Therefore, the tactics and procedures discussed in this book do not take into account laws and regulations. If the rule of law is functional, all government regulations and laws should be abided by.

All manufacturer's cautions, warnings, and instructions should be heeded insofar as it is operationally possible to do so. This book is not a guide for basic operation of individual airframes, nor does it contain exhaustive, liability-driven warnings. Use common sense.

Any person applying any concept discussed in this book does so at their own risk and the individual is responsible for their own education, their safety, and that of others while engaged in unmanned aircraft flight. **Failure to understand basic flight principles, operating requirements, or other guidelines/regulations may result in legal charges, loss of the aircraft, mission failure, injury, or death.**

DISCLAIMER: the content of this book is *not* intended for normal, peacetime commercial or hobbyist operations. Obey all FAA/government regulations.

- Unregistered drone usage (over 249 grams) is illegal.
- Unlicensed drone usage may be illegal.
- Using drones to support criminal activities may be illegal.
- Arming drones is illegal.
- Building explosives without an ATF license is illegal.
- Shooting down, jamming, hacking, or otherwise interfering with drones is illegal.
- Spoofing or jamming GPS signals is illegal.
- Intercepting communications and using frequencies outside of their approved scope is illegal.
- Disabling identification features or lighting is illegal.
- Low-level flight and operation in certain areas/manners may be illegal.
- All readers are responsible for safe flight, satisfying all legal requirements (licensing, education, registration, etc.), and reading all applicable manufacturer's information.

Sections discussing lethal, injurious, or destructive attack methods are intended as thought exercises in contemplation of use of sUAS by small paramilitary units. Military readers who may not have official doctrine on sUAS were taken into account when writing this work. Units of measurement are typically given in US customary units and metric, although altitude is largely referred to in feet as per aviation custom.

Definitions

AGL: Above ground level (vs. altitude above sea level—ASL).

AO: Area of operations, which would include your neighborhood, part of town, or immediate surroundings.

BLOS: Beyond line-of-sight (in this work the term includes, and is used to refer to, beyond the radio horizon as well as out of sight).

BVLOS: Beyond visual line-of-sight (out of eye contact only, does not include beyond the radio horizon). May be within RLOS (radio line-of-sight).

COTS: Consumer-Off-The-Shelf or commercially available consumer-grade drones.

EW: Electronic warfare *or* early warning.

LOS: line-of-sight. In some contexts, it may mean "loss of (radio) signal."

LRE: Launch and Recovery Element; launch and landing recovery team responsible for physically handing the aircraft.

LRP: Launch/recovery point.

LSS: Low, Slow, Small. Mini or micro-UAVs used at the tactical level, typically either consumer grade off-the-shelf (COTS) commercial products or similar to them.

MGRS: Military grid reference system (MILGRID), the US military/NATO location reference system which uses a combination of letters and numbers to geolocate positions within a few meters.

NLOS: Non-line-of-sight

OP/LP: Observation post/listening post.

RAM: Rockets, artillery, and mortars.

RC: Radio controlled, usually in reference to toy or hobbyist RC aircraft.

RLP: Ready launch point; a staging point where the drone can land unattended to preserve battery life before launch on a time-critical mission, such as an ambush.

RLOS: Radio line-of-sight; radio signals cannot be exchanged by the aircraft and controller beyond this.

RPV: Remotely Piloted Vehicle.

UA: Unmanned Aircraft; synonym for *drone*.

UAS: Unmanned Aircraft Systems. This term is broader than the aircraft itself but includes the drone itself, the ground controller, launch and recovery equipment, and any additional communications systems.

UAV: Unmanned Air Vehicle; synonym for *drone*.

UCAV: Unmanned Combat Air Vehicle ("killer drone"). This is any UA that carries weapons. Used in a technical context or a synonym for a "killer" drone. Includes ""kamikaze"" "suicide" drones and can include loitering munitions. "suicide" drones could be best described as self-steering bombs. Vernacular usage outside this work is trending more towards larger aircraft that are substitutes for manned fighter/attack/bomber planes.

sUAV: Small Unmanned Aerial Vehicle. Generally, what is meant in this work by the generic term "drone." These are what is meant by Group 1 vehicles.

UAW: Unmanned Aerial Warfare.

Part I: Small Unmanned Aerial Systems

Ch 1. Introduction

In a civil conflict or during the aftermath of a major destabilizing event (SHTF) drones will play a huge part in both self-defense and any violence. In 2021, I published *Suburban Warfare* and discussed how small drones (quadcopters) would be weaponized ad hoc for attack roles. In 2022, following the Russian invasion of Ukraine, we saw this happen and for the reality of small-drone warfare to quickly become nightmare fuel. What is happening in Ukraine with drones is transformative to warfare and the integration of small unmanned aerial systems (sUAS) is already leaving the pioneering stages.

Militaries have quickly seen what small drones can do both for and against them. Proliferation of unmanned aerial systems will occur rapidly. The advantages to terrorists and partisans is also obvious, already experimented with somewhat by drug cartels and ISIS. Citizen defenders will also be able to leverage UAS to strengthen their defense in times of domestic unrest and also must plan for this asymmetrical aerial threat.

The greatest advantage UAS has is as a poor man's air force. Helicopters are out of the question for much of the public or small militia groups, but an off-the-shelf consumer (COTS) grade drone, or Unmanned Aerial Vehicle (UAV) could be a large force multiplier. The benefits a drone can give defenders, small units, and irregular forces could make the difference in a defensive situation or conflict.

This book looks mainly at two groups: civilian defenders who are protecting a neighborhood or property against lawless unrest and how small paramilitary units might employ UAS. The scenarios envisioned where employment may incur include widespread riots and looting, a major disaster scenario akin to Hurricane Katrina in New Orleans, a general state of anarchy due to governmental collapse, or a civil war.

The second element looks at how partisan groups or the military, at the squad to company level, may use drones against their adversaries or the population. Many uninvolved persons will be caught in the crossfire of wars, large and small, so drone warfare bears consideration by the prepared citizen. Another audience is the common soldier and Marine who may find themselves confronted by small drones (sUAS) in the international wars which appear to be brewing on the horizon.

General specifications

Various models of sUAS exist, including large-scale remote controlled fixed-wing aircraft. This book focuses on consumer drones, which are overwhelmingly quadcopters. These are the cheapest, most ubiquitous, and easiest to fly. They are sold and owned in large numbers.

Consumer quadcopters can reach typical altitudes of up to or exceeding 1,500 feet, average top speeds up to 30 MPH (48 km/h), have a range of up to five miles (8km), and loiter/endurance times of up to thirty minutes. Exact specifications will vary.

Please note this data varies from model to model. Manufacturers may have set a 400 foot altitude restriction for the United States in the firmware, but some models do have the capability to fly at altitudes of conventional aircraft. Firmware restrictions can be removed by the end user with varying degrees of complication and success.

Some models have modes that can be pre-programmed to travel a pre-set path (user defined pattern) or even be set to autonomously track a moving target. Cameras can be in ultra-high definition, use extreme zoom, see at night, and utilize thermal vision all while transmitting the feed back to the operator in real time. Multiple cameras may be included, such as a First Person View (FPV) forward-facing or navigational camera, a digital windscreen, and an undermounted gimbal camera of up to cinematic quality.

Virtually all drones are capable of audio and visual surveillance; video can be day/night/thermal although audio will likely be degraded due to distance and the hum of the rotors. Camera quality depends on the model; larger drones can loft telephoto lens equipped cameras. Consumer cameras that can be used with drones typically lose video quality at distances in excess of a quarter mile or more (400m).

Payloads can be carried by drones, up to around five pounds (just over 2kg) maximum in some models. 1.5 pounds (half a kilo) seems to be the most common safe maximum payload for COTS sUAS models. Homebuilt versions could be made to carry far more and professional models do. Note that carrying any payload decreases range, speed, and endurance. Payload mounting points can be, and have been, used for offensive purposes.

Note that all of this will vary depending on the exact model in use, however, these are very rough parameters that can be expected of drones that are commonly sold commercially.

Characteristics and utility

For the partisan and prepper, drones are excellent intelligence, surveillance, and reconnaissance (ISR) tools. If used just for an aerial picture of one's surroundings, they are little more than flying periscopes. UAS's utility is in *how* it is used. Video feeds can be used to direct maneuver forces in real-time, locate targets and provide guidance to other weapons, perform battle damage assessment (BDA), serve as airborne radio repeaters, and attack the enemy.

Drones can provide real time intelligence from "impossible" perspectives that someone with a pair of binoculars in a tall building or on a hill can't see. The area that one can actively surveille expands with the drone's height and mobility advantage. They allow loitering and tracking of mobile targets. Ground units can be supplemented or supported by aerial observation.

UAVs are first and foremost passive collectors of intelligence and instruments of command and control (C_2). Their ability to be an "eye in the sky" provides ground forces with **reconnaissance, surveillance, damage assessment,**

target acquisition, and **troop guidance**. The first three are all forms of intelligence gathering.

A drone can provide a tabletop like experience to a commander that enables him to guide or deploy his troops in the most effective manner given the real time threat picture he sees. Live aerial imagery permits the steering of forces in anticipation of, or in reaction to, what the enemy is doing, instead of making guesses about an old intelligence picture or assumed enemy course of action. Some dangers of this are overreliance on drones, overemphasizing the overhead picture versus what subordinates are doing on the ground, and micromanagement.

Drones are inherently stealthy platforms because of their relatively small size and quiet motors. Electric motors present in most COTS drones and multicopter designs reduce the sound signature even further. Small size, neutral colors, and low or no thermal signatures make visual acquisition difficult. This makes them less obtrusive than a manned aircraft. Ukrainian experience has shown that drones can be practically undetectable at night by eye or ear.

The low speed, maneuverability, and in the case of multicopters, hovering allows stealth characteristics to further decrease the probability of intercept. Terrain-masking flightpaths, hovering or peeking from behind cover, pop-up attacks and reconnaissance, and very low/slow flight are all advantages that manned aircraft do not have. A skilled pilot can take advantage of these characteristics to maximize the survivability and undetectability of his UAV.

Coupled with being able to dodge behind

concealment or being as small as a large bird, very high in the sky, drones may not be seen at all. The lack of experience and awareness on the modern battlefield, as evidenced in very recent conflicts, also lends a psychological advantage as the ground combatant is not (yet) expecting such observation or an attack from above.

Radar struggles to track UAVs as they have smaller radar signatures than manned aircraft due to their size exclusive of any RCS-reducing features. Composite airframes and the very small size of sUAS make them very radar resistant. Additionally, their ability to fly very low in the "grass" or the margin of muddled radar returns from the ground interferes with radar distinguishing ground returns from a drone.

Being highly maneuverable allows frequent deceptive or evasive course changes and the ability to exploit gaps in radar and/or visual coverage. Very small drones are too small for large SAMs[1], intended for manned aircraft, to shoot down, even if a radar or IR lock could be gained. Very small drones present a target that is too small, too fast, and possibly too maneuverable for effective small arms and anti-aircraft artillery fire to hit.

Drones can afford to be patient to search out targets. They can loiter, orbit, and change altitude to get a better look. Helicopters even in a slow hover don't have the same advantages. They are loud (troops can hide before it arrives overhead) and conspicuous; rotor wash stirs up dirt, dust,

---

[1] Surface to Air Missiles

and snow. Their greater bulk makes them a larger target for ground fire and require larger safety margins in orbits, hovers, and maneuvers.

Fast-movers (jets) with greater speed and altitude requirements have less ability to observe targets on the ground. Forward air controllers are needed to spot for attack jets for close air support (CAS) to be really effective. Modern sensors in two-seater aircraft make a huge difference but planes and helicopters still suffer from cost, endurance, and human risk considerations.

A drone can be its own spotter and strike aircraft, fulfilling both a CAS role and intelligence gathering at the same time. A drone can be sent on an armed reconnaissance mission to find targets of opportunity and attack them. Drones are excellent for this because it is cheaper than a manned attack aircraft and doesn't risk a human life. The macabre novelty of grenade bombing is a new way to demoralize and impede one's enemy.

UAS brings a new threat of surgical strikes on the battlefield, targeting precisely those enemies which may present the greatest threat or hindrance at the moment. Before, pockets of resistance that weren't large enough for artillery to hit had to be outmaneuvered and killed by infantryman at great risk. Take for instance a squad protecting a machine gun emplacement. Now, a drone, possibly launched by the maneuvering unit, can attack and neutralize that small pocket faster, more accurately, and more efficiently than a blanket artillery barrage.

Killer drones, also known as ""kamikaze"" and "suicide"

drones, or loitering munitions combine the first-person view of a drone with the precision of a missile. More small missile than drone, these are true hunter-killers. All it needs is the general location of a target so it can fly off, conduct its own reconnaissance, and then execute a terminal attack. The improvements these munitions offer over conventional missiles are greater maneuverability and less reliance on third-parties to provide target fixes.

Loitering munitions are like flying bombs or flying artillery/mortar shells; many look like an angry, oversized can of novelty peanuts that shoots out a "snake" (the munition). They can be launched from these portable tubes into the general area of an enemy target without precise guidance beforehand or manually guided the same way as a larger missile.

The lower tech end of this is an ordinary drone equipped with a warhead or bomb on it and flown manually into a target. While civilian or partisan groups will struggle to have sophisticated loitering munitions like the AeroVironment Switchblade, nor small guided missiles, modifying drones to satisfy the same mission requirements is guaranteed.

Note that these "flying bombs" are not the same as grenade-dropping, reusable UCAVs[2]. ISIS in Iraq is believed to have pioneered using drones for attack purposes with Mexican cartels imitating the tactic. Loitering munitions, while similar in purpose, followed a different development

---

[2] Unmanned Combat Aerial Vehicle

track through conventional major military research and development programs.

However, it is not impossible that separatist movements or partisan forces supported by foreign nations could have access to these weapons and it is highly likely that homebrew killer/attack drones will be made by irregular forces. A bomb that could be flown past security and defenses to destroy a high-value target, such as a critical utility node, would be a terrorist's delight. Ukraine is an excellent example of how COTS technology can be leveraged to aerially harass and attack an enemy, so why wouldn't a small group use UCAVs to its advantage?

Classification of UAVs

Group 1 sUAS or Micro-UAV 1

Federal law defines sub-249 gram unmanned aircraft as "micro" drones. These micro-UAVs do not require registration in the US or most countries. They range from toys to hobbyists' racing drones, to a novice cinematographer's flying camera. Top-of-the-line micro-UAVs could make a helpful adjunct to a mobile unit.

Table 3-1. UAS groups

	Speed / Altitude	Characteristics
Group 1 Micro / Mini UAS	Normally operates below 1,200 feet AGL at speeds less than 100 knots	Generally hand-launched. Real time video and control. Small payloads; focus on reconnaissance, surveillance, and intelligence operations. Operates within LOS of user (limited range).
Group 2 Small Tactical	Normally operates below 3,500 feet AGL at speeds less than 250 knots	Launched in unimproved areas by a small number of personnel. Medium range and endurance. Payload focus: reconnaissance, surveillance, and intelligence operations; may add weapons. Requires LOS to ground control station.
Group 3 Tactical	Normally operates below 18,000 feet MSL at speeds less than 250 knots	Launched in unimproved areas by a small number of personnel. Range and endurance vary significantly. Payload focus: reconnaissance, surveillance, and intelligence operations; may add weapons. Requires larger logistics footprint than Groups 1 and 2.
Group 4 Persistent	Normally operates below 18,000 feet MSL at any speed	Can be used both strategically and tactically. Requires a runway for launch and recovery. Extended range and endurance. Payloads: reconnaissance, surveillance, intelligence operations, and ASM weapons. Operates at medium-to-high altitudes.
Group 5 Penetrating	Normally operates higher than 18,000 feet MSL at any speed	Strategic-level asset. Requires an improved runway for launch and recovery. Greatest range, endurance, and airspeed. Payloads: suite of optics for targeting and weaponry for engagements. Operates at medium-to-high altitudes. Logistics footprint similar to that of a manned aircraft.

AGL	above ground level	LOS	line of sight	UAS unmanned aircraft system
ASM	air-to-surface munition	MSL	mean sea level	

Table 3-1 drone classes FM 3-01.44 SHORAD

They are smaller, lighter, and faster to deploy than larger models. A very small drone can be easily carried along and used to augment the patrol where a larger drone providing overwatch is not available or to clear or recon areas in lieu of sending in a man. Heavier drones being man-packed will slow a patrol down, will take longer to launch and recover, and will hinder mobility if attacked.

Virtually all preppers, partisans, and small military units will be using Group 1 micro/mini UAVs or Group 2 small tactical UAVs (sUAS). Most will be off-the-shelf and take the form of multicopters, quadcopters, and small, fixed-wing aircraft the size of the RQ-11 Raven. This book looks almost exclusively at Group 1, especially quadcopters. This group strikes a good balance between price, availability, and ease of use. Though they have limited payload and endurance (not persistent) they are agile and can be unobtrusive.

COTS drones operate within line-of-sight and operate within an approximate range of 3 miles (5 km). Ranges of up to 10 (16 km) miles are touted, but these are often maximum communication ranges with OEM controllers and antennas. These range figures do not consider endurance nor advanced equipment and techniques to extend range. Remember that the drone must get to the target, conduct its mission (orbit), and return. At 30 MPH (50 km/h) it takes 20 minutes to go ten miles (16 km); a thirty-minute battery life is insufficient for a round-trip.

Groups 1 and 2 are the smallest and hardest UAVs to detect and consequently pose the greatest threat. Their small size makes distant visual detection hard, and their low noise signature is well-masked at any appreciable distance or altitude. While the aircraft themselves may not be armed, they are not harmless. The greatest weapon mankind has ever devised has been the radio. Video from the drone (and location data) can supply targeting information to indirect fire or allow a commander to direct ground troops for an attack.

Group 3-5 UAVs (i.e., Predator/Reaper drones) are not able to be heard or seen ordinarily on the ground. These usually fly at an altitude of several miles, are painted in low-visibility colors that blend in with the sky and are often operated at a stand-off distance rather than directly over any ground targets. UAVs in these classes will almost exclusively be operated by national militaries by remote relay. Killer drones/loitering munitions form their own class that doesn't fall within the scope of the Army classification above.

RC vs. drone

The history of consumer drones begins with early hobbyist unmanned aircraft in the form of radio-controlled (RC) *model* aircraft. These models are essentially small unmanned airplanes whose flight controls are manipulated by a radio controller. Until very recently, installed cameras or other sensors were extremely uncommon in these aircraft. Most were used for aerobatics or racing at model airplane fields. Though model aircraft have much in common with early drones and the technologies are now converging, this work does not look at model aircraft.

Model aircraft are differentiated for the purposes of this book by the fact that they are intended primarily for entertainment as a hobby. Drones are more flexible. While drones can be raced, do aerobatics, and be used for "fun," they have a broader application of personal and commercial use, most commonly photography. Strictly speaking, both could be called "drones," but your quadcopter might be useful to perform surveillance during a riot whereas your neighbor's model plane can only fly around.

What sets apart a "drone" from a model aircraft, in this

context, then? Well, at the risk of oversimplifying and upsetting hobbyists, RC model aircraft are basically big toys whereas drones can be used for more than simply performing exciting flight maneuvers.

Drone	Model aircraft
Mostly battery powered	Mostly combustion/jet engines
Probably a quadcopter	Probably fixed-wing
One or more cameras	Likely has no cameras
Intended for photography	Intended for stunts/racing
Uses GPS for semi-autonomous flight	Does not have GPS and not autonomous
Almost always 2.5 GHz and 5.8 GHz comms	Almost always VHF comms
Recreational and commercial users	Almost always recreational users

Quadcopters and multicopters

Quadcopters are by far the most popular form of consumer grade drone and perhaps the most prolific UAV in the world. Using four rotors to lift, stabilize, and propel the aircraft like a helicopter, these drones are capable of vertical take offs and landings (VTOL) and hovering. Note that in this book *quadcopter* will be used though it can almost always apply to drones with more than four rotors, the *multirotor* or *multicopter*.

UAS vulnerabilities

The main disadvantages of UAS are:

- Too dependent on GPS especially beyond line-of-sight (BLOS).
  - Limited BLOS ability for micro-UAVs and COTS sUAVs.
  - Vulnerable to jamming and interference.
  - COTS UAVs have known frequency ranges (i.e., Wi-Fi).

Limited range: Requires a line-of-sight (LOS) to the control operator/ground station, resulting in ranges of 1-10 miles' (1.6-16km) distance, further made problematic by low endurance due to battery capacity (about 30 minutes).

Lack of freedom of maneuverability: Cannot fly non-line-of-sight (NLOS) missions or where control/GPS signals are obstructed by terrain or structures, such as ducking behind a building or ridge. Must overfly buildings.

Poor susceptibility to damage: While drones are often small, hard to hit targets, they have zero armor protection and not much in the way of system redundancy.

Weather sensitivity: Affected by or inoperable in high winds, cloud cover, precipitation, or other weather conditions. Waterproofing can be a problem.

Sensor limitations: Visibility is restricted to whatever the camera is pointing at with poor situational awareness due to a restricted field of view. Some aircraft may not have night/infrared (IR) cameras. All cameras are ineffective in heavy cloud, fog, smoke, or dust/sand.

Radio frequency (RF) interference: Drone radio signals

are easily detected in known portions of the radio spectrum which leaves them vulnerable to jamming, spoofing, interception, or hacking. The nature of radio signals is such that they cannot be hidden which allows the aircraft and pilot to be located by a technically sophisticated adversary.

Logistics: For individuals, drones can be cost-prohibitive. Replacement parts or resupply may be difficult or impossible in a domestic or revolutionary conflict. Electricity is needed to frequently charge many models.

GPS reliance: UAVs are reliant on GPS for operating BLOS, for accurate positioning, and stability. GPS-denied environments, deliberate or natural, will be problematic for COTS drones.

Nerfing: The manufacturer may have imposed firmware limitations to ensure regulatory compliance, necessitating, or prohibiting, modification.

Drawbacks to operational usage

Some of the operational drawbacks to drone usage are:

- It can draw unwanted attention.
- The characteristic buzz is now immediately recognizable as a drone.
- If you are trying to remain as clandestine as possible, a drone may negate your other efforts to remain undetected if they are followed back to their point of origin to identify the owner.
- Interest in a location can alert an enemy to a potential attack.
- Regular surveillance patterns can be exploited.
- Can be shot down, hacked, or jammed.

- They are not a replacement for patrols, observation/listening posts (OP/LP), surveillance cameras, or general situational awareness.

Nerfing

"Nerfing" is a term originally from the video game community that refers to developers changing elements of the game in the name of obtaining balance, but often to the detriment of gameplay in players' opinions. It is derived from the soft, blunt NERF balls and darts. It has come to mean making something worse often trying to make it idiotproof or acceptable to critics. Speed governors in automobiles are one example of mechanical nerfing.

Drones are nerfed by their manufacturers to limit what kind of problems ignorant or unethical pilots can cause, which in turn may make for bad publicity for the manufacturer. This self-imposed limitation makes it more difficult for mishaps or misbehavior to occur. Self-regulation to avoid mandatory government regulation or even outright bans is commonplace in various industries. DJI brand drones are notorious for having strict limitations on their machines.

Firmware limitations

Many commercially available consumer drones are easy to fly thanks to firmware that uses AI and other advanced features. The downside is that many manufacturers have placed restrictions on their products, from geofenced restricted areas to altitude limitations. Drones may require an Internet/cellular connection before launching or regular updates to remain functional.

Certain flight behaviors may be prohibited. An inexperienced user with no hard curbs on the firmware may fly the drone into illegal areas, in violation of FAA regulations, or beyond the parameters of the airframe.

To overcome this, a user serious about unconventional use needs to look into disabling these limitations and restrictions. There are ways to "jailbreak," or circumvent, the firmware or overwrite it entirely. Someone who does not understand the firmware may "brick" the drone in the process. Doing so will likely void the warranty and may constitute a criminal violation in some areas.

While usage of jailbreaking software or manually modifying the hardware or firmware should be on-hand *prior* to any conflict with its potential technological embargoes, actual removal of restrictions should be saved for when the rule of law is more flexible, and the danger outweighs the legal repercussions.

Generally speaking, without use of jamming or spoofing technology, the only way to impose altitude restrictions or geofences is through the aircraft's firmware. This makes nerfing something that the OEM does, not the government. A DIY drone with open source or self-designed firmware would not be subject to these limitations.

Remote ID

Remote ID (RID) is a radio transponder system that openly broadcasts over Wi-Fi bands a drone's location, altitude, and speed, as well as the location of the pilot. Its short-range signal should not be detected any further than the drone's telemetry and video signals can be detected. A drone cannot be publicly identified by its unique identifier remotely, only by physically matching the broadcast ID number to the serial number.

If using a COTS drone in a defensive or combat application, RID is a liability because it broadcasts real time location data that could be used to pinpoint the aircraft and the pilot. If deniability is an issue, the unique identifier can be matched against the serial number if the pilot and the aircraft are captured. In operational terms, RID cannot be easily disabled without potentially rendering the drone unusable.

AeroScope

Similar to RID is DJI's proprietary AeroScope detection system with a putative range of over 12 miles (20km) to up to 31 miles (50km) under ideal conditions. This is limited to DJI products and is effective because DJI has by far the largest share of the civilian sUAS market. AeroScope works by detecting signals being transmitted from its own models in a manner similar to RID but using its own existing protocols.

AeroScope receives a radio packet dubbed "DroneID" approximately every second. It is not a secure signal and could be intercepted by anyone with the proper equipment to receive it. Information AeroScope reveals are:

- Model identification
- Serial number
- Real time altitude and speed
- Real time location of the drone via GPS

- Pilot's location via GPS

AeroScope is not making inferences; it is being fed actual data with the above information. This method does not exempt the requirement for RID and only works for DJI products. For non-DJI products, substantially similar information can be deduced by the system as it intercepts and analyzes the received signals by "popular" models but *not* receiving the "DroneID" packet.

The popularity of DJI-brand drones extends even to the battlefields of Ukraine where Ukrainian officials were complaining that DJI's AeroScope in Russian hands was being used to find and kill UAS pilots.[3,4] AeroScope enables its operator to find the location of a drone pilot. Once the position of the pilot is known, artillery or missiles can be fired at that position to kill the pilot.

Ukrainian technicians utilized a product called CIAJeepDoors that modifies the

firmware to deactivate remote identification on their DJI airframes. This would not eliminate the ability of AeroScope or other devices to triangulate a pilot based on the

signals transmitted to the drone but makes the process much more difficult as the

proprietary embedded information is no longer broadcast.

Misconceptions

---

[3] https://www.c4isrnet.com/battlefield-tech/2022/10/17/how-ukraine-learned-to-cloak-its-drones-from-russian-surveillance/
[4] https://www.youtube.com/watch?v=UZXzMUxfR6c&t=30s

A drone launch *could* alert your opponent of imminent offensive action, although the author believes this fear is overwrought. The phrase "when the balloon goes up" refers to anti-aircraft barrage balloons being launched prior to a WWI air attack or observation balloons being launched prior to a Civil War battle, depending on which etymology you choose to believe. This can be mitigated by skillful use of altitude and deceptive flying techniques.

Increased intelligence and awareness outweigh the disadvantages of the attention it might cause. The suppressive effects of a drone can be exploited as well, turning its overtness into an asset. Stealth can be leveraged if a drone is kept high, used in a noisy environment, remains out of easy visual spotting distance of the enemy, and uses visual obstructions to hide behind. A wise user will not launch and recover the drone from the same place, if possible, and not from their immediate property, using terrain masking as much as possible.

The argument that "drones will advertise your presence" and thus shouldn't be used is naïve. Even if you have a really great hidden retreat in prepper paradise, eventually someone is going to stumble across you. Smart people aren't going to huddle inside their perimeter with no intelligence on what's going on in the outside world. Stupid people will do that and die. Use of UAS to gain intelligence is an exercise in risk management.

There are a lot of things that can give you away. Someone with Google Earth can look on the map and note your location for post-SHTF exploitation. Smoke from your chimney or fire could give you away. Bad guys might stumble across your patrol. Whether your drone advertises that you have "resources" or not, bad guys will try to steal from anyone they can, "rich" enough for a drone or not.

This whole debate reminds the author of caliber wars (9mm vs. .45). Everything has its own unique advantages and disadvantages. In SHTF or war, one will want to have the choice of every advantage possible tempered by the common sense that something, such as launching a drone, might be tactically inappropriate at that moment.

As for the argument that EMP (electromagnetic pulse) will make drones useless, EMP hasn't been shown to affect small devices, especially if they are powered down and indoors. An EMP is a very long shot anyhow. A more likely scenario is a cyber war or anti-satellite attack. If there was an EMP attack or nuclear war, GPS satellites and the electrical infrastructure to charge a drone will almost certainly be destroyed.

The GPS system relies on satellites and ground stations. In a major peer-to-peer war with Russia or China, GPS will be a target. The US military may also disable GPS or degrade accuracy of the signal. Without GPS, some features of a drone like "return to home" and pre-programmed flightpaths may not function at all. Some models may refuse to fly without GPS input, and all will have to be controlled manually by the pilot sans any speed/altitude data from the satellites.

A loss of grid electricity or modern delivery systems does not have to be crippling. Anyone planning to use a drone seriously in extreme contingencies needs to have multiple spare battery packs and alternative electricity sources. A generator or solar panel system and a way to store the electricity once generated (batteries or power packs) is a must. Spare parts can be ordered prior to SHTF and kept on-hand as one would stockpile things like high-wear automotive items that might be unavailable.

Drones also don't replace tried and true methods. Just because one has a magic flying thingy doesn't relieve the need to walk the perimeter, send out patrols, or perform inspections in person. Technology is not a substitute for using God-given senses to further investigate suspicious circumstances. Drones can't see everything and *will* change the behavior of those that they observe in ways actual humans may not.

The biggest obstacle to drone employment is cost, followed by owner piloting experience. Not everyone has the money to buy quality drones and all the peripheral accessories. Flight experience is also critical, and some persons might just not have the technological proficiency and aeronautical ability to fly a drone.

Drone swarms and should an average person fear being killed by a drone?

Is the average person likely to be killed by a drone? It is *highly* unlikely unless you are a combatant in an anti-government insurrection or a guerilla war. Though the odds are increasing as UAS tech proliferates since I published my first thoughts on drone warfare in 2021, it is still improbable that the average person needs to worry about getting droned.

In a future destabilized America immersed in urban combat, most deaths will be caused by famine and disease, followed by gunfire, as in most wars. Drone warfare will occur because it is a useful technology for war. In application, it is little different than modern militaries using attack aircraft, helicopters, precision guided munitions, or indirect fire weapons (rockets, mortars, and artillery—RAM). It's just that drones make this kind of thing suddenly accessible to anyone which makes it scary.

Drone swarms are large-scale mass attacks by small, explosive-laden UAVs intended to terminally crash into a target and detonate. The number of aircraft is intended to overwhelm any defenses to ensure a kill. Drone swarms have emerged as a powerful tool in military operations, particularly in the area of precision strikes, but they are not what the reader might assume.

To date, drone swarm strikes have been little more than miniaturized versions of cruise missile or air strikes that employed numerous platforms approximately the size of aircraft launched air-to-ground missiles. In practical terms, this is nothing that the world hasn't seen before. In September 2019, Houthi rebels in Yemen attacked Saudi oil facilities at Abqaiq–Khurais, with a swarm of over 25 drones and resulted in significant damage to the oil processing plant.

In the Abqaiq–Khurais attack, the drones used in the attack were Iranian-made and were likely a mix of both the

Qasef and the Delta Wave models. The Qasef has a range of about 150 kilometers and can carry a warhead weighing up to 30 kilograms. The Delta Wave is a smaller UAV that can be launched from a tube and has a range of about 15 kilometers. A stand-off air strike could have accomplished the same thing except that these "suicide" drones can be launched from the ground or sea, so no aircraft radar signature is generated.

Many readers will have in their minds a horror-movie image of a swarm of very small, explosive laden drones flying through an open window and chasing a person down. This fear, which theoretically possible, is unfounded. Drones will be problematic mostly as a reconnaissance and command and control tool. One should be more worried about a looting gang launching a drone to see who is asleep before the 3 AM attack than someone flying a drone with C4 through their bedroom window.

For the average reader, even those who fancy themselves partisans or guerillas in a domestic conflict, the chance of assassination via drone swarm is low. A single UCAV hit, conventional air strike, or midnight commando raid is far more efficient. Also, the technology to implement the "exploding hummingbird" style strike is so niche only top-tier governments could utilize it and even then, is the reader important enough to justify such a thing?

Ch. 2 What can UAS do for you?

Most of the roles a drone can be used in blend together, so they aren't an elegant delineation of missions but a broad variety of possibilities. We are using *some* military terms and descriptions as a baseline, but this is not a field manual, nor an intelligence gathering manual, so the explanation of battlefield concepts will be relatively superficial as we focus more on civilian-adapted applications.

After all, a drone is about remotely seeing stuff to expand an intelligence profile or to make plans to attack or defend. A reconnaissance flight can easily transition to a surveillance mission which ends in either a direct attack or providing targeting support. Some of the advantages drones can provide to neighborhood defenders are:

- Perimeter surveillance.
- Reconnaissance (scouting).
- Threat awareness.
- Real time route advance reconnaissance.
- Unarmed overwatch.
- Deterrence/suppression/distraction.
- Battle damage assessment (BDA) and casualty confirmation.
- Secure communications delivery.
- Small package delivery.
- Short term airborne radio repeater.
- Inspecting suspicious packages or vehicles.
- Tracking a moving target (person or vehicle).

The author features the use of drones being used to the advantage of good guys post-SHTF in the VCSO EMP series of novels.

The advantage drones have over manned aircraft is that drones fly a lot lower and a lot slower, giving them more time to make more detailed observations and have an easier time of maintain visual contact while maneuvering more easily for better perspectives. As mentioned elsewhere, they also democratize airpower. Roles UAS excels in:

- Intelligence
o Reconnaissance and surveillance.
- Maneuver support
o Real time information on enemy activities to ground combat forces in battle.
- Fire support/targeting
o Identifying targets, providing target coordinates, and designating targets.
- Command and control
o Situational awareness of enemy and friendly movements and activities.
- Attack
o Direct attack on targets or ad hoc precision weapons.
- Movement support
o Scouting for ambushes, roadblocks, IEDs, or mines, etc.
- Security
o General surveillance of an area or perimeter and scanning for approaching threats.

Drones are really doing three things: putting a moving camera in the sky, taking humans out of harm's way, and provide force multiplication. Having a new vertical perspective increases intelligence collection and enhances situational awareness doing it faster and over larger areas/distances than a man on foot because a drone can fly and look over obstacles.

UAS gives the citizen defender or partisan overhead imagery support (surveillance and reconnaissance) and airborne attack capability. They can locate a target, gather intelligence on it, monitor it until the best time to strike, and when they do strike, the ground forces can be supported in real time by the drone's camera feed. Additionally, a UAV[5] armed and equipped properly (assuming access to explosives) can engage in aerial attacks (bombing), perhaps giving a semblance of long-range fires to a group without military-grade weaponry.

Drones provide a vertical perspective, essentially rendering the understanding of the "battlefield" in the third dimension. An adversary can no longer hide behind something between he and the observer thanks to the look-down perspective of a UAV. UAS is also a force multiplier; formerly, someone would have to go out and look behind the bushes to see if an enemy was hidden there. Now, a drone can do so without risking a human life and potentially attack if it finds an enemy without having to deploy a whole squad, giving a force multiplication effect.

Drones are a helpful addition to traditional capabilities; they are not a substitute for human intelligence and ground reconnaissance. Technology needs to be regarded as an enhancing complement to conventional means, not a

---

[5] "a UAV" vs. "an UAV": using "a" contraindicates the grammatical rule to use "an" before a word that begins with a vowel, however, "an" sounds awkward and is not used in the vernacular. UAV the initialism begins with a yu- or ʊ sound, which is a consonant if UAV is considered a standalone word rather than purely an initialism.

convenience for laziness.

Detailed examples of potential UAS applications

Reconnaissance
- Offensive reconnaissance to locate targets to attack
- Defensive reconnaissance to look for threats to a static position (encampment, position, property, neighborhood)
- Scouting the route ahead of a vehicle, convoy, or patrol
- Physical intelligence collection (grabbing and recovering light objects, such as portable radios)

Surveillance
- Static property surveillance from dynamic angles without physically sending a person.
- Increase the distance, angles, and areas of observation beyond that of a ground-based human observer
- Maintain visual contact with subjects of interest
- Determine the identity, composition, intent, equipment, and activity of subjects of interest

Targeting
- Provide target coordinates or locations
- Assist ground personnel to navigate to a target (maneuver)
- Designate targets for guided weapons (i.e., laser guidance)

- Conduct battle damage assessment (BDA) after the engagement

Communications

- Communications relay (airborne radio repeater; RETRANS)
- Electronic signal detection and interception.
- Radio frequency jamming (voice communications)
- Drone telemetry rebroadcast (airborne repeater or node)
- Emergency lightweight logistics resupply

Attack

- Bombing (dropping grenades or other explosives)
- Improvised precision guided munitions
- Purpose-built ""suicide" drones/loitering munitions and substitute guided missiles

Situational awareness

Some uses of drones for situational awareness/perimeter surveillance seem obvious, like artificially giving a defender increased height for greater observational distance, but they are much more than highly placed eyes in the sky. Drones:

- Have the ability to look straight down and see around visual obstructions versus line-of-sight only for a static observer.
- Can maneuver around terrain, structures, trees, or other visual obstructions affecting your line-of-sight.

- Create time-lapse videos to identify any sign of intrusion on your perimeter or property.

Drones are not restricted to observations from an aerial static location, as an observer in a high tower or on a hill is. Nor are they bound to an eye-level view from the ground that a person is. They can go behind obstacles, fly over buildings, and fly very low to inspect things behind things like fences. They can easily inspect dangerous or denied areas.

Drones can be programmed (depending on model) to "patrol" a geofenced loop. By watching past videos or using software to analyze the footage, changes can be detected over time. Perhaps a camouflaged observation post has been constructed just outside your fence line.

Threat awareness is about monitoring for potential dangers beyond your immediate perimeter. This is an indefinite distance but assume that it is the maximum range your drone could fly, or the distance you could walk in an hour. An example is scouting a nearby major intersection or roadway that attackers or refugees may use for activity. Put most simply, awareness via drone is getting to a high position, looking down, and seeing what's going on without needing high terrain or a building.

Intelligence, surveillance, and reconnaissance (ISR)

Reconnaissance is more specific than general surveillance or awareness. The term here is used to mean targeted inspection, observation, or study of a particular event, activity, location, or persons/people. In other words, you want to know something specific. This also includes preparation for an attack or defense.

In my book *Hard Favored Rage*, a drone is used, flying at high altitude and partially concealed in low clouds, to create a detailed map of an enemy camp and gather valuable intelligence. A drone can perform a pre-attack survey and also support the attack (or defense) itself by providing real time updates on enemy movement.

Spy planes often fly over wide swaths of territory photographing everything beneath them for later intelligence analysis. Drones can do this too. Firmware modification to override any restrictions on distance from the user could allow you to program a flight plan that takes the drone out of line-of-sight communication to perform a reconnaissance mission. Of course, the drone would be on its own and midcourse updates or evasion is impossible. This will require a functioning GPS system or sophisticated internal navigation.

Monitoring and overwatch (screening)

In Iraq and Afghanistan, vehicle convoys and foot patrols often had helicopter or Predator/Reaper drone support to alert the soldiers and Marines to what was happening around and in front of them. One could remotely clear intersections, curves in the road, behind hills or obstacles, for ambushes. Imagine that instead of having to send a team on foot to check out some wrecked cars in the road, your drone can simply do a fly-by to see if guys with guns are crouching on the other side. Other examples include:

- Inspecting obstacles for booby traps.
- Clearing likely ambush points.
- Inspecting ideal positions for snipers.
- Watching for the approach of enemy forces.

UAS support for overwatch and screening was vital to American troops in the last thirty years. Even without the ability to fire on the enemy, eyes in the sky passed on timely tactical intelligence that often saved the day. For instance, an unarmed drone performing screening could allow you to detect and respond to an ambush or flanking maneuver before it occurs. A checkpoint could be given advance warning of a breach attempt.

Unfortunately, while COTS UAVs can pass on warnings from what they see, they cannot provide fire support like helicopters or Predator/Reaper drones can without modification. Limited attack capabilities can be added as modifications or entirely new platforms can be built to provide armed recon.

Communications and delivery

Like carrier pigeons, drones can deliver written or recorded messages securely to allies across contested or inaccessible terrain. Messages would need to be encrypted in the event the message is captured or the drone is shot down.

Another use is as a flying short term airborne radio repeater. A ham skilled with a soldering iron could rig up a lightweight repeater that could potentially cover a 50 mile

(80 km) radius from a height of 1,500 feet AGL (depending on terrain). This would enable long-range line-of-sight communications if a grid-down disaster (or sabotage) has rendered conventional repeater towers out of commission. Its utility would be limited by the duration of the drone's batteries.

Small packages of urgently needed material could also be delivered via drone. Large consumer quadcopters can carry up to five pounds in some cases (with a severe range/endurance reduction), enabling emergency delivery of critical goods. When American troops were surrounded by Germans in a battle in France, empty leaflet shells were loaded with desperately needed medical supplies and fired on the American position. Unfortunately, most of the supplies were damaged on impact.[6]

Drones can take this idea and deliver things a bit more gently. Isolated homes may be resupplied in a number of drops. A fighter trapped behind cover might get needed ammunition or water dropped to him. Drones could even drop smoke grenades in the open to provide concealment to ground forces.

Physical intelligence collection

Ukrainian forces published video of a drone grabbing a radio in the 2022-2023 war.[7] Taking the footage at face

---

[6] 30th Infantry Division at Hill 314, Mortain, France, August 1944.
[7] Sophia Ankel, "Ukraine boasts that it used a drone to steal a radio from a dead Russian soldier, letting it listen in on enemy

value, a quadcopter hovers over a portable radio lying in a field near an abandoned fighting position and a dead soldier. The retrieval drone has a servomotor controlled hook dangling from a cable that looks as if it might be about ten feet (3m) long. After playing a short game of the claw machine, the drone grabs the radio by the antenna and flies off with it.

To summarize, drones can serve as physical intelligence collection platforms by using remote hooks. If the CIA can lift part of a Russian submarine from three miles below the ocean surface, drones can be used to pinch small items for later intelligence exploitation. With a payload of just under five pounds or two kilos, a skillfully maneuvered quadcopter could snatch radios, maps, documents, and other small items.

If this is indeed a Russian radio, it does have some intelligence value for Ukraine. As news articles state, Ukraine claimed the radio was still working and they were able to monitor Russian communications for nine days. It is likely that after nine days Russian units using the same frequencies either moved out of the area, changed an encryption key, or changed their frequencies. Unless the radio traffic was encrypted, having possession of the enemy's radio wasn't necessary to intercept their communications.

The loss of a radio allows intelligence to download the

---

plans, *Business Insider*, Jan. 17, 2023
https://www.businessinsider.com/ukraine-says-stole-russian-radio-drone-could-hear-enemy-plans-2023-1 &
https://www.youtube.com/watch?v=2sNJxWi3N4Y

radio to analyze its channel plans and any encryption contained on the radio. For elements using unencrypted radios this isn't much of a loss as the information transmitted over the air in the clear can be intercepted and listened to anyway. Revealing a channel plan is more of a boon because it makes the signal intelligence (SIGINT) team's job easier.

In the case of a captured radio, all the analyst has to do is tune to the channel labeled RED41 on the LCD screen. Tactical communications instructor and US Army Special Forces veteran NC Scout, in his book *The Guerilla's Guide to the Baofeng Radio*, stresses that one does not "program the memory of a radio you intend to use for tactical or clandestine purposes."[8] COMSEC[9] procedures help alleviate the risks in losing a radio. In combat, people will lose their gear and die.

The lesson for drone operations is that they can do more than spy on people and drop explosives. Quadcopters are useful physical intelligence collection platforms as long as they have the payload capacity and mechanism to grab objects. Defenders and soldiers need to account for this potential and not leave sensitive materials lying around. What may be relatively safe in a rear command post might not actually be safe from a drone, though abandoned/lost gear being collected is understandably unavoidable. On the positive side, the extremely low approach and hovering required to recover the gear makes it easy to shoot down or

---

[8] *Guerilla's Guide*, p. 21
[9] Communication security

simply grab the airframe.

Ch. 3 The Changing Face of Ground Warfare

The rapid technological advances of the 21st century, particularly with the revolution in consumer-grade small drones, has made the battlefield a fully vertical one. Widespread aerial surveillance and reconnaissance has brought ground conflicts under the eyes of the Gorgon where the only limitations to near-constant and total observation are money and enough aircraft. Quadcopters have taken aerial hunting and attacks out of the domain of scout helicopters and delivered it to the squad-level.

UAVs have replaced manned aircraft in many roles while opening doors of unimaginable horrors that are as shocking to the 21st century mind as the first infantryman in a trench to be killed by an airplane. As smokeless powder, the repeating firearm, tanks, and radios created bloody maneuver warfare, drone warfare will in greater ways alter how we think about fighting and picture battlefields.

Watching grenades, mortar bombs, and other improvised explosives being dropped on Russian troops in Ukraine is heavily reminiscent of black and white footage of WWI aerial bombardment. During the Great War, tactical bombers were in their infancy and battlefield aerial attack was little more than throwing hand grenades or lawn-dart like bombs on the troops below. Effect on target and accuracy relied on judgement and mainly luck. The ordnance was crude and the tactics primitive, but it didn't take long to become a crucial part of warfare.

In future conflicts, be they full-scale international wars,

civil wars, or domestic unrest, people will be killed in increasing numbers by drones. Their ease of use and lack of risk to the pilots will make killing easier, enabling those who cannot or would not be soldiers or insurgents, to participate in violence. Drones are the new threat as IEDs were and will be used in similar ways to both sniper attacks and bombings against civilian, military, and government targets.

Combatants without drones or defenses against them will be at a marked disadvantage. UAS superiority or even supremacy, where counter-UAS (CUAS) defenses are a nuisance to totally ineffective, can be achieved when one side is more technologically advanced than the other. This is possible by one party being a government or multi-national force, such as ISAF in Afghanistan, or a domestic combatant with superior financial or logistic resources.

The rise of drone technology and CUAS systems will level the playing field to parity where neither side can claim dominance of the skies. Parity will be achieved through the propagation of UAS as a force multiplier *and* a force projector as well as the evolution and ubiquitous integration of CUAS. While legacy views of drones in conflicts has been an extension of post-WWII airpower or an adjunct to surveillance and reconnaissance, miniaturization and proliferation promises to alter centuries of ground warfare in the ways previous iterations of disruptive technology has.

Phases of sUAS in warfare

IOC: Initial Operating Capability

- Basic use of small drones; IOC or experimental phase.

- Mainly isolated ISR for reconnaissance.
- Limited or no strike capabilities.
- Not ubiquitous.
- Mainly COTS technology or military prototypes.
- Acquisition and replacement scarcity may limit deployment for fear of loss and replacement challenges.

A good example of the sUAS IOC phase would be Iraq. ISIS showed how a non-state actor could integrate UAS into its operations, both for ISR and attack, though this was a nascent capability. The Donbas war prior to the 2022 invasion of Ukraine also showcased the first real front-line use of COTS sUAS by national militaries and the years prior allowed Ukrainian forces to leverage that experience against Russia.

In this phase, a side has not developed any real doctrine or use for sUAS. sUAS is a useful, but not reliable tool to augment the traditional ways of doing things. Experience is gained in this phase as the technology is so new to the world let alone militaries. COTS airframes are often repurposed, most often by non-state actors, or COTS designs are used as the basis for military airframes. The curiosity and cost of the technology may limit usage due to a lack of familiarity and availability, though governments are better suited to replacing any lost drones.

Integration
- Widespread use of sUAS for ISR at the tactical level.
- Strike capabilities are still limited (dropping hand grenades or mortars) but commonly used.

- Effect of strikes are largely psychological rather than altering the course of battle.
- Well-equipped forces are using purpose made military models.
- Troops have not fully adjusted to the use of sUAS either by them or against them.

The integration phase is what we have seen from Ukrainian forces in the 2022-2023 war. UAS has left the experimental phase and proceeded on to an operational prototype model of employment. In the 2003 war, the RQ-11 Raven gained widespread attention for ground troops to be able to conduct their own aerial reconnaissance without needed helicopter support.

Use in this phase is widespread and tactics have rapidly evolved into a pre-doctrinal stage. Attacks are primitive in most cases but get better constantly, paving the way for innovation and sounding out future concepts. sUAS is not decisive but can have significant effects either directly or through supporting roles. The psychological effect on troops is still shocking and disturbing as training has not caught up with the aerial threat.

In Ukraine, we see of course ISR usage but at the sub-unit level. Attack roles include support for long-range fires and "suicide" drone attacks. The most infamous use of sUAS has been to literally hunt individual soldiers which has inflicted untold deaths but has not been shown to win any battles yet. Larger strike weapons, often of the loitering munition class employed against vehicles, have been much more effective and devastating. COTS technology is pervasive but use of military sUAVs is as widespread.

Ubiquity

- COTS units have been largely supplanted by purpose-made/military-grade models.
- Drones for ISR use are widespread down to the platoon level.
- All ground forces must assume they are under enemy observation at all times.
- Loitering munitions are in common use with small units, replacing modified sUAS for attack.
- Larger UCAVs are used in roles traditionally reserved for strike aircraft.
- Strikes occur on small units up to major command centers and logistic depots.
- Psychological effect on troops is that they are not safe from a drone strike anywhere, at any time.

In the mature phase, UAS has become ubiquitous in warfare. COTS drones have been replaced by aircraft of similar function but purpose-made for military use. Use of sUAS for ISR is standard with small units and so is attack. Reliance on manned aircraft and long-range fires can be decreased, but not replaced (augmented). Solid doctrine for employment of sUAS and CUAS has ben deployed. Operational planning and training consider the use and effect of sUAS.

Use of airpower in Vietnam would be a good analogue to the mature phase of sUAS warfare. By the 1960s, air-ground coordination had improved so that infantry could come to depend on the fire support of aircraft. Units like the Air Cav might scout out NVA/VC units from the air and attack using only helicopter support. Air attack was not a novelty but something that was expected and actively mitigated through the use of tunnels or the complicated procedures along the Ho Chi Minh trail.

The poor man's air force

In our contemporary age, technology evolves at a rapid rate. Advancements are steppingstones and mastery of one element allows revolutions that were impossible even to imagine not long before. Warfare also creates a great drive for innovations and ingenuity. UAS is an outstanding example of that drive.

What began as crude guided bombs or aerial targets turned into pilotless surveillance and killing machines. We've gone from unmanned planes, to flying cameras, and arrived at semi-autonomous flying ordnance. A missile that can be fired before it even knows its target exists is terrifying. All of these changes and the democratization of high tech into the aerial realm gives citizen defenders an advantage during domestic unrest and adds a new dimension to warfare.

Drones are the poor-man's air force. On the smallest playing field, quadcopters have brought much of the same to the squad/platoon level in militaries and to the citizen or insurgent. Smaller militaries that are unable to afford the same planes and guided weapons that larger, wealthier militaries can, now have the capacity to offer broad air support and wage aerial campaigns through UAS.

UAS has increased sortie rate/cycle times over manned

aircraft as no crew rest is required, maintenance is less extensive, and refueling/rearming is faster. Lower maintenance may come at the cost of a slightly higher operational failure rate but there is no loss of a pilot. The price of a UAV is less than a manned aircraft and the loss of investment in the pilot's training.

Aside from financial cost, military risk calculus has changed. Losing an expensive manned aircraft and a pilot is also a consideration in the escalation of small conflicts into larger wars. At the international conflict scale, larger, manned aircraft are seen as signs of a serious, more involved clash while a drone is, at the time being, not seen as a major commitment of armed forces.

Removing men from the equation via the employment of UAS broadens the politicians' and generals' options. Drones can be used in higher threat environments because there is no pilot's life to risk, and the cost of the drone is less than a fighter or attack plane. Drone warfare can therefore be more aggressive, persistent, and daring than conventional air forces.

Earlier doctrine regarding the use of unmanned aircraft focused heavily on risk reduction for human pilots. No longer would a wild weasel have to risk his life conducting SEAD[10] missions nor would we lose pilots by the dozens trying to deliver imprecise munitions on a heavily defended target. The losses of the Vietnam air war surely were foremost in the minds of those developing doctrine for UAV missions.

---

[10] Suppression of Enemy Air Defenses

Autonomous aircraft, slightly smaller than fighter jets but bearing much in common with them, would fly as wingmen to manned aircraft. "Heavy" targets would be suppressed, making the airspace safe for human flyers. Air superiority UCAVs would win dogfights by outmaneuvering traditional fighters that were not bound by the G-limits of the human body. The doctrine was not so much an evaluation of what unmanned aircraft could do, but how existing air missions could be better executed without a pilot in the cockpit.

With the Global War on Terror and the surveillance capabilities of Predator and later Reaper drones, the ability to use these aircraft to radically shape war began to change. What began as mainly a reconnaissance platform evolved into a limited prompt strike vehicle. Why spend hours watching for a target only to call in an air strike when the drone could fire a Hellfire missile itself? The ability of high-endurance aircraft to conduct both the ISR and strike roles was quickly realized.

While ISR, air strike, and CAS had been a part of modern air force's missions for at least the last half-century, the persistence that UAVs brought was a major change. Stealthy platforms loitering high above the battlefield could lurk undetected in ways that helicopters and manned aircraft could not do before. Ground troops could have real time airborne intelligence without the same costs as from manned missions and armed drones watching over the soldiers could provide limited air support if necessary.

Drones can be an effective adjunct in conflicts but drone warfare, like manned air warfare, alone cannot achieve victory. All warfare is about what happens on the ground; forcing your enemy to accede to your demands because his troops are dead, his supplies are gone, and his country is ravaged. War is about destroying an enemy's ability to wage it and his morale to continue it.

Even naval warfare is no exception as it interdicts and disrupts overseas trade and supply, harming a nation's economy and war effort. What air attacks can do is kill troops on the ground, destroy war material to degrade fighting abilities, and provide valuable intelligence support to commanders. Aerial warfare is a sideshow that makes for dramatic stories and young men's dreams but victory in the air in and of itself is not a final victory. UAS will be an important part future conflicts, both used by air and ground forces, but drones will never supplant armies.

Manned vs. unmanned aircraft

Until the advent of drone warfare, aerial attacks on ground troops have always been relatively impersonal. With the exception of high altitude bombers, like the B-52 Arc Light missions of Vietnam) troops often had warning of an air attack, even if their precautions were ineffective. The planes and helicopters could be heard coming. Constant aerial dominance was difficult to keep up because aircraft can't stay up forever. For much of the 20th century, night air attacks were technologically limited as well, giving a respite after dark.

To paraphrase C. S. Lewis, manned aircraft are not capable of torment without end. Pilots must sleep. The aircraft cannot lie silent in wait or materialize out of seemingly nowhere. Airframes, ground and aircrew, ordnance, and fuel are all expensive commodities that must be husbanded. Unmanned aerial warfare does not have a respite, even if only from a psychological perspective.

Drones are creeping, silent, stalking wraiths that strike seemingly out of nowhere to the terror of ground troops. Ambush can come from the skies at any time with virtually no warning. A soldier never knows when he is under observation from above, death waiting to fall upon him. Aerial warfare and high altitude surveillance have always brought this risk, but small unmanned aerial systems (sUAS) made what was once impersonal very personal.

Silent death from above goes against decades of modern warfare experience and invalidates untold eons of human experience that expects ambush to come from another man at eye level. Small drones are so horrible because, like a sniper hiding in the jungle, the operator chooses the time of attack and the target on an individual level against what most soldiers have been programmed to expect by instinct and training. A soldier might hide from a sniper, who may miss, or out-maneuver to kill him, but a soldier is often as helpless beneath a killer drone as a fieldmouse running from an owl.

While drone attacks can indeed be mitigated and aren't necessarily as pervasive or persistent as one might fear, the psychological effects are something else. In some cases, attack footage shows the clear surprise that troops feel as they spot the drone. Habits on the ground also tell of soldiers who may be doing everything right from a pre-UAW[11] standpoint only to die when their horizontally oriented camouflage and cover fails them. One must feel quite powerless to know a grenade can be dropped on you out of the blue when you are seemingly behind the front line.

Partisans, preppers, and terrorists

Quadcopters in battle will proliferate and become ubiquitous reconnaissance tools and weapons. The defense industry will begin designing and marketing purpose-built military quadcopters, adaptations of COTS civilian drones will be common among irregular groups, and workshop builds will grow. The advantages to small units and domestic actors—criminal, terrorist, and defender alike—are too much to pass up.

Partisans, rebels, and guerillas can access the air without support of a major financial benefactor or a sympathetic foreign government. They will have precision strike capabilities, if only slightly less crude as the pioneering armed drones of ISIS were. Most importantly, UAS gives irregular forces airborne ISR capacity, aiding them in battle (ambushes), easing reconnaissance, and aiding attack behind enemy lines.

On the civilian front, how UAS can be used to extend one's sphere of defense is evident. Height has always equated a better tactical position and a drone will permit beleaguered neighborhood watches or assistance groups

---

[11] Unmanned Aerial Warfare

trying to survive the aftermath of a disaster or civil war greater situational awareness. While we envision UAVs being used by "good guys" to fight mobs of looters or marauding gangs, the risks of lethal or malicious use by bad actors has to be considered.

When adversaries have a similar level of offensive parity, one side will seek to leverage any additional technical advantage over the other. For example, if all parties have guns, one side may seek machine guns while the other develops a bomb-building capacity. Two equally armed and capable militias will not rely on luck for victory over their enemy but will pursue overmatch to put them in the superior position, such as having artillery support.

Drones are an example of tie-breaking technological superiority but one that is also easily subject to an arms race. One side gets a drone to spy on the other, so Side B uses drones to guide their maneuvers. After that comes explosive-laden drones used as a poor-man's smart bomb. The limiting factors with UAS altering the face of a domestic conflict are financial resources, technical capabilities, access to explosives, and the availability of the aircraft or components. Foreign actors could easily introduce all of the above into a domestic conflict to bolster their proxies or achieve other ends.

The use of drones in Ukraine to hunt and kill soldiers individually is a sobering wakeup call. In a dense urban environment, drone attacks may occur with little warning like the echo of a shot and the fall of a body is the herald of a sniper's attack. Imagine remote robberies by air, with the perpetrator safely concealed hundreds of yards away from the victim. A quadcopter flies up carrying an explosive or firearm, the operator announces via speaker his demands, and the loot is either flown away.

Imagine drones being used in street gang warfare. A drone could be used to reconnoiter a neighborhood to see where the homies are hanging out. Then a hand grenade is dropped on a group of rival gang members standing on a corner. Drive-by shootings place those on the street, in front yards, and in the front rooms of homes in danger; drones would erase any illusions of safety away from these places.

Alternatively, backyard gatherings and parties would become vulnerable. Congregating in front yards or streets is hazardous due to the possibility of a drive-by shooting, but many backyards require someone to infiltrate the gathering or to assault it—both are usually too risky to try. A drone changes the geometry of possible attack. Off-limits territory becomes penetrable through flight.

Terrorism is often cited as a danger from UAS but the evil imagination of how a lone wolf could manipulate one is often overlooked. The mere application of explosives could be enough to create disruptive or serious effects.

A drone attacking a dispatch center or similar unfortified command/operations center could easily render it non-mission capable with minimal effort and explosives. Many modern emergency response dispatch centers are aboveground with windows and skylights for natural light. Construction of these facilities may be no more substantial than a concrete tilt-up building. An unprotected facility could be attacked by one or two drones delivering explosives to the windows or skylights. The blast effects and glass injuries would incapacitate the staff. Even if casualties were light, the damage would prevent or severely hinder continued operation.

Psychological operations and effects

UAS will have unintentional effects on people and will be used to engage in psychological operations (psyops). In 2019, Greenpeace used a drone to drop a smoke grenade on a nuclear-material storage building in France. Though no harm was done, a similar attack could send a message that a damaging attack using the same vector is possible and unstoppable, thereby harming the adversary's morale. Actual attacks in rear or "safe" areas remove the illusion of safety of behind the lines or in a high-security area.

Long-range precision strikes by manned aircraft from high altitude and artillery fires are impersonal methods of killing at a distance that have little to no warning. The difference between those and UAS is that the latter is new threat and one that is incredibly personal. To see a robotic flying machine, even if it is controlled by a person, stalking individuals is the stuff of nightmare. As experiences in Ukraine have shown, the mind of the soldier has not yet adapted to the threat posed by UAS.

UAVs, above a certain altitude (dependent on the size of the drone), are practically invisible to the human eye and silent. These hovering or orbiting drones performing surveillance or reconnaissance are like an omniscient "all-seeing eye" that is an impersonal representation of death. Vertical attack takes advantage of surprise because few people look up or expect attacks to come from above. Paranoia and fear set in. No place is safe.

Sound is another powerful factor. The distinct buzz of drone motors becomes a kind of "whispering death" that signals the imminent or constant threat of attack. Nazi weapons also produced sonic effects that terrified people on the ground.

The V1 "buzz bombs" that struck London in WWII were a quivering sort of buzz that is, to the modern ear, like a poorly running two-stroke mini-bike. The peculiar buzz was due to the nature of its pulse-jet engine design. Shortly before the explosion, the engine would suddenly cut out, leaving a dreadful silence as the now-quiet bomb dove on its target. After the silence an explosion would follow. Survivors said the worst part was the silence between the engine cutting out and the explosion because one never knew if they would be hit.

A video[12] out of Armenia shows an incoming "suicide" drone that created a loud, highly pitched whirring sound as it made its terminal dive. The sound was remarkably like the "Jericho trumpet" sirens attached to Junkers Ju 87 Stuka dive bombers from WWII. In the video, the soldiers immediately hit the ground when they hear the engine, audible for about 10 seconds before impact, just like the reaction of allied troops hearing a Stuka in a dive. Though

---

[12] https://twitter.com/AuroraIntel/status/1311728844773130241

the Stuka's siren was intended as a psychological weapon, drones' engine noise will come to be associated with small-munitions attacks.

Asymmetric threats

Firebombing

Drones can be used to initiate arson fires, whether wildland or of structures. The chief advantage to fire-starting drones offer is no human presence at the crime scene. Arson cases are often made when evidence left at the ignition scene or a nearby sighting leads back to the suspect. The greater the distance an arsonist has from where the fire starts, the less of a chance that incriminating evidence is deposited or there are witnesses.

An arsonist with a drone could be up to several miles away from where the fire begins. Remote ignition can give him a greater degree of precision over the fire's initial progress. For a given topography and wind conditions, the ideal ignition point, or multiple points, may not be feasible to reach on foot or by vehicle in a reasonable amount of time. Air drops could start a flame line coordinated to take advantage of fuel beds, wind, and geography to maximize destruction, overwhelming firefighters.

In dry areas, drone ignition would be a boon to the disturbed arsonist, the terrorist, and the guerilla. The potential size, certainty, and anonymity of such a wildfire would be undeniably attractive. If the cost of the airframe is offset, the time and opportunity costs make it a "cheap" attack vector. Methods range from an incendiary device released from a servo-motor to a road flare being duct-taped to a cheap, unregistered drone, ignited, then crashed.

In an urban environment, drones can be used in similar was to set buildings alight. Fire can be used as the weapon itself or to flush persons out for either air or ground attack. One can survive in a blast-damaged home, but not as it burns down around their ears. Even before the advent of drones, the tactic of firing a structure to force out or simply burn alive the occupants was practiced with little more than torches.

A window could be shot out and a UAV flown in to deposit an incendiary. Ruins could be easily fired to deny their use or scatter an entrenched enemy. Homes or buildings could be targeted in terror attacks or in dedicated raids on a particular objective. Logistics are another target, from ammo dumps, to warehouses, to crops in the field.

Fire tends to be a difficult thing to protect against. Even a blast hardened structure may not be particularly fire resistant. Take the average wood-framed American house. A home may have special bracing installed and a blast shelter built but it remains vulnerable to ignition by incendiary devices and wind-driven fires. Note that even if a modern home is built to the latest wildfire standards with flame resistant materials, a device could be precisely positioned in a weak spot that will defeat the precautions.

Maneuverable munitions

"Suicide" drone, "kamikaze" drones," and loitering munitions are terms used for a UAV that is terminally guided into a target, whether by an operator or autonomously. Hi-tech weapons can be like small missiles that can orbit before striking, the way a bird of prey wheels in the sky watching for a rodent to emerge from a den.

The low-tech version of these new weapons is a low-cost expendable drone that has been optimized for delivery of an explosive. ISIS is believed to have created the first such weapons by fastening IEDs to COTS drones. As discussed here, a *"suicide" drone* is not a quadcopter that drops grenades. Imagine an exploding quadcopter that can fly over a wall, get below an anti-drone net, and then fly through the target's window—a flying IED.

Missile-based *loitering munitions* might not be able to hover like a quadcopter, but they will be much faster. These agile smart-bombs combine a mortar's non-LOS attack capability with the flight characteristics of a missile in addition of being able to orbit and maneuver. Loitering munitions are:

- More portable than a mortar, lighter than a rocket launcher.
- More maneuverable than both a mortar and a rocket launcher.
- Have more explosive power and a lager lethal radius than a grenade.
- Can be detonated to negate the effect of cover (airburst or maneuvered around obstacles).
- Relatively rapid speed makes them difficult to shootdown.

If the quadcopter releasing grenades is analogous to hand-thrown bombs from biplanes, these killer drones are the equivalent to the infantryman's own portable guided missile.

A mortar is a smoothbore weapon that launches an explosive shell, known as a bomb, in a high-arc parabolic trajectory for indirect fire support of ground troops. Mortars are popular forms of artillery that are usually (depending on caliber) man portable down to the platoon level. Capable of firing at maximum ranges of up to approximately 4 miles (7km) these weapons predominately fire unguided high explosive rounds but are capable of firing guided bombs in some cases.

Whether guided or unguided, a mortar bomb is limited to its ballistic arcing trajectory. Terminal accuracy can be as precise as one wants but in the same way a rifle bullet cannot turn a corner, a mortar cannot reorient mid-flight and fly horizontally through a window. Man-portable missiles can fly horizontally but cannot fire indirectly. "Suicide" drones can do both.

Popular military models include the five pound (2.5kg) AeroVironment Switchblade 300 which is launched from a small tube like a mortar. An operator then provides guidance from a nose-mounted camera until impact. Range of the Switchblade 300 is seven miles (11km), and it has an adjustable blast radius. It can loiter before impact and has a "wave off" feature that can be activated up to two seconds before detonation. A single Switchblade costs $6,000; less than a tenth of a $100,00 Hellfire missile.

Cost is probably the only barrier to wider integration to major militaries. However, it is still cheaper than the Javelin missile, which costs $78,000 per missile and $100,000 for the launcher. US troops fielding Switchblades and similar UCAVs in the near future is well within the realm of possibility.

Another troubling possibility is the use by enemy forces or terrorists. There is no technological barrier to another sufficiently advanced adversary building loitering munitions. China or Russia could build and deploy them on the battlefield. Homemade "suicide" drones could be employed by terrorists or partisans to attack targets they would have been hard-pressed to attack before. Electrical systems, utility grids, and other critical facilities could be easily sabotaged by drone attack.

Munition drops and flying bombs into targets is bad enough, but as the cost barrier comes down, these weapons will certainly replace the grenade-dropping quadcopters as the infantry assassins from the sky. The level of disruptiveness that these weapons will cause has been likened as "the new IED."[13] As American tactics in the Global War on Terror were shaken and changed by both concealed and suicide bombs, so will military tactics be changed by the flying smart bombs any patrol can carry.

---

[13] Shaan Shaikh in: Ken Dilanian, "Kamikaze drones: A new weapon brings power and peril to the U.S. military," NBC News, Dec. 6, 2021, https://www.nbcnews.com/news/military/kamikaze-drones-new-weapon-brings-power-peril-u-s-military-n1285415

What's the difference between an attack drone, a loitering munition, and a "suicide" drone? While there is no defined terminology as of yet, a "suicide" drone as envisaged here is like a quadcopter with a bomb on it; an airborne IED. When the bomb explodes, the drone is destroyed, unlike an attack drone, which flies off after releasing a warhead. A loitering munition is built off of missile technology, and eventually explodes on-target, but doesn't have to fly straight to the target like a missile. An attack drone could be considered a grenade-dropping drone.

What Northern Ireland can tell us about the threat of airborne IEDs

In Northern Ireland during The Troubles, the hardening of police stations (barracks) against car bombs and snipers resulted in PIRA attack methods changing. Many were modified or constructed over the years to incorporate greater protection. As the barracks were fortified, vertical attacks became necessary to get over the perimeter fencing and walls. Thrown Molotov cocktails and grenades gave way to mortars. In addition to changing the geometry of the attack vector, mortars provided standoff capabilities, allowing greater chance of anonymity and escape for the PIRA team.

Mortars were effective early on because while the barracks may have been protected laterally, their roofs could not be shielded. Fortification measures included reinforcing roofs. As physical hardening was expensive, it was cheaper to empty top floors to absorb blast, shrapnel, and debris without risk to personnel. More cost-effective measures included identification and surveillance of known and likely firing points while bases were equipped with mortar alarms and safety drills.

Highly maneuverable explosive-laden UA can defeat layered protection and target weak points. In the future, a terrorist with a killer drone could use its ability to fly in a non-ballistic trajectory to circumvent these outmoded defenses. Whereas a mortar might be harmlessly deflected by a hardened roof, a "kamikaze" drone may crash right through the glass of an office window and detonate in the offices of an anti-terrorist investigation unit.

Drones offer new attack geometry to defeat unidirectionally oriented defenses. The non-ballistic flightpath, maneuverability, and remote operation of UAS all offer far greater advantages to terrorists and insurgents than a mortar while adding greater precision. For groups who are challenged with obtaining military equipment like a mortar tube and bombs, a drone with a homemade explosive circumvents this disadvantage.

While the PIRA had to source its heavy weaponry internationally, often with the help of illegal arms dealers or foreign intelligence agencies, drone technology eliminates that problem for the modern insurgent. A modicum of chemistry knowledge is needed to create explosives and a hobbyist can modify a COTS airframe to carry out the mission. Though modified consumer-grade UAVs can never supplant military-grade weaponry, the ability and danger is there nonetheless.

Lethal raids aren't the only offerings that would have been a helpful addition to the nationalist terrorists. UAS reconnaissance and surveillance could have gone a long way as they were meticulous planners who learned from their mistakes. Since PIRA couldn't do BDA first-hand, they needed to gather any information by observation from beyond the police lines and by word of mouth. A second drone filming the attack would not only gather valuable propaganda video but also take care of the BDA aspect.

In addition to BDA, human intelligence was critical to terrorist operations. A large network of observers and informers were used to conduct clandestine activities including espionage, counter-surveillance, and attacks. Manpower needs could have been reduced, increasing the level of security with fewer potential leaks. More thorough and remote observation may have helped defeat shadowing by Special Branch investigators.

Though it should go without saying, had the PIRA had UAVs during The Troubles reconnaissance would have been *much* easier and attacks far more deadly.

Mercenary drone teams

UAS has a relatively high cost barrier to entry. Cheap, short range drones of sufficient quality to add to a defensive or insurgent group cost a few hundred dollars to begin with. Large quadcopters like the DJI Phantom cost several thousand dollars with more capable multicopters approaching or exceeding ten thousand dollars. Additional batteries, replacement parts, and communication gear all add to the price tag. A credible UAS force with the ability to attack will not be affordable for most small groups.

Drone teams for hire is a potentiality. A team of enthusiasts could pool their equipment and expertise to serve as a for-hire UAS reconnaissance and attack service. Anyone who could afford their services would have an instant unmanned air force. Ukraine's specialist drone unit, *Aerorozvidka*, began as the collective effort of private citizens before nationalizing under the military.

Individuals with the financial resources might offer their services either for pay or in exchange for joining a group that might offer protection. Such arrangements might appear appealing to those with the need and finances to contract for UAS service, but complications follow.

For-hire drone services may be destabilizing by giving one group an "unfair" advantage over the other. Financial motivation could allow compromise by an adversary into providing intelligence on, or substandard "service" to, their customer. Mercenary UAS may be sponsored by, or under the control of foreign or criminal interests who pursue ends other than that of their erstwhile employer.

Less connection to the community or cause may make hired UAS operators more liable to commit atrocities. A profit motive may drive the video-gamification of war (see below) where attacks are conducted to provide the most compelling footage. Whatever the outcome, any combatants who do not have a direct moral and political stake in any conflict are a liability for escalation and barbarism.

Propaganda

Possibly the first use of small drones in combat by irregular groups was for propaganda purposes. ISIS pioneered the use of drone footage for their supporters and to recruit. As propaganda, drone videos are brutally effective. It combines the macabre with a spectator sport. The YouTube comments section on a random Ukrainian drone attack video is filled with dehumanizing comments about Russian soldiers, calling them "orcs", and other vile statements. Partiality aside, it is as if the people leaving the comments are watching a video game rather than young men actually dying.

Whether or not the attacks are effective, the videos showing successful attacks certainly pander to bloodthirsty audiences. Of course, misses, failures, and shootdown videos are seldom posted, mostly successful and dramatic kills. What gets out to the public is a stream of hapless soldiers being slaughtered. This exaggerates the impression of success.

Street gangs, if they had the financial and technological resources to use weaponized drones, could make hay from even a single successful attack. Drive-by shootings are videoed now. Dropping a grenade on a cluster of rival gang members in an area they believed to be safe would have devastating effects on rival morale. Conversely, just one successful attack in such a novel way would be galvanizing to the attacking side.

Video-gaming footage in which an enemy is killed in an ironic, vicious, or impressive display of skill is very popular.

Such dramatic kills is known as being "pwned," a misspelling of "owned," implying that the other has been utterly dominated. Real killings in combat would have very powerful propaganda effect due to the combination of a friendly triumph, a visually impressive event, and the immersive, high-def, depersonalized view of drone footage.

With this video-gamification of warfare, it is not hard to imagine a decentralized weaponized drone war where lone operators went hunting for targets, cooperating perhaps with other drones to film their ambushes. During the Siege of Sarajevo, "Snipers' Alley" attracted not only partisan snipers, but those that simply wanted to try their hand at killing, even a journalist turned-war tourist.

Drone killings might be done in a combat zone for "fun" rather than any tactical advantage. Even without imagining the worst, a smaller scale effect will certainly develop. Add on a profit motive and it might even be possible that we see mercenaries joining UAS teams to kill for pay. Entrepreneurs may solicit the public to not just have a message written on a munition for a price but paying in order to fly a mission and kill remotely themselves.

Politically, drones have been used by activists as well. In 2019, Greenpeace used a drone to drop a smoke grenade on a nuclear-material storage building in France. Though no harm was done, a similar attack could send a message that a damaging attack using the same vector is possible and unstoppable, thereby harming the adversary's morale. Actual attacks in rear or "safe" areas remove the illusion of safety of behind the lines or high-security areas.

Ch. 4 Lessons From Ukraine

Ukrainians call them "mosquitos." A quadcopter flies slowly high over the treeline watching as Russians soldiers walk slowly through the woods, feeling safe far behind the front line. The drone waits until the men are in a clearing. The pilot gauges the wind and selects his aim point. A servo releases. A grenade or mortar falls. There is a puff of smoke and dust. Russian soldiers now lie dead without knowing they were ever targeted by the near-silent "mosquito."

Military sUAS began its maturation in Ukraine, beginning as ISR platforms in the 2014 conflict and the following war of attrition. By late 2022, drone warfare had been democratized as it entered its adolescent phase. Videos gone viral show how UAVs have turned the impersonal nature of drone warfare from intelligence and limited high-value strikes into a stalking, relentless hunt of individuals by snipers of the air.

Ukraine's specialist drone unit, *Aerorozvidka* was begun by volunteers in 2014 who were civilian UAS enthusiasts. It is now officially integrated with the military and is tasked with development, testing, and designing UAVs. The unit got its start making a propaganda film using a DJI Phantom, perhaps the most popular drone in the world.

DJI is so common on both sides, that on some battlefields, the appearance of any small quadcopter that *may* be engaged in reconnaissance is shot down, without verifying if it is friend or foe. While DJI products, intended for commercial photography, worked well for ISR they left much to be desired in attack roles. Other brand drones too small to carry a payload are used for psychological operations to fake Russians into thinking they are about to be attacked by an armed UAV.

For Ukrainians, the use of drones is a constant learning process that evolves the best tactics, techniques, and procedures (TTP) while spurring on the development of effective UAS. Civilians from all walks of life have participated in the drone war from becoming pilots, building munitions, constructing indigenous UA, to 3D printing parts. It is here where the crude attempts to put small munitions on drones went from experimental to production-prototype stage.

It was innovation that allowed consumer UAVs to become an unconventional attack vector. A COTS accessory intended for more innocent missiles, water balloons, or small packages was used as the warhead release mechanism.[14] Grenades were modified by replacing the standard detonator with an impact-fuse initiated by a nail mounted in Play-Doh shaped to make a nosecone. 3D printed fins and tubular bodies were added for stability.

Over the year-plus course of the war, armaments have been refined. Small drones drop modified frag grenades; the larger copter drones drop modified anti-armor hand grenades, rifle grenades, or RPG warheads. These are as

---

[14] Andrew E. Kramer, "From the Workshop to the War: Creative Use of Drones Lifts Ukraine," *New York Times*, Aug. 10, 2022, https://archive.is/VKMMk#selection-407.0-407.66

capable of killing a tank as Javelin missiles as long as the warhead is able to detonate inside the crew compartment and cause a secondary explosion of the ammunition magazine. Russian tanks utilize an autoloader system which means rounds must be stored in the crew compartment, rather than in a separate protected container in the hull.

Accuracy comes from the drone itself coupled with the low altitude the munitions are dropped from. Aim is experience and a bit of timing to calculate the proper lead of a moving target. Multiple munitions allow the pilot to adjust his aim and drop again in the same sortie without having to return to rearm.

Some Ukrainian UAS units prefer to gather targets and intelligence by day, then return at night to strike. They note that it is "impossible" to see their aircraft at night and the darkness makes much closer approaches possible than in daylight.[15] The low noise profile and the advantage of flying at altitude makes it quite possible for victims to have no advance warning of nighttime attacks, more so if there is any background noise such as traffic, a battle, or idling engines. Claimed successes include halting entire convoys by attacking the lead vehicles, stranding the rest, which were then picked off over several nights.[16]

_____

[15] Specialist Ukrainian drone unit picks off invading Russian forces as they sleep," *The Times* (London), March 18, 2022, https://archive.is/Hzftx

[16] Julian Borger, "The drone operators who halted Russian convoy headed for Kyiv," *The Guardian*, March 28, 2022, https://www.theguardian.com/world/2022/mar/28/the-drone-operators-who-halted-the-russian-armoured-vehicles-heading-for-kyiv

Drone attacks come with little to no warning such as the screech of an incoming artillery shell or the increasing throb of a helicopter's rotor blades. It is frequently said that the Russian troops never knew what hit them, so drone attacks are often mistaken for artillery strikes. The failure, either by carelessness or poor training (perhaps both), to take the UAS threat seriously is markedly evident. Very few, if any precautions such as proper camouflage, air guards, or even aerial awareness (looking up), are practiced.

A masked Ukrainian drone pilot claimed to "train" Russian soldiers[17] to make it easier to drop more lethal thermobaric grenades more accurately and with greater survivability from lower altitudes. He tricks Russians, described as "orcs," to stay in their positions by dropping a fragmentation grenade outside the position. To avoid shrapnel, the soldiers stay in their foxhole, assuming they are doing the correct thing, only to be killed by a grenade better suited to confined spaces.

Given the revelations about the poor training and leadership of Russian troops, combined with conscripted replacements being rushed into combat off the street, the startling lack of caution is quite probably one of inexperience. These soldiers have likely not learned either through indoctrination or experience how to properly camouflage their positions, move while on patrol, and maintain an air guard. Counter-UAS (CUAS) precautions

---

[17] **www.reddit.com/r/CombatFootage/comments/** 11vmpbr/ukrainian_drone_operator_describes_the_proces s_of/

may not even be taught by the Russian Army and if so, the lessons not widespread or applied.

Ignorant, undisciplined troops or civilians will likely react in the same manner, careless to the threat from above and indifferent to its dangers. Even veteran troops may have trouble with the realities of drone warfare, but their experience may give them an instinct to pick up on danger or to better apply learned precautions. Citizen defenders and guerillas with a non-military background will need to have an agile mind to adapt to the drone threat.

Attack video analysis

Note: An article with links to the videos referenced in this section will be available on my website, www.donshift.com, and www.americanpartisan.org. These videos are composites of various recons and strikes by Ukrainian forces against Russian troops.

Video 1[18]

Soldiers are below, not under, cover in a trench/foxhole. They would be out of sight to direct observation from other ground troops and thus below the line of fire. The only way to attack the men, as long as they stayed down, would be indirect fires: grenade launchers, a mortar, or artillery. However, they had zero overhead cover or concealment so the UAV could find them easily and attack directly by

---

[18] https://www.youtube.com/watch?v=_0tyR2oC1wY

dropping a grenade.

Effective overhead camouflage may not have disguised the position, but even with knowing there was a fighting position below, if the pilot was unaware of the presence of soldiers beneath, say camouflage netting, he may not have dropped ordnance. Most UAS passive-countermeasures are about fooling the pilot/sensor operator. One soldier only reacts when he sees the drone release its warhead.

In the second segment, two soldiers are lying prone behind what looks like a small shell crater. They are probably just below the line of fire in a small depression. It's little low spots like this on a battlefield that have provided safety to countless soldiers since the invention of firearms. However, they cannot hide from a drone above.

The UAV in this case has the ability to perform real time overhead reconnaissance to look for hiding soldiers just like this and instantly attack them when located. The benefit of UAS in this situation versus a helicopter is drones are much quieter, practically going unobserved. In this attack the soldiers don't even notice, let alone react, to the presence of the drone.

In the third segment, a line of soldiers are moving behind cover, at least in one direction in what may be a natural gully or eroded and overgrown trench. The approach is a textbook use of a terrain feature to move into position safely. Unfortunately, they are being observed by what appears to be possibly two drones. While an observer at ground level may not see them, the drone sees everything. As some men get into position, they are struck by artillery fire that the drone was spotting for.

Video 2[19]

A drone observes troops moving in mostly-leafless trees in a late-autumn forest. Their uniforms are relatively effective, though they are darker than the ground and do contrast, but their movement makes them readily apparent more than the color clash. Had they been motionless against patches of ground that matched their uniform they likely would have been much harder to spot.

In part two, a soldier is lying on his stomach in a foxhole. A grenade drops a few meters to the side, the shrapnel hitting a comrade who does not appear to be sheltered. The soldier in the foxhole is apparently unharmed by the blast, but he has no protection from above. A second grenade is dropped precisely into his foxhole. Amazingly, he is able to get up and run away, but he and another comrade are offed by a drone that drops a grenade directly on one of the soldiers.

Finally, soldiers lounging are easily visible in their uncamouflaged position and mostly plain green uniforms and kit. Two soldiers in a foxhole are dropped on. Of note is their drab green uniforms clashing with the dark brown soil and the tan leaf litter/winter killed vegetation.

---

[19] https://www.youtube.com/watch?v=j9XWOX0DwWs

Video 3[20]

Soldiers notice the drone and run to hide beneath the trees which are fully leafed enough to offer some obscurity, although the operator can guess their general location. A grenade is dropped, and the blast radius is enough to cover the area where the men are suspected of hiding. A grenade is dropped on what appears to be a dark green poncho or tarp blowing in the wind. Camouflage needs to be effective, not move unnaturally, and blend in with the terrain.

Video 4[21]

Soldiers enter a "bunker" which is really just a section of trench covered over with a layer of soil on top like a bridge. The covered area is about the size of a bedroom. One of the open sides is partially closed with debris or a tarp. A grenade is dropped where the covering is not complete. That side should have been fully enclosed with sandbags or earth.

Next, a grenade is dropped into what appears to be a vertical shaft of an underground bunker. The hole is easily visible as a dark black spot on the edge of a fallow field. As this was taken in November-December, the trees that formerly covered the hole have now lost their leaves. Not far away, more bunker entrances can be seen. These bunkers

---

[20] https://www.youtube.com/watch?v=VWH84-kNiJl
[21] https://www.youtube.com/watch?v=o7Y6ON__mrw

are well-built with sandbagging visible. Dead and denuded tree limbs indicate that there was natural camouflage at one point in time, but no longer.

Video 5[22]

The pilot drops on an open trench, no protection let alone concealment from above. In another scene, we see what appears to be an aboveground position or slightly excavated. It is very conspicuous because of the number of tarps and debris around it. Human sign is everywhere and very obviously contrasts with the surroundings. The non-camouflaged black tarps and tires especially stand out. It looks like a pile of garbage in the middle of a winter orchard.

Lessons

Awareness

Situational awareness is the key to staying alive. "Up" has to be considered a threat direction without the forewarning that an approaching manned aircraft gives. Soldiers *must* get into the habit of constantly looking up and scanning the sky, the same as scanning their sectors at ground level. Incoming drone-delivered munitions offer little to no warning of an attack such as the screech of an incoming artillery shell or the distant report of cannon fire.

---

[22] https://www.youtube.com/watch?v=1wqn4qHHhXQ

In nearly every case, the soldiers move without the slightest hint of awareness that they are being observed. Russian troops exhibited a failure to take the drone threat seriously by neglecting to post air guards, allowing them to be surprised. They have likely not learned either through indoctrination or experience how to properly camouflage their positions, move while on patrol, and maintain an air guard.

Russian soldiers do not appear to be trained to deal with the UAS threat. Discipline and camouflaging seems to be lax to non-existent. CUAS and organized responses do not appear to be something line troops have received any instruction on and no equipment for. Even when they do act intelligently by moving behind cover or in low ground, it is no protection from a UAV with its look-down perspective.

Overhead covered positions

With the UAS menace overhead, static positions of future wars will return to WWI style underground bunkers. The foxholes and bunkers in the videos are well-protected from long-range small arms fire and moderately protected from artillery fire. However, they offer no overhead protection and are poorly camouflaged. There are three factors at work: 1, the position is open to allowing a munition in; 2, the blast protection is inadequate; and 3, the camouflage is inadequate.

Shelters, if discovered, will be subject to recon by fire in the form of precision grenade drops on the openings due to low-cost of the flight and the ordnance. An open excavation allows the grenade to drop right in. Blast-resistant overhead cover is needed for fighting positions and blast deflectors or 90° angles are needed at horizonal entrances. Static positions and excavations need to be well camouflaged against overhead observation.

Open trenches are a thing of the past. They are way too obvious and are easily spotted from the air. Their size makes effective camouflage and blast protection difficult. Fixed fighting positions are equally vulnerable though probably safer than a trench network if the position is small, well concealed, and camouflaged properly.

Vertical openings to the sky are dangerous; horizontal ones to the ground less so, although an explosive detonated just outside the opening can send shrapnel inside. "Bomber" drones are accurate enough, owing mostly to their ability to precisely position themselves, to drop explosives down chimneys. Chimneys must not be open to the sky and if they are, should have some sort of grate to eliminate the possibility of anything being dropped in.

Many soldiers when attacked by a drone use the same self-protection procedures for any explosive attack; they go prone or find cover. This worsens the problem by fixing the target potentially in a point where a grenade blast is magnified, such as a foxhole. By contrast, running seems to have spared more than a few lives. Pilots must chase and re-aim on anyone who runs, so it is easier for them not to follow the runners and instead attack the slow or freezing soldiers.

Camouflage

The main factor in spotting a position seems to be a lack of camouflage. Excavations and human sign (trash, artificial materials) stands out. Shelters need to be dugout for both camouflage (especially in winter) and overhead protection from UCAV-dropped grenades and bombs. Concealment from the aerial perspective appears to be nil.

Airpower in Ukraine also seems to be less than what NATO might bring to bear. Why worry about covering over your fighting position or bunker if the Ukrainian air force has been destroyed? Ten years ago, the Russian soldier might have been fine with this attitude, but not today when drones can get very low and slow to search around in the weeds. HD cameras, low altitude, and deficient camo discipline does not mix.

Vertical camouflage must change to reflect the same attitude as for horizontal camouflage. Positions should not be detectable above an altitude of the treeline (ex. 50 feet/15m). A dark green winter parka might meld with the forest background at several hundred meters over the open sights of an AK-74, but when walking across a brown field of dry grass, a human is a dark, contrasting shape over the lighter backdrop.

Proper camouflage clothing that blends in with the ground from an aerial perspective is needed. Humans think of camouflage in a horizontal sense because that's how we've fought since time immemorial. We want to blend in with the brush, grasses, trees, and rocks as we see them, and humans can't fly. Camouflage from above, that is blending in with the ground as it looks to someone or something looking down, is new.

Winter deciduous forests are practically transparent to drones. Humans and positions can be easily seen through the bare branches. When winter comes and deciduous trees drop their leaves, concealment and camouflage must be adjusted to compensate for the lack of a tree canopy. Winter is a very vulnerable time to overhead attacks by drones for this reason. A shaded, semi-hidden position in July needs to be moved or improved in October.

Lower signature

Signature management is important. Garbage, tire tracks, and the parts of a shelter below the line-of-sight of the enemy across no-man's land might not be visible from ground level, but they sure are from the air. Russians don't seem to clean up their trash well. Litter is highly visible from the air and tends to expand the signature of their perimeter as it is blown or tossed around.

The interior or roofs of shelters are also important. Sure, an enemy a hundred yards away cannot see the walls of your trench or the color and texture of your roof below the parapet, but a drone can. Wattle supporting trench walls shows up well as it contrasts with the earth. A sheet of plywood for a roof is conspicuous in a semi-natural area. If you must use objects like tires in your shelter construction, cover them with dirt or other natural-appearing camouflage. All surfaces need to be camouflaged or at least have neutral contrast to the earth or groundcover beneath them.

Another immediately apparent sign is tracks in a field; large mechanized units will leave a lot of them and in some cases completely tear up grass cover. Tire tracks, tread tracks, and obvious signs of mechanical excavation indicate the presence of men. The age of disturbed ground can be estimated with some accuracy. Machine-made marks in the earth have to be covered with shovels or by marching through it until the highly identifiable vehicular signature is obscured.

Large groups of people in crowds or queues are more visible versus dispersed individuals; do not cluster in the open. Do not stack manmade objects in a natural area where they would be out of place. Convoys and proximity to military vehicles in the open is extremely hazardous as the vehicles are easier to spot. Do not park vehicles near your shelter whenever possible; keep them away at least 100 feet (30m).

Attacks

Grenades dropped on vehicle hoods detonate at head and torso level. Ground level detonations increase shrapnel and blast deflection plus hardened vehicles are less susceptible to ground-level explosions. Armored vehicles must have their hatches closed at all times except when occupied and in such cases, there needs to be an air guard on watch.

Drones can afford to be patient to search out targets. They can loiter, orbit, and change altitude to get a better look. Helicopters even in a slow hover don't have the same degree of advantage. Drones' characteristics reward an operator's patience as he hunts, looking for the right angle or telltale that reveals a hidden soldier.

Motor noise is often buried under environmental or battle noise or the UAV is flown too high to hear. Attacks at night are essentially undetectable. The lack of awareness and detectability is actively exploited by armed drone pilots.

Ch. 5 Communications

All the drones this book focuses on communicate via terrestrial radio waves. They do not use satellites but transmit directly between the controller and the aircraft. The pilot's remote controller sends commands to the drone, such as flight inputs or camera movements, and the drone sends back information such as its location, altitude, and battery level along with a video stream.

Most COTS drones use radio frequencies in the same ranges as Wi-Fi or Bluetooth to communicate (microwave). In addition, some drones also have the ability to communicate using cellular networks. This allows the drone to transmit data over long distances, but these should not be expected to be available, or even secure, in war, a civil unrest, or domestic conflict.

Frequencies

COTS drones most commonly utilize UHF (Ultra High Frequency) and SHF (Super High Frequency) between 900 MHz and 5.9 GHz. The most popular consumer models communicate using Wi-Fi protocols in the 2.4 GHz and 5.8 GHz range. While there is no technological requirement that these bands be used, the clustering in these bands is to take advantage of unlicensed frequencies for consumer devices (noted as ISM, or Industrial, Scientific, and Medical).

Common unlicensed unmanned aircraft frequencies

26-28 MHz and 72 MHz (Radio Control Radio Service-RCRS)

   433.05 MHz-434.79 MHz (UHF Short-Range Devices-SRDs)

915 MHz (often described as 900 MHz ISM)

1.3 GHz

3.3 GHz

863-870 MHz (European 868 MHz SRDs)

2.4 GHz-2.4835 GHz (2.4 GHz ISM)

5.725 GHz-5.85 GHz (5.8 GHz ISM)

Very early drones and RC vehicles used the 27-69 MHz range set aside by the FCC for consumer radio transmitters. RC drones that do not relay video to the operator commonly use the 900 MHz range. 900 MHz does not offer sufficient bandwidth to reliably transmit HD video. The GHz frequencies can transmit both control signals/telemetry and video.

Modern COTS sUAVs commonly use the higher 2.4-5 GHz frequencies often in a dual-band configuration. For example, for a DJI Phantom 4, the published operating frequency ranges are 2.400-2.483 GHz and 5.725-5.850 GHz. Dual-banding helps to reduce interference or latency and the firmware can automatically select the most reliable frequency. Most COTS drones use the 2.4 and 5.8 GHz ISM bands. The 5 GHz range spans from 5.170 GHz to 5.835 GHz but often is referred to as just 5 GHz or 5.8 as the UAV frequency range is 5.725 GHz to 5.85 GHz.

A higher frequency does *not* equate to a faster signal. All radio waves propagate at approximately the speed of light regardless of frequency. Frequency itself refers to how many times the wave oscillates or cycles. Since this cyclic rate is a fixed value, it becomes the location on the radio spectrum as we know it on the radio dial. The higher the frequency, the larger the bandwidth is for passing data (video) giving better ability to penetrate semi-opaque obstructions like vegetation.

Penetration does not refer to being blind to obstructions. A large building will stop UHF/SHF radio waves from penetrating to the other side, but because the wavelengths at the higher frequencies are physically smaller, they are able to more easily go through any openings than higher frequencies. Think of this as a rat squeezing through a tiny hole. At the superlatively low frequencies, the waves are measured in kilometers and will pass through the Earth itself. A 5 GHz drone signal will merely be small enough to maybe find a way through tree branches, for example.

2.4 GHz	**5 GHz**
A physically larger radio wave	A physically smaller radio wave
Increased	Relatively decreased

range	range
Lower data transmission rate	Higher data transmission rate and less latency
Less directional	More directional
	Less chance of interference in urban areas

A problem with the 2.4/5 GHz frequencies is that so much technology shares these bands. The "Wi-Fi frequencies" can suffer from interference in urban areas where wireless routers are in use. This is alleviated by Frequency Hopping Spread Spectrum (see below), but interference does still occur.

All of the frequencies for COTS drones are line-of-sight (LOS) only and have a typical range of 1-4 miles (1.5-6km) although this is limited by terrain and equipment, not physics. Range can be increased with more powerful transmitters, altitude, and higher gain antennas. In fact, the only limitation on transmission range is terrain and the curvature of the Earth as only a line-of-sight is required if the signal is strong enough. After all, 50 Watts from 12,5000 miles above the Earth is sufficient to send a GPS signal to your phone. However, without modification consumer drones are not optimized for much more than a few miles' range.

Frequency hopping

Frequency Hopping Spread Spectrum (FHSS) is a technique that is used to spread radio signals over a wide frequency range. It helps to ensure reliable and secure communication in (RF) noisy environments including jamming. FHSS, in addition to being used by UAS, is commonly used in wireless systems such as Bluetooth, Wi-Fi, and military radio systems.

In FHSS, the carrier signal hops or changes its frequency according to a predetermined pattern. The main advantage of FHSS is its ability to resist interference and jamming. Since the transmission frequency changes constantly, it is difficult to jam the communication without precisely tracking the frequency hops or knowing the pattern.

Before we can understand how FHSS works, we must understand what a carrier signal is. A carrier signal is a powerful radio wave that is modulated to transmit information more efficiently. By itself, it does not carry information, such as voice or data traffic, but is superimposed with information (modulation) that *does* contain information. On an AM radio, this would be the center of the radio station's frequency.

The carrier wave is generated at a specific frequency that is selected by the transmitter within a predetermined range. The communication channel is divided into several sub-channels, each with a unique frequency range. The transmitter generates a pseudo-random sequence, which is also known as the hopping sequence. The sequence is determined by an algorithm or code that is known to both the transmitter and the receiver.

A drone's communication system includes an FHSS

transmitter that generates a carrier signal at a specific frequency. The transmitter uses the hopping sequence, known to both the drone and the controller, to switch the carrier frequency. The carrier frequency is changed according to the hopping sequence, hopping from one sub-channel to another in its pseudo-random manner.

The pilot's controller is synchronized to the sequence. It hops its frequency to match the drone's carrier signal and receives the data signal, which is then demodulated to extract information such as the drone's location, altitude, and video feed.

By using FHSS, the UAS can resist interference from other devices operating on the same frequency band. Because of the nature of the typical drone frequencies, unintentional interference can occur without using FHSS. It also provides a secure and reliable communication link between the drone and the remote controller, which is essential for security and to mitigate the risk of intentional jamming.

FHSS is resistant to jamming because the in-use frequency constantly changes. Several factors enable resistance and frustrate the attacker. Since the frequency of the carrier signal is constantly changing, it becomes difficult for an attacker to jam or intercept the signal. In terms of electronic warfare, FHSS basically creates a moving target.

The spread spectrum technique spreads the signal in such a way that it appears as noise to an attacker trying to jam or intercept the signal. The technique makes it difficult for an attacker to distinguish the signal from background noise. It is possible to distinguish it, but the jamming operator must have the skills to recognize the signal on a RF spectrum analyzer.

As both the transmitter and the receiver are synched, an attacker must know the sequence and be synchronized with it to intercept or jam the signal. With COTS products, this may be known or deduced from analyzing other models, so the best security comes from an independently developed sequence algorithm.

Though FHSS is not encryption, it can also be combined with encryption techniques to provide an additional layer of security. The data is encrypted before being transmitted over the airwaves, making it difficult for anyone intercepting to understand or decode the information even if they manage to find the signal.

Although FHSS is resistant to jamming or interception, it is not entirely immune. A major weak spot in UAS, especially COTS drones, is that the frequency ranges are known. Combined with the above weakness that the sequences can be deduced; commercial products are weaker than the technology allows for. Techniques to jam FHSS are:

- **Wideband Jamming:** This involves transmitting a high-power signal over a wide frequency band. This makes it difficult for the receiver to detect the hopping signal, as the noise signal is present in all frequency bands. It works best in situations where the precise frequencies are not known.
- **Partial-band Jamming:** This involves transmitting a high-power signal on a specific frequency band, which is used by the transmitter. This causes interference with the signal and makes it difficult for the receiver to detect and decode the

signal. In this situation, the general frequency range *is* known, such as with COTS drones.

- **Follow-the-Hopper Jamming:** This is using a receiver to detect the hopping sequence used by the transmitter. A low tech version would be listening to a scanner as an adversary changes channels on his radio, then listening for his voice again on a new channel. The jammer then uses this information to jam the next frequency in the hopping sequence, making it difficult for the receiver to detect the signal.
- **De-synchronization:** If the jammer can cause the FHSS transmitter and receiver to become unsynchronized, it can disrupt the communication link. This can be achieved by transmitting a strong signal on the carrier frequency or by interfering with the timing signals used by the FHSS transmitter and receiver.

The latter two require the most sophistication from an attacker. Overall, jamming FHSS requires a high level of technical expertise and sophisticated equipment beyond the skillset of most.

Wideband jamming requires the least experience and uses the simplest equipment. Individuals knowledgeable about electronics and radio communications should be sought out to provide EW (electronic warfare) capabilities to a defense team.

GNSS and GPS

Drones use global navigation satellite system (GNSS) technology—most commonly GPS—to determine their position, velocity, and altitude. GNSS is a constellation of satellites that transmit signals to receivers on the ground, which use those signals to calculate the receiver's location. The drone's GPS receiver uses signals from multiple satellites to triangulate its position.

GPS (Global Positioning System) is by far the most common and reliable GNSS. Other worldwide services include the Russian GLONASS and European Space Agency's Galileo. China's BeiDou and similar Indian and Japanese systems are geographically limited to Asia.

GNSS is taken for granted today. Many people cannot navigate outside of their familiar routes without it. It has become integrated into our entire economy and technological systems mainly because it is a highly accurate timing signal. Accurate time is necessary for high-speed worldwide communications and many commercial transactions.

It should be assumed that all drones can provide accurate location data, either by conventional geographic recognition or providing latitude and longitude (GPS). Civilian GPS is accurate to within about 10 feet (3m) which is sufficiently accurate for long-range fires like mortars or artillery. An overflight by a UAV should be considered being targeted for attack.

GNSS denied environments

In a future war, GNSS may be unavailable locally or the satellites could be destroyed, so a GNSS denied environment is possible. Without accurate GNSS location, many drones will not function or will have their ability to safely operate seriously degraded. Loss of the GPS system is probably the greatest threat to sUAS operations at the sub-national military level. Even without destruction, government actions could be problematic for precise navigation.

GPS in particular, but each GNSS constellation has the ability to have its signals degraded to reduce accuracy. In the United States, this function of GPS is called *Selective Availability*. Selective Availability was ended in the United States as of May 2, 2000. It can be reintroduced at any time, including in specific geographic locations, and it would not be surprising to see it reintroduced in the area of a domestic conflict.

An error of approximately 50m (164 feet) laterally and 100m (328 feet) vertically were deliberately introduced in order to prevent precise targeting of weapons by non-allied militaries. Timing errors were programmed in order to create the variation in accuracy. This deviation creates a circular area of uncertainty where the receiver could be anywhere in a given circle, not necessarily in a specific "false" location.

A reintroduction leading to a degradation in accuracy would still make artillery fire a possibility or allow a "suicide" drone to be automatically piloted to the target area where a man-in-the-loop visual guidance system completes the terminal phase of attack. The lack of GPS would inhibit precise autonomous navigation, altitude determination, and features such as auto-land, but not the overall operation, of UAVs. Commercial models may suffer more than homebuilt versions.

While the United States may choose to degrade the

signal, say in the event of a civil war, commercial drones that support GLONASS or Galileo may function fine. Russia would have a vested interest in maintaining accurate GNSS signals over the US in order to prolong or steer a domestic American conflict to its advantage. Both China and Russia may find it within their interest to sell or provide GLONASS receivers or capable drones to supplant GPS reliance entirely, thus negating the US Space Force's efforts.

INS (no GNSS/GPS)

Multipath and loss of signal are the causes of poor accuracy of, or no, GNSS signal in urban areas or high-relief terrain. Multipath errors occur when radios signals reflect off of nearby surfaces, such as buildings, trees, or other obstacles, before reaching the receiver. When the reflected signals arrive at the receiver, they can create interference. With GNSS, this causes the receiver to calculate the wrong position information. This is because the receiver may collect both the original signal as well as the reflected signal, which can result in two or more signals arriving at the receiver with a slight delay.

Loss of signal is easily explained by flying into an area with no clear view of the sky such as a canyon or streets below tall buildings. Hollywood writers may be shocked to learn that GPS does not work underground.

In addition to GNSS, drones may also use other sensors such as accelerometers, gyroscopes, and magnetometers to improve their navigational accuracy and stability. For example, accelerometers help the drone detect changes in velocity, while gyroscopes measure changes in orientation. Magnetometers—basically a compass—can help the drone detect the Earth's magnetic field, by which it determines its heading.

Accelerometers, gyroscopes, and magnetometers are all parts of an IMU (Inertial Measurement Unit). When navigating without the external position information provided by GNSS and relying only on onboard sensors, this is called an inertial navigation system (INS). Not all COTS drones are equipped to operate safely autonomously or solely by these methods. They suffer from a lack of accuracy as the system is basically navigating by dead-reckoning.

INS combines computer calculations and tracking over time of the IMU data to improve accuracy. Smaller and cheaper IMUs are not impossible to reach at a cost-effective level for workshop builds, but there is little need for autonomous flight, so existing tech is focused on being sufficient for auto-landing or RTH. Fully autonomous flight without GNSS is outside the scope of most COTS products but is not technologically impossible.

Line-of-sight

Unless one has a satellite, drones can only be operated in strictly line-of-sight (LOS), meaning that the controller must have a direct, unobstructed path to the UAV and vise versa. Radio waves do not penetrate solid objects like hills and buildings and so LOS is often used to describe direct paths for high-frequency radio bands. Many other natural and artificial obstructions block, degrade, or deflect signals. In varied topography, there will be terrain and objects that get in the way to interrupt communication between pilot and aircraft.

- **BVLOS:** *beyond visual line of sight*; the pilot is unable to see his drone, but radio communications are maintained. Civilian aviation regulations require sUAS remain in eyesight of the pilot at all times.
- **RLOS:** *radio line-of-sight*; <u>direct</u> radio contact, similar to visual line-of-sight, but the UAV may not be seen by the naked eye.
- **BRLOS**: *beyond radio line-of-sight*; drone is out of <u>direct</u> radio range or behind/below an obstruction.
- **BLOS:** *beyond line-of-sight*; this combines being out of visual and direct radio contact. The drone is out of view of the pilot *and* does not have a direct path via radio to the controller, either because it is flying at long-range over the horizon or has descended below something that blocks the view/radio signal. For large, military UAVs that operate over hundreds of miles, this would be *over-the-horizon* or *OTH*.

Drones cannot fly out of radio contact behind terrain or obstructions unless they are capable of autonomous flight. Even then, a pilot will lose his video feed and the ability to control the aircraft in real time. A pilot cannot stand on one side of a city block and fly the drone out of sight behind a row of buildings. As soon as the drone descends below the roofline signal with the controller will be lost.

When the control signal is lost, a drone goes into several autonomous recovery modes including:

- Return to Home (RTH) mode, where it flies to the preprogrammed recovery point or where it took off from.

- It hovers in place until the batteries run out and it crashes, or communication is reestablished.
- It auto-lands right where it is, perhaps using obstacle avoidance to not crash or maybe it lands somewhere it shouldn't.
- The drone attempts to climb in order to reestablish a LOS for communication.

sUAS and the Group 1 aircraft used by small military units, insurgents, and civilians will all require additional components and support to fly BLOS, if at all. The vast majority of sUAS users will need to maintain direct radio and visual contact at all times.

Long-range communication is done via satellite or from ground-based relays on high terrain. US military drones (and those of other similar first-world nations) communicate and are controlled primarily through satellite relays. Smaller nations with large UAVs like Azerbaijan but no native satellites use long-range terrestrial transmissions which limits operation range to a few hundred kilometers.

These Group 3 and up (most commonly Predator and Reaper) drones are controlled remotely from a control center in safe locations, such as Creech AFB in Nevada, using remote uplinks. Telemetry and video is sent back to base and commands are sent to the drone. Such drones are usually capable of being controlled remotely over short-range radio from their in-theater airfield. NLOS flight, such as over hundreds of miles or around the world, is not within the scope of this work.

Flying BVLOS, beyond *visual* line-of-sight means that there is still a direct radio connection, yet for reasons of distance, atmospheric conditions, or obstructions (with the right gear), the drone cannot be visually seen. It must be noted that FAA and other government regulations require that sUAS be flown within eyesight of the pilot at all times. In a conflict environment, the legalities don't matter and BVLOS is technically feasible.

BLOS is possible over terrestrial radio. Range is limited by the radio horizon and the altitude of the transmitter, but the physical limits of radio waves on the radio horizon exceed what sUAS is capable of. Long-range BLOS is enabled by using radio repeaters either in aircraft or mounted on prominent topography or buildings. The higher a transmitter is, the greater distance the signals can reach and the better angle into obstructed terrain it has.

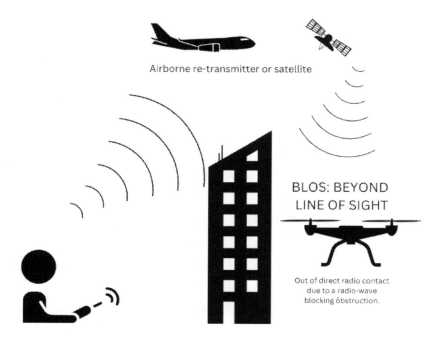

Airborne re-transmitter or satellite

BLOS: BEYOND
LINE OF SIGHT

Out of direct radio contact
due to a radio-wave
blocking obstruction.

For insurgent forces, operation of such a transmitter would be unlikely and would make an excellent high-priority target for enemy destruction. Partisan forces who can defend the terrain around the repeater could make good use of one or a network of them. These would enable long-distance operation of UAVs and possibly down into high-relief terrain or cityscapes.

The flying repeater drone

The Ukrainian *Kvazimachta* ("Quasi-mast") is an unmanned aircraft that only hovers in one spot. Indeed, the Ukrainians don't even consider it a drone, but literally like a flying radio antenna mast. It is a static airborne flying repeater and camera platform, capable of both surveillance and radio retransmission.

It can achieve a 230 foot (70m) altitude which equates to a theoretical horizon of over 18 miles (30km). As it is static, it is vulnerable to CUAS and artillery, though it can be rapidly relocated if necessary and if destroyed, can be replaced much more easily than a fixed tower.

It hovers while dangling a powered tether that allows up to three days' flight before maintenance is needed. If being used for passive camera or RF surveillance, the tether relieves the need for transmission of radio signals, eliminating the possibility of its signals being triangulated (unless it is being used as a repeater). There is no technical reason why it couldn't be used as a flying telemetry/radio repeater for other UAVs.

Something similar could be constructed and even be

maneuverable instead of static. The gimbal camera payload could be removed for a flying repeater (node) to create a high-flying link to allow other UAVs to fly NLOS at low-level. The flying repeater could move to keep up with the advancing low-level UAVs. An electronic warfare (EW) receiver package could be used for ELINT or SIGINT to spy on enemy radio transmissions.

Extended range NLOS drone operation using repeaters and mesh net

Problem: Buildings and terrain block drone telemetry and controller signals so a drone must maintain a radio line-of-sight to their pilot, which limits how they can be operated.

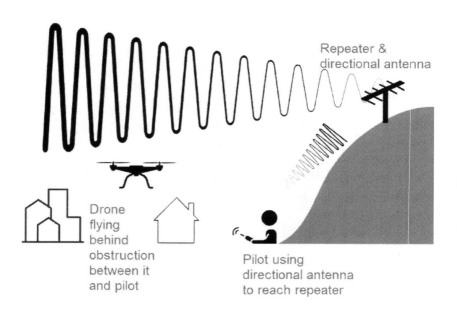

Repeater & directional antenna

Drone flying behind obstruction between it and pilot

Pilot using directional antenna to reach repeater

Small unmanned aerial systems (sUAS) such as consumer-grade drones using off-the-shelf technology are limited to line-of-sight (LOS) operations only. While range can be extended by the use of increased transmitter power, higher gain antennas, and use of frequencies better adapted to particularly urban environments, the laws of physics cannot be overcome. Drones cannot be operated behind terrain features or structures without a direct (radio) LOS to their operator.

This inhibits the ability to operate sUAS at low-levels in narrow terrain or dense, urban settings. Without airborne control nodes or satellite control that major militaries have, civilian defenders in a domestic conflict, first-responders, or small-scale military users cannot exploit the full possibilities of sUAS capabilities as loss of communication occurs before range/endurance is exhausted.

In an urban area, sUAS now have to be flown either no lower than rooftop height or the operator has to get "up" in order for his signal to clear buildings. A SWAT team drone pilot who wants to look into a window on the far side of a building can only see vertically down over the top of the building. He must shift his position, potentially into the line of fire, to the far side if he wants to communicate with the drone as it descends behind the back of the building. Alternatively, a better angle can be obtained by flying at a longer distance and looking obliquely, but this is a compromise.

Changing positions constantly is potentially risky in a combat/hostile situation, delays the delivery of timely intelligence, is cumbersome, and can be exhausting. Accepting less-perfect solutions, such as a bad view into a hostage taker's window, may compromise mission success.

Due to legal restrictions, the ability to integrate with repeaters is constrained. While range can be extended by the use of increased transmitter power, higher gain antennas, and use of frequencies better adapted to urban environments, the laws of physics cannot be overcome. Even where repeaters are possible, a single rebroadcasting transmitter may suffer from dead zones.

Solutions

Legalities aside, a small, lightweight, modular, end-user customizable remote-operable repeaters and mesh nets that can be quickly deployed can end "dark zones" for non-line-of-sight (NLOS) operation.

Properly placed nodes in well-chosen points could create areas of radio reception beyond the LOS of the operator enabling flight in previously radio-blind areas. A tethered UAV could be flown with a node as an airborne repeater as well. These nodes should also be able to communicate together as a network so only one node ("master") requires a direct LOS to the controller. As long as each node in the network can communicate with either another node or this "master" node, much of the network can be deployed NLOS to the controller.

An overwatch UAV at higher altitude, carrying a node as an airborne repeater, visually monitors the low altitude drone while remaining both within the LOS of the "blind" drone and the controller. A squadron of drones could all network together, providing mobile coverage, rather than having simply statically deployed sensors.

A small military unit expecting combat in an urban area could deploy nodes to strategic points to create areas of radio reception. Law enforcement could deploy nodes around the perimeter of a building to enable the pilot to fly completely around a building at low-level from behind cover. Maneuverability would be greatly enhanced in an urban area where drones could be operated out of LOS behind buildings or in narrow "urban canyons." Militaries could operate from behind cover—i.e., behind a hill, over a ridgeline—and search and rescue units could descend into "blind" territory like canyons.

Take for example a military unit assaulting an urban area. Prior to the attack, the unit sends out drones to deposit a master node on a tall building. From there, other nodes are deployed at lower levels in strategic areas across the town out of sight of the UAS operator. A network now exists to where the drone can operate throughout the city below the skyline, behind buildings, and down to street level.

The SWAT operator from the above example could fly from the safety of the command post and descend the drone directly in front of the window for a clear view in; something that currently may require the pilot to place himself in potential danger. Operational visibility could be enhanced beyond the usual "top down" view that a pilot often has. Search and rescue teams could send a drone out over varied terrain from their command post as well. High altitude or confined valleys and defiles could be searched more rapidly and safely than sending a high angle rescue team.

Starlink

Starlink, Elon Musk's SpaceX satellite Internet constellation, was being used for drone control in Ukraine. In February 2023, SpaceX announced that it took undisclosed measures to deny access to its satellites for offensive purposes, including drone control.

The company stated the receivers it sent to the country were intended for citizens to keep connected, not offensive purposes. Russia was accused of attempting to jam Starlink signals to deny its use in Ukraine.[23]

Starlink was used as the satellite uplink for its Group 3 PD-2 drones.[24] The satellite uplink allowed for long-distance telemetry and high-bandwidth video to be transmitted securely over the horizon. These tactical drones are smaller than American Predator and Reaper drones but boast similar ISR and attack capabilities. The PD-2 is capable of

---

[23] James FitzGerald, "Ukraine war: Elon Musk's SpaceX firm bars Kyiv from using Starlink tech for drone control," BBC News, Feb. 9, 2023, https://www.bbc.com/news/world-europe-64579267

[24] Nick Allen and James Titcomb, "Elon Musk's Starlink helping Ukraine to win the drone war," The Telegraph, March 18, 2022. https://archive.is/UCJwH#selection-1315.1-1315.58

flying at 84 MPH (140km/h), has an altitude of nearly 10,000 feet, and up to 10 hours of endurance.

sUAVs (Group 1) are too small to accommodate the necessary 228 square-inch (1500cm^2) dish. Multicopters remain RLOS capable only, though, having a large UAS program could allow for orbiting, fixed-wing relay UAVs to act as flying repeaters in addition to other innovations.

Civilian, insurgent, or partisan satellite control is unlikely in most domestic conflicts. While it is not impossible that a business or government may offer satellite services for insurgent uses, it should not be counted on. As we have seen, SpaceX has decided to limit use of their service for offensive purposes without any overt government action. Even if no official mandate is given, the private sector can deny access to those they deem undesirable as they choose. Behind-the-scenes corporate coercion or cooperation during wartime is not unknown.

Starlink's usage in a war zone is made possible by broad support from the international community. If the shoe were reversed, and Ukraine seen as the pariah by the world community, it is highly doubtful that Starlink would be permitted to remain in business as long as they allowed their technology to be used in warfare. Any such business would be subject to legal and international sanctions making any profitable or benevolent offering non-viable. For example, if Musk attempted to provide Starlink to Russia or a group waging a guerilla war against the US government—however objectively moral the insurgency may be—this would result in charges against Musk and civil forfeiture of his businesses.

This may vary depending on the political nature of warfare. One party who is judged to be politically acceptable by the national or world community may receive exemptions to continue providing their service. Functionally this would be indistinguishable from national-level wartime aid. Regardless of international sanctions, governments or militaries may offer this service to a faction they support openly or clandestinely.

Indirect or direct interference by belligerents is a real possibility. Russia attempted to interfere with Starlink satellites over Ukraine. Jamming of satellite signals or using other means of electronic warfare on the satellites themselves is certainly technically feasible. Beyond that, cyber attacks or even direct kinetic attacks on the satellites or their control facilities are not out of the question in a major war.

Whether or not satellite control is available, it shouldn't be counted on. It surely is not secure, as the company or governmental entity offering the service will almost certainly be compromised to one degree or another. Redundancies also have to be factored in as the communication loop between the drone, satellite, and the operator can be jammed or spoofed. At a much larger scale, anti-satellite warfare cannot be ruled out if China, Russia, or the United States are parties to the conflict. A survival or military strategy should never depend on not being deplatformed.

Part II: Defense

Ch. 6 Drone Defense: Counter-Unmanned Aerial System (CUAS)

Defense

Counter-UAS defense (CUAS) is a form of *area defense* to protect a small geographic area, be it a neighborhood, a camp, or a ground unit's position. The goal is to deny enemy UAS the ability to observe, target, or attack by neutralizing his drones. CUAS is mostly defensive in nature, although it could apply to any proactive attempts to destroy an enemy's UAS capabilities.

There are three layers of counter-UAS defense: *detection*, *passive* defense and *active* countermeasures. CUAS begins with early warning (detection) and progresses to destruction of the air threat. It is more than just blowing up or crashing drones. The intent of CUAS is to deny the enemy the ability to gainfully use his UAS; anything that accomplishes that is a CUAS tactic.

All combat is about what happens on the ground. Society has a tendency to glorify fighter pilots but ignore ground attacks or even logistics where the real battles are won. The "cool" factor of shooting down drones cannot be allowed to overtake the mission of self-defense, most of which will be on the ground. Enemy UAS mitigation will be more about acting smartly rather than drone zappers. Proper survival techniques and operational security are paramount at avoiding compromise from drones. "Drone guns" cannot be the only defense.

CUAS tactics, from purely advisory in nature to active destruction, are:

1. Camouflage, hardening, redundancy, etc.
2. Electronic detection and early warning.
3. Air guard and visual observation.
4. Radio frequency interference with UAS (jamming, spoofing).
5. Destruction of UAS (shootdown or destructive interference).
6. Discouragement of drone warfare.

Note: The solutions discussed in these chapters are intended to address solutions that are practical. Not every possible method is discussed. Due to the wide difference in electronics and ever-changing nature of technology, specific solutions and "how to" will be generalized.

Passive countermeasures

Passive defense starts with *avoidance* which should be self-explanatory; don't be observed by the drone in the first place. If they can see it, they can hit it. If they can hit it, they can probably kill it. The takeaway from videos from Ukraine and the Nagorno-Karabakh wars should be to remain unseen and under (not just behind) cover.

Detection is the second part of avoidance. No longer can combatants take for granted that any attack from above will be pre-announced by the sound of artillery or approaching aircraft. Eyes and electronics must be fixed on the sky. Detection methods which are detailed in their own chapter include:

- Employing air guards (observers on "drone watch" detail); and,
- Creating an early warning (EW) system.

Passive measures are force protection measures that do not involve engagement of the enemy or their UAVs. Passive defense is about avoiding discovery and mitigating the threat if discovered. Mitigation can include both reducing casualties in the event of an attack but making any intelligence or targeting data gathered by a UAV less effective to the enemy commander. In short, don't be detected, limit the adversary's opportunities for detection, and limit what the enemy sees during his observation.

To mitigate the damage that can be done if observed, several kinds of measures can be taken. They include:

- Dispersion
- Deception
- Camouflage
- Hardening
- Redundancy

Dispersion is the spreading out of vehicles, personnel, or positions to limit what can be readily observed. This makes it more difficult to get an accurate estimate of numbers or unit size. An enemy may over or under-estimate the number he is facing or the size of the defended area. Proper spacing is also a part of redundancy—it is more difficult to attack if targets are spread out.

Deception limits what information is given by observation or misleads the adversary as to strength, equipment, and intentions. Obscuring identity, numbers, behaviors, and capabilities can limit what intelligence can be gathered. This would include covering or removing license plates, creating fake positions, disguising weapons, etc. Deception operations such as feints or misleading movements are included along with decoys (equipment, positions) and signal emitters/emulators (spurious radio signals).

A decoy is something that one wants to be seen, or, if it is seen, draws the enemy away from, or to a different conclusion, from whatever is being protected. This could be a unit moving clumsily and obviously in a opposite direction from the covert unit or creating poorly hidden fighting positions when the real ones are better concealed. A key component in deception is showing something that the enemy wants to see and that he expects to see without it looking too obviously staged.

Camouflage is intended to prevent detection in the first place through concealment. Camouflage includes hiding, blending, and disguising. Hiding is concealment from observation. Blending is looking like part of the natural background and most often what we think of when we think of camouflage. If this fails, camouflage then is a mitigation technique to disguise personnel, weapons, and equipment. Disguising, or decoying, is fooling the enemy's eyes or sensors into seeing something other than what they are seeing to conceal identity, purpose, or abilities.

Hiding can be as simple as freezing and ducking when a drone is observed. Good practices are to minimize the time spent potentially exposed and lower signatures (dust, light, noise) to make detection more difficult.

Hardening is making facilities and fighting positions more resistant to attack. One of the biggest lessons from Ukraine is the lack of overhead cover. Not only can the hapless troops not hide from the grenades falling from drones, but they have no protection to run to. Ducking in a trench or foxhole makes sense if artillery shells are bursting around you because, in theory, the shrapnel can't reach the bottom. Not so with a drone that can drop a grenade into a pickle barrel.

Outside shelters should be dug into the ground, where possible. This will also economize on sandbags or other containers. The spoil should be used to reinforce the roof or any gap between the roof and the ground used for firing. The roof needs to be stout enough to support several feet of earth or sandbags. Camouflage the shelter.

To be effective, overhead cover has to be able to withstand the warhead impacting directly. This means both enough earth or rock above and support for the weight of the overburden and to not collapse when there is an explosion. Hardened roofs can be gotten around by a canny UAV pilot.

Bombing just outside a shelter is a common tactic in Ukraine as there is often nothing to shield the interior. The position has to be constructed in such a way that a munition detonated at the entrance can't penetrate into the shelter area. This will require covered entrances with at least one, if not two, 90° turns to deflect the shock wave and shrapnel. 45-90° turns in trenches are more important than ever.

Outdoor shelters should have a camouflaged grid or screen to "catch" or detonate warheads above the shelter. Similar screens can be placed around the sides as well. The intent is that any explosion occurs several feet away from the actual sheltering surface instead of against it—the screen will not stop any shockwave or shrapnel. Such screens can be made of dense metal grids, dense fencing, or failing that, metal frames reinforced with stout wire lattices. All screens must have openings smaller than 40mm and should be easily replaceable after a blast.

Indoor shelters should be beneath a stout table or purpose-built reinforced structure nearest the center of the building on a ground floor. This structure should have a layer of sandbags on top to stop any shrapnel. The shelter frame should be strong enough to support a portion of the building structure in case of a collapse. This shelter should have sandbag sidewalls to protect from lateral attacks or concurrent gunfire.

Many prisons now have nets or cables to keep out drones that attempt to deliver contraband. These are not blast protection. Such an idea is possible for small spaces, but not feasible to protect a home. Floridians can put a cage around their pool, but no one is caging a house. As described above, small screens can protect small defensive fortifications, but not large areas.

Redundancy is the ability to recover from an attack or a forced change in plans. Spacing, such as five meters apart on patrol so one burst/grenade can't take out multiple men, is one method. Having plenty of men who can replace casualties is a start for any fighting unit or neighborhood defensive team. Extra equipment to replace what might be lost, for example after a "suicide" drone attack on a fuel tank, will help ameliorate any incurred damage. Never have all your eggs in one basket.

Dynamic passive measures also include detection, through observation and electronics. Every defender needs to employ air guards (observers on "drone watch" detail) and create an electronic early warning (EW) system integrated into communication (radio) networks to disseminate the information to all potentially affected parties, not just leadership or the "warrior" cadre.

EMCON

EMCON, or emissions control, usually refers to limiting radio transmissions to avoid interception and triangulation. It can also cover emitting any kind of electromagnetic energy, including light, and sound. Radio transmissions should be limited to only that which is necessary, sent at the lowest power possible, and using a directional antenna, preferably transmitted a good distance away from the main body of any unit.

Light discipline, including not using lights in darkness but also eliminating "shine" or sun reflection from faces, glass, or equipment needs to be considered. It must be remembered that many drones, even consumer grade ones, have infrared cameras so IR illuminators and lasers must be as tightly controlled as white light. This includes blackout style headlights, face paint, covering windows of parked vehicles, using mud or other obscurants to dull shiny materials or easily recognizable equipment like sandbags, etc.

Detection

Vigilance and dissemination gives one the earliest warning of a drone so it can be passed on to everyone else. As the saying goes, "knowing is half the battle" a proper defense can't be had without detection, otherwise you're running hoping you can sprint outside of a grenade's lethal radius in three seconds instead of being in a shelter to begin with. Action must follow detection; detection is of limited utility if nothing is done when a warning system acquires a hostile or unknown UAV.

Even if shooting down drones is not desired or necessary a detection capability *is* a necessity. An observer (someone looking up, equipped with binoculars and other optics) is the basic method. The ground cannot be the main focus (i.e., an enemy's route of advance and approaching traffic, etc.). "Up" is as dangerous as the perfect ambush site.

Where possible, integrate technology (electronic detectors) with human observers. These work in parallel with each other to compliment hi-tech and no-tech. Observers both visually detect aircraft and confirm drone signal interception. The network members are responsible for passing on reports between members and friendly forces.

Detection doesn't have to be entirely electronic or guys lying on their backs looking at the clouds. Probable launch/recovery points (LRPs) or ideal control locations can be identified through applying terrain analysis, map reading, and aerial/satellite imagery review. Anyone attempting to identify these zones should be familiar with the basics of UAS operation and launch/recovery.

Few private consumer turnkey solutions exist for electronic drone detection. Products like Hack RF One with various firmware packages can do the job but these will require some familiarity with radios and electronics. True easy-to-use solutions are very expensive and rarely sold to anyone other than government/military users. Electronic detection can be done by the knowledgeable amateur with a proper antenna, a software defined radio (SDR), and radio spectrum analysis software.

Note: Observation (air guards) and electronic detection are detailed in separate chapters.

Active countermeasures

Most people will see a video of a drone being knocked down by a thrown bottle or some redneck with a shotgun taking a hovering quadcopter out of the sky and assume CUAS is that easy. In a combat environment, drones will rarely be low, slow, and dumb targets for such lucky means to work. The drone shootdown videos that many will have seen are mostly either demonstrations or involve some sort of neighborhood dispute, not evasive or high flight.

These "kills" aren't challenging, they're lucky shots. Drones are most often shot down while hovering; being stationary makes the shot easier. The pilot may also be distracted by his camera picture and never see the shooter.

The Army Short Range Air Defense (SHORAD) manual cautions "UASs are small and elusive. They usually fly low. Altitude can vary. Once in the target area, they may fly an orbit attempting to stay out of engagement range..."[25] A smart pilot will keep his UAV moving and evade to keep from being taken out by a lucky shot.

Drone technology has advanced so quickly that what were essentially small, unmanned aircraft that could be shot down using conventional anti-aircraft artillery or missiles just ten years ago have become a fraction of that size, often smaller than the missiles themselves. Quadcopters have very small radar cross sections (RCS) and virtually no infrared (heat) signature, making it very difficult for missiles to lock on to them. Battery powered Group 1 drones are basically invulnerable to man-portable SAMs like the Stinger.

The larger the drone, the easier it is to kill using conventional anti-aircraft means (machine guns/cannons/missiles). The smaller it is, the harder it is to kill because of the size and the lack of anything to home in on for conventional missiles. Using bullets, cannon shells, and shot are difficult propositions as well because of the size, speed, altitude, and maneuverability of a drone. Even a world-class skeet shooter could be stymied by a maneuvering drone.

Active air-defense against drones—CUAS —is kin to

---

[25] FM 3-01.44 Short Range Air Defense (SHORAD), p. C-3

Short Range Air Defense (SHORAD), which encompasses air-defense against drones but mainly manned aircraft. Active defense is a hostile act that damages, destroys, or nullifies UAV capabilities. Active air defense can be further defined as attempting to shoot down or electronically force a drone to crash.

Two methods exist: kinetic and non-kinetic. Using electronic means to interfere with the operation, flight, or data transmission of a drone is non-kinetic. Non-kinetic involves jamming the GNSS/command signals or "hacking" the signals to provide false inputs, either to cause the aircraft to crash or behave in a manner unintended by the operator.

In urban environments, the kind of countermeasures used in more sparsely populated or more permissive environments are less likely to be used due to the potential for collateral damage. Stray bullets and damaged drones falling over a city can kill innocent people. Jamming can affect ordinary civilian communications.

Kinetic countermeasures include shooting down the drone via lasers or a projectile, using a killer drone to collide with the enemy drone, or using a net or something to ensnare the aircraft. An extension of this is attacking the pilot.

Any dedicated CUAS weapon or device has to be relatively unobtrusive, so the pilot doesn't see it and avoid it. Deterrence value is fine, but one may want to hide it and kill the drone sometimes. It has to be quick to deploy and able to rapidly acquire and engage the target. Reloads, if any, should be rapid. Desirable CUAS weapon characteristics are:

- Unobtrusive to avoid a pilot taking evasive maneuvers during the immediate preparations to engage.
- Capable of being concealed or looks like something else (i.e., a jammer that could just be a radio).
- Is portable and easily aimed/traversed to track maneuvering targets.
- Has a range of at least 100 yards/meters.
- Must not rely on a stationary or "compliant" flightpath but can engage high speed, maneuvering targets.

Once a drone is observed, it needs to be immediately reported to all affected parties (friendly personnel, command units, civilians). It should be assumed hostile until proven otherwise. Once confirmed hostile, shootdown attempts can begin.

A hostile drone that has just been launched or in the process of launch should be targeted ASAP before it is able to gain altitude and begin maneuvering. Launching crews and operators should be a priority for attack. Attacks might include area weapons and indirect fire on the launching area or more precision attacks (sniper) on the pilot. Once downed, the wrecked drone should be captured for intelligence exploitation, or an ambush can be setup to wait for the enemy's recovery attempt.

Drone air-to-air combat

Shooting down a drone with a gun is not going to work against a pilot who is anticipating anti-drone fire, actively evades, flies smartly, and keeps the drone out of range. This means that the fight will need to be taken to the offending drone. Anti-drone air superiority will become a thing. Some options for air-to-air CUAS are:

- Crashing any UAV into the adversary's drone.
- Using small, cheap micro-UAVs as a sacrificial interceptor.
- Using RC jets as interceptors.
- Using model rockets as missiles.

Aerial use of jammers is problematic because of the high likelihood that the offensive jammer will also affect the intercepting drone instead of only its intended victim.

Aircraft were first used in military applications for reconnaissance, then bombing. Naturally, the countermeasure was to develop fighter planes that specialized in shooting down aircraft. While fighter vs. fighter combat has captured the imagination and hearts of fighter pilots all over the world, the actual job of air superiority is to deny the airspace to the enemy. If fighter jets are waiting to shoot down his bombers and transport planes, he can't use his air force to support his ground troops or bomb the enemy.

Net dropping drones have also been demonstrated but the question of feasibility and how realistic a successful snaring might be is questionable. Armed drones dropping grenades on the target UAV would need a proximity fuse on their munitions which would fall unguided and be easily evaded by the target. A gun-armed drone would need a FPV camera to serve as the gunsight and while dogfighting. Though gun kills have accounted for the majority of aircraft shootdowns to date, the concept appears to be untested with UAS.

Though it would be expensive to have a lot of remote control planes and drones, it is possible to use drones against drones. Note however that one would have to fly their remote control aircraft physically into the drone to knock it out of the sky. For a small UAV, this will be a suicide mission resulting the loss of the airframe in all probability.

A light and cheap drone that can climb to a decent altitude and fly fast would probably be the ideal interceptor. Practice can be done with easily repairable drones. An experienced drone pilot may be able to accomplish a mid-air collision without much rehearsal. The kinetic impact should be all that is required to crash most consumer quadcopter types.

RC aircraft are ideal interceptors due to their speed, maneuverability, and most importantly their level of control. Larger jets may be more durable and resilient to collisions which could allow skin-to-skin kills to be survivable for the interceptor. In WWII, isolated aerial ramming attacks occurred over Germany and Japan. Aircraft designs like the Lippisch P13 and the Northrop XP-79 were intended to ram aircraft, using strengthened wings to slice through fuselages.

RC planes (piston engines and propellors) may be cheaper than RC jets but will have a slower speed, meaning greater interception times and less velocity on impact. RC jet flight time is short, up to 10 minutes for most models, but their greater speed equals less flight time to target and more velocity, thus a higher probability of kill, on impact.

The greater speed of jets may conversely make maneuverability more difficult against a slow moving target such as a quadcopter.

Missiles

Informed supposition from conflict journals indicate that Ukrainian drones (of unknown size) that have been shot down by Russia often exhibit major damage. Burn marks and the extent of the damage indicate an old-fashioned shoot down by a missile or AAA. Based on the fact that these were hit by missiles would tend to indicate these were probably Group 3-4 large UAVs. On the other hand, Russian drone wreckage was found relatively intact, indicating they were disabled with more advanced electronic means.

While large, Group 3-4 size drones can be easily shot down by fighter aircraft or surface-to-air missiles, domestic adversaries will likely lack both. Consumer-grade drones are small enough that their size and lack of a heat or significant radar signature negates the use of missiles to target them. An F-15 or Stinger missile simply can't be used to shoot down a DJI Phantom.

Due to the low radar and thermal signature of UAVs, missiles are a no-go for COTS type sUAS. Sourcing or building missiles is unlikely, though unguided or minimally guided rockets are a possibility. Model rockets could be adapted for kinetic kills (no warhead) though guidance is a problem for the above reasons and the cost/complexity of building a sensor.

Early surface-to-air missiles (SAMs) used command

guidance with the operator tracking flares or the smoke trail. Accuracy was not that great and without a lead-computing sight it will be hard to control a rocket against such a small target as a drone. A small nose-mounted camera, similar to an FPV drone, could be used to guide the missile into the target by a human. The lack of a warhead and proximity fuse will require a contact kill.

DIY anti-UAV missiles might start with a model rocket body, perhaps using G-O class solid fuel motors, and a seeker or camera for guidance. Using a maneuverable rocket kit, creating adjustable fins or thrust vectoring, the rocket could then become a guided missile as it steers into the target. This could be put into a tube for transportation and weather protection. Deployment would consist of opening the tube up, locking the seeker on the target, and igniting the motor.

Anti-radiation missiles are typically used against SAM radars, but any sufficiently strong radio signal could, in theory, be used to guide a missile in. These passive seekers home in on the drone's telemetry and video signal. A radiation homing seeker could interface with a small computer that would also control either a thrust vectoring device or control surfaces to maneuver the missile.

A similar model could be constructed for ground-to-ground use. A rocket-missile adapted to a more ballistic trajectory and probably larger (and thus heavier) with a small warhead could be used to target static jammers or drone pilots. Technological barriers to be overcome would include a miniaturized warhead, powerful enough to inflict damage but light enough to fly, and the guidance system.

Alternatively, this could be a laser guided missile. The missileman would simply use an optic to aim an infrared laser at the drone, which an optical seeker in the nose of the missile would track. All the operator would have to do is keep their sight centered on the drone until the missile impacted. Again, the laser tracking and guidance system would be a technological barrier.

What is a success?

A shootdown kill is not the only way to succeed at CUAS. The goal of air defense, or CUAS, is to delay, disrupt, destroy, or influence the enemy's activity or his course of action. Break his UAVs, make his job harder, or discourage him until he quits sending drones. Successful CUAS defense:

1. Forces the pilot to increase altitude or take evasive maneuvers and leave the target;
2. Causes a mission abort;
3. Captures the drone;
4. Physically damages the drone, resulting an abort; or,
5. Damages the drone and causes it to crash.

What is a "mission abort?" A mission abort is when a pilot chooses to discontinue his mission and land the drone because of damage, to avoid harm, because of electronic interference, the element of surprise is lost, or other enemy actions make it unlikely the mission will succeed. Anything that accomplishes this is a success, although the desired outcome (destroying the drone to prevent it from flying again) is a lesser degree of success.

Damaging or destroying the drone is ideal. Not only is the platform lost, but for small units or groups, even individuals, the loss of a drone is expensive and something that is not easily replaced. Hence, pilots will be eager to spare their aircraft when possible. Drones are full of sensitive components. Their composite bodies and rotors don't stand up well to being shot at. Damage does not have to be total. A destroyed gimbal camera makes the UAV unsuitable for ISR.

Discouraging drone warfare

Direct assault, when tactically feasible and prudent, can also target the operator and launch crews. Neutralizing trained drone operators and capturing/destroying their equipment hinders the enemy's ability to use drones in the future. Launching crews and operators should be a priority for attack. Attacks might include areas weapons and indirect fire on the launching area or more precision attacks (sniper) on the pilot.

Patrolling, or better yet controlling, terrain where a pilot may be located denies easy vantage points. This includes hilltops, ridgelines, promontories, and other high terrain. Tall buildings or ones with good sightlines may also prove to be good locations for UAV pilots. When unable to occupy or patrol them, keep them under visual and electronic surveillance. Remember that UAS itself can be used to augment, but not replace, human foot patrols.

Dealing with the pilot

As manned air superiority missions entail shooting down the enemy fighters first, UAS denial must focus on eliminating or at least severely curtailing the ability to operate UAVs. The easiest way to do this is to target the operators as training takes time and eliminating experienced men are a more finite resource than equipment. A dead or captured pilot can't be built from parts on the shelf or ordered online. Ostensibly, a modern military would place a priority on capturing UAS teams and interning them as POWs. In more realistic terms for domestic conflicts or those between parties not subject to, or abiding by, the Geneva Convention this would be killing UAS crews.

Snipers may be an analogue to UAV attacks. Snipers characteristically strike from ambush "out of the blue" with no warning or indication of their presence, using fieldcraft to remain hidden, their enemy unaware of their presence, until shots ring out. A sniper will use tactics to draw more soldiers into the kill zone or trap them there. Many war films have highlighted and dramatized the work of snipers and their effect on morale so extensive examination is unnecessary.

Quadcopters in Ukraine are already becoming terrifying killers that strike with little warning (similar to IEDs, mines, and booby-traps). Drone attacks have the same hallmarks of surprise, high difficulty in counter-attacking, negating the effect of cover, concealment, and movement. The psychological effect of drones on morale in relation to snipers/IEDs cannot be understated and this effect is likely to grow as drone warfare proliferates.

After being proverbially decimated by a sniper or trap, troops have often acted poorly in contravention with traditional honor and good discipline, resulting in war crimes. Summary execution of a captured enemy (the sniper) is in violation of the laws of war and contravenes most militaries' ethics, but it can be found in every conflict by every belligerent. The US Army has this to say on the subject:

"Historically, units that suffered heavy and continual casualties from urban sniper fire and were frustrated by their inability to strike back effectively often have become enraged. Such units may overreact and violate the laws of land warfare concerning the treatment of captured snipers. This tendency is magnified if the unit has been under the intense stress of urban combat for an extended time. It is vital that commanders and leaders at all levels understand the law of land warfare and also understand the psychological pressures of urban warfare. It requires strong leadership and great moral strength to prevent soldiers from releasing their anger and frustration on captured snipers or civilians suspected of sniping at them."[26]

The Army goes on to discuss adherence to ethics

---

[26] FM 3-06.11 Combined Arms Operations in Urban Terrain, p. 6-5

and the laws of warfare in the treatment of snipers. It goes on to admonish:

> "Under the law, it is forbidden to kill, wound, or harm an enemy who, having laid down his arms or having no means of defense, has surrendered. A sniper who has been captured, or who has surrendered, must not be harmed. It does not matter how many friendly casualties he has caused or how long he waits before he surrenders...Under no circumstances should a captured person be mistreated or killed in retaliation for sniping, regardless of how many casualties he may have caused."[27]

Ideally, we would like to live in a world where honor supersedes emotion, and any captured enemy can be treated well. We do not and neither do we live in a world where technological CUAS solutions are going to be widely available.

Some soldiers will become emotionally invested in the operators and pursue them out of revenge. Examples of excess include:

- Disproportionate uses of force to kill operators in combat (i.e., indiscriminate artillery fire).
- Summary execution.
- Torture and mayhem.
- Beatings.
- Retaliation against family members.

---

[27] Ibid.

- Enduring public humiliation and ridicule (the stocks).
- Mutilating the dead.
- Gibbeting dead bodies with placards indicating a UAS affiliation.
- Killing civilians drone owners without evidence of any use in battle (UAS *franc-tiréurs*).

Excesses will occur and it must be unequivocally stated that in addition to being war crimes, these acts are moral outrages that violate time-honored traditions of honor.

Nevertheless, they will occur and the prospect of being subjected to dishonorable horrors may limit and dissuade future use of these weapons or restrict their role. The sheer viciousness may be calculated by commanders to serve a broader strategic purpose than an outlet for their troops' combat stress.

The sad reality is that much of a CUAS strategy will focus on deterring UAS crews and drone pilots at the individual level. This means killing them or terrorizing them when captured in order to demoralize other UAS teams, discourage replacements, or make the prospect of being caught as one too horrifying to take the role. Teams will need to be made a priority to kill or capture in any battle due to the force multiplication they can provide to their side.

The noble side in a war that does not take excesses with its UAS prisoners may find its own UAS crews that are taken captive will be subjected to various atrocities. The level of professionalism, discipline, education, and fatigue experienced by the enemy will all play into treatment. An unprofessional, brutal force of cartel or gang fighters who have been ripped to shreds by UCAVs may have no restraint when it comes to killing their tormentors.

More appropriate methods of dealing with UAS crews specifically involve targeting them using ordinary combat methods. These include:

- Making them a priority for capture.
- Prioritizing fire and maneuver missions to kill the crewmen.
- Employing snipers against UAS control positions.
- Using artillery or recharge/rearming support sites against UAS control or LRPs.
- Booby-trapping known LRPs or unprotected drone storage.
- Using psychological warfare operations such as publicly disseminating photos and identities of known UAS crewmen.

These methods still neutralize or demoralize the crews but remain within what is considered acceptable in modern western warfare. The end goal of all of this is to discourage the use of UAS, especially armed UAS, in warfare.

State level

For the average terrorist, it is impossible to shootdown a US military Class 3-5 drone. Predator and Reaper drones are effectively immune except while on the ground or perhaps on takeoff/landing from forward airbases (depending on the weaponry the enemy has). These aircraft are operated on takeoff/landing from local control vans and while on-mission remotely from stateside bases like Creech AFB.

Attacking the operators is the only feasible way for most unsophisticated forces to attack these drones while engaged in flight. While it would be within the means of a group like the Taliban to use rockets, mortars, a ground assault, or suicide bombers to attack a forward base, this is highly improbable in CONUS. However, the concept of attacking the operators remains valid in the United States.

Using Creech AFB, a half-hour north of the outskirts of the Las Vegas suburbs, as an example, terror tactics against drone operators and support personnel could do tremendous psychological damage. A direct attack against the base would be largely fruitless; while a sniper or suicide bomber *might* kill personnel entering the base, any attack on the base would be unlikely to succeed. Off-base terrorist tactics would be more successful.

Intelligence operations could identify drone pilots and sensor operations for later assassinations. The families of said personnel could be targeted while their servicemember is on-duty. Military personnel in uniform off-base could be attacked. Gathering places where large numbers of servicemen from the base in question could be bombed. All of these kinds of attacks would be demoralizing and require an increase in security. While it may not materially degrade offensive drone operations, it is an unconventional counter-offensive. Though it goes beyond the scope of this work, should the US become embroiled in a hot war with a foreign nation, this kind of asymmetrical attack may be executed by foreign agents.

Infrastructure

UAS can be hampered by destruction of the infrastructure necessary to support it. The mainly electric drones cannot be recharged if the power grid is down. Solar panels, wind turbines, and generators would be high priority targets to disable electric sUAS. For combustion or jet engined UA, fuel transporters or fuel tanks would need to be struck.

Replacement parts or resupply can be intercepted or captured. Dual-use technologies like 3D printers that can make airframes, rotors, weapon release mechanisms, etc. could be embargoed, destroyed, prohibited, etc. Depending on the level of control one side might have, precursor components like certain electronics and circuit boards might be interdicted. The reader may recall the period in the mid-2000s when garage door openers were, an item of interest being sent to Iraqi insurgents to construct IED remote detonators.

Embargoes

In a large-scale domestic conflict where third-party nation states and even NGOs are involved in supplying factions they support, traditional means of cutting off outside supply chains will be difficult. 3D printing and similar technology and smuggling of dual-use components makes interdiction of drones and parts problematic even for state customs officials.

Indigenously developed UAS will be increasingly common because in a small-scale or domestic conflict, parties may not have the support of the world community or the ability to purchase defense-contractor airframes and loitering munitions. What is needed will probably have to be adapted or built locally.

In the case of ISIS using COTS drones and technology, the primary solution was to stem the flow of commercial UAVs and associated parts to the conflict zone. With the world largely aligned against ISIS, this was not something that was all that politically hard to accomplish. Governments essentially created an embargo of drones to the ISIS-held areas of Syria and Iraq, additionally working with companies to implement various other solutions to prevent abuse of their aircraft.

Intelligence agencies have long supplied weaponry to guerillas. Providing drones and components clandestinely would be novel only because of the involvement of UAVs. State-sanctioned supply in defiance of international efforts has occurred by Iran to the Houthi rebels in Yemen and to Russian in the 2022 Ukraine conflict.

Traditional smuggling is always another possibility. Smugglers or cut-outs could obtain the aircraft or components for importation to the conflict zone. This may or may not be funded or encouraged by the above outside elements having interest in the conflict continuing or escalating. Vast amounts of effort by law enforcement and intelligence agencies went in to tracing ISIS, Al Qaida, and insurgent forces' access to not only drones, but explosives and bomb making components throughout the war on terror.

In a world where global order has broken down, international cooperation will be scant. The kind of supply chain disruption by police and intelligence agencies across borders that we saw against Middle Eastern terrorists will be a thing of bygones. Nations who do crack down on export of UAV systems to conflict zones may only do so superficially or with the other hand be undermining them clandestinely.

Homebuilt UAVs will largely negate any embargo. One drone in Yemen was built out of sticks that supported the control board and the flight motors. 3D printing enables the easy creation of fuselages, frames, propellers, and many other components. Electric motors and wiring can be sourced legally for wholly legitimate purposes that can't be interdicted, which are then diverted to UAV construction.

Probably the most difficult parts to source would be the computers and circuit boards themselves as they can't be home built. However, components can always be scrounged and repurposed if a builder is creative and innovative enough. Most likely, small microcomputers (Raspberry PI is the most famous) would be obtained through sub rosa means or even openly and then diverted for reprogramming and integration. As proponents of 3D printed guns say, "You can't stop the signal."

Ch. 7 Electronic Drone Defense (CUAS)

Electronic warfare

Electronic warfare (EW) is about control of the radio portion of the electro-magnetic spectrum, most commonly spoken of in the form of electronic attack (EA). This often includes jamming, to deny the enemy use of radars and radios, and deception to control the information he receives. Deception includes sending misleading signals in the open to spoofing electronic signatures that provide false data to an enemy's sensors.

Electronic CUAS begins with early warning (detection) and progresses on to destruction of the air threat. Electronic detection can extend the range that drone activity can be detected beyond the local visual horizon which may be obstructed by vegetation or buildings, which allows for greater reaction time. An electronic CUAS system scores a success through:

- Causing a mission abort;
- Physically damaging or destroying the UAV through jamming/spoofing;
- Rendering the drone ineffective (jam, forced landing/RTH); or
- Hijacking and capturing the drone.

The tools necessary for electronic CUAS, including detection:

1. Antenna optimized for the target frequencies (ex. 2.4/5 GHz UHF/SHF)
2. Software defined radio (SDR)

3. Spectrum analyzer or software, preferably part of the above SDR
4. Jammers (GPS and control signals)
5. Spoofers (GPS and control signals)

At the small unit/individual level, many news stories in the past years have showcased various electronic devices, often called "anti-drone guns" intended to disable hostile or threatening sUAS. These man-portable devices have been used in the Middle East against ISIS and other forces as well as in Ukraine. Allegedly, Ukrainian forces have downed hundreds of drones using US-provided CUAS systems by GPS-signal jamming or microwaving the UAVs' electronics. It's unknown what exactly has been provided but these devices could vary from drone guns to vehicle mounted EW systems.

It must be noted that man-portable units are not suitable for use against higher flying drones but are almost totally for use against Group 1 COTS drones. Regardless, the principals of jamming, spoofing, and hacking remain viable against all levels of threats. The defender's technological sophistication and intelligence on enemy UAS is the limiting factor.

A properly constructed device with directional antennas can have greater range than most civilian-available firearms and better accuracy than all but the best shooters. It should be noted that criminals sporadically do use communication jammers (cell phones, usually) to hamper the ability of victims to call for help. This is common in South Africa. EW and a UAS jammer could be an addition to future sophisticated criminals' MO.

Note: This chapter does not cover specifics or every possible way of detecting or interfering with a drone. The subject is far too broad to go into exhaustive detail. Additionally, the variation in individual electronics and the constant changes in technology, as well as the availability of certain programs, code, and components makes it impossible to provide accurate instructions on "how to do X" that will hold up over the life of this book. Individuals without the skills to figure it out on their own won't be helped by a book and those who *do* have those skills won't need a book.

Jammers and spoofers

Arguably the most effective way of stopping a drone is by interfering with its communication abilities, including jamming the operator's command link or GPS signals locally. Jamming is an interruption of the legitimate signal by a more powerful spurious signal. Whereas a legitimate signal often includes information (data/voice), a jamming signal is electronic noise. Due to the higher power from the jammer, the receiver cannot distinguish the real signal from the spurious one. The most basic form of jamming is keying a microphone on a radio at the same time as someone else is transmitting.

Wideband jamming is the most common form of jamming. The airwaves are blasted across all frequencies believed to be in use with such powerful radio waves that they overpower the control/telemetry signals. The receivers of the aircraft and base station cannot distinguish each other's signals from the high spurious noise threshold of the jamming unit. Generally, one needs 30% more power delivered from the jammer than is being sent by the legitimate transceiver.

Wideband jamming can be achieved using various methods, including the use of high-power transmitters and noise generators. It can be effective against a wide range of communication systems, including those used by drones, as it disrupts multiple frequency bands simultaneously (electronic collateral damage).

Narrowband jamming involves transmitting a signal over a limited frequency range, targeting only the frequency band of the desired signal and blocking or interfering with the communication on that band. Unlike wideband jamming, narrowband jamming is more precise and can be used to target specific frequencies or signals without affecting others. Narrowband jamming would be used when the target frequency or range is known and wideband used when the frequency is unknown, and the possible range is very large.

An RF (radiofrequency) jammer requires a power source to generate the RF signal. An oscillator is a component that generates the RF signal at the desired frequency. An amplifier increases the power of the RF signal to a level sufficient to disrupt the target signal *at the receiver* (jam the receiver, not the transmitter). Additional components include control circuits, antennas, and a cooling system to prevent overheating and ensure reliable operation as the components can generate a lot of heat.

Power is dictated by the size of the transmitter and power supply in the jamming unit. An antenna of sufficient gain is necessary to make the most efficient use of the wattage being pumped out. A 20 watt desktop VHF/UHF wideband jammer advertises a 200 meter range with a 100 watt version up to a kilometer. Commercial models advertise ranges of approximately a quarter-mile to half a mile (500-1500m).

Jammers are line-of-sight devices and need to be able to directly "see" the UAV. Like with legitimate radio signals, terrain, buildings, and vegetation obstructions will inhibit the jamming signal. Drones can be jammed using radiofrequency (RF) "rifles" that send a directional radio beam at the drone. Omnidirectional radial antennas can provide area protection from drones as well.

Jammers may be difficult to purchase due to shipping restrictions and price. Some devices capable of drone or GPS jamming are available out of the box and do not require extensive technical expertise but may suffer from low signal strength and poor antennas. One such product is the Hack RF One with additional aftermarket antennas and software. Homemade models can be built if one has the technical expertise.

A weakness of jammer/spoofer systems is that like any emitted RF energy, they can be detected and localized. Once an emitter has been triangulated, it can be struck by anti-radiation homing weapons or attacked conventionally.

A counter-jamming system in common military use is frequency hopping. Upon detection of jamming (or in non-malicious contexts, interference) an unjammed frequency can be automatically selected and switched to.

In UAS, jamming overwhelms the drone's receivers either overriding the pilot's control signal, the video feed, or depriving the drone from receiving GPS signals, hopefully, causing it to become unstable and crash. Failing that, a loss of contact with the controller will cause many types of drones to return to their launch point, however, this generally requires the ability to receive a valid GPS signal. A loss of GPS may also cause the drone to lose orientation and crash, however, if the control signal remains unjammed the operator may just fly it away.

A jammer will have one or more of the following effects on a drone:

1. Loss of its control signal and hovers until the signal is re-established;
2. Loss of its control signal and auto-lands in its current location;
3. Loss of its control signal and RTH;
4. It becomes unstable and crashes; or,
5. A runaway occurs (flies off uncontrolled in a random direction).

There are two kinds of jamming applicable to UAS: GPS disruption and control/telemetry signal disruption. One can deny the UAV a valid GPS signal or the control signal (and data/video feed from the drone) can be disrupted. GPS jamming creates a signal on the GPS frequencies that is much more powerful than the real frequency, preventing the receiver from getting its location data. A control jamming signal overwhelms and superimposes itself over the control signal so legitimate commands are indecipherable. It is best to jam both GPS and control/video signals for maximum effect.

Jamming Pro: non-destructive, potentially highly directional (less collateral damage), longer range than shotgun shells.

Jamming Con: can cause interference with other devices or friendly UAVs, crashes could cause collateral damage, jamming gives away the location of the jamming transmitter.

Commonly used drone control frequencies are 900-915 MHz, 2.4 GHz and 5.8 GHz. Most COTS hobby drones use 2.4 GHz for video transmission and 5.8 GHz for control signals/telemetry. These two bands are unlicensed, have high bandwidth, and channel spacing; all advantages that are shared with other popular services in the same band as Wi-Fi. Bandwidth is 80 MHz for 2.4 GHz and 20 MHz for 5.8 GHz. Spread-spectrum frequency-hopping is common.

As many COTS drones communicate via Wi-Fi, a Wi-Fi jammer would probably disrupt control many, but not all, modes of commonly owned UAVs. Inadvertently this occurs by installing a high-gain antenna intended for a 5 GHz signal on a 2.4 GHz router which overpowers other nearby wireless routers. The signal isn't getting any more powerful, it's that the antenna more efficiently radiates what power is available.

Wi-Fi is not the only band range that drones communicate on. One typical commercial jammer covers six bands utilizing 50-100W transmitters to target the most common frequency ranges and GNSS, including:

- 433 MHz
- 868-928 MHz
- 2.4 GHz Wi-Fi
- L1 GNSS 1570-162 MHz (GPS, GLONASS, GALILEO, and BeiDou)
- L2 & L5 GNSS 1160-1290 MHz (GPS, GLONASS, GALILEO, and BeiDou)
- 5 GHz Wi-Fi

This is a static unit that operates out of two small-cooler sized Pelican-type cases and radiates using six (one per band) approximately half-meter long antennas. The unit advertises a nominal maximum range of 5 miles (8km). A smaller man-portable unit advertises 10W transmitters and a 1,968ft (600m) range.

Jamming devices must be used in concert with signal detection and triangulation methods. If the target transmitter (controller/UAV) is not visible, electronics are necessary to locate the drone and the pilot as directional antennas require the jamming operator to know where to aim. Otherwise, only omnidirectional wide-area jamming can be used for non-visible threats.

There are two types of jammers that can be used: *omnidirectional* and *directional* jammers. Omni devices are often used in static positions for no-fly zones (i.e., the White House). Defenders could use these to create a bubble of protective jamming

143

around their perimeter or it could be mobile, moving with a convoy or ground team. Omnidirectional jammers can be left off an only switched on at the approach of a hostile UAV.

Directional jammers are almost always a component of a "drone gun" and transmit the jamming signal in a concentrated pattern. This can increase range, the effective received signal strength, and is far more precise than a circular omnidirectional pattern. Directional antennas also lower the risk for unintended collateral jamming.

What antenna should be used? Omni antennas are ideal for protecting static locations or when the avenue of approach is unknown. Directional antennas are preferred for "drone gun" jammers, spoofers, and when it is desirable to constrain a jamming pattern. Note that a wide-area omni jammer is more likely to reveal the location of the jammer through radio direction finding than a directional "drone gun."

An RF "drone gun" requires a dedicated operator who may not be able to carry a separate weapon and relies on a line-of-sight to the drone. They are less likely to reveal the EW operator's position or cause unintended jamming.

- Jammers are illegal and can only be purchased on the gray or black markets.
- Electronic "fratricide" and collateral damage to civilians may occur as friendly or civil receivers are inadvertently jammed.

144

- Jammers will not allow the CUAS operator to take control of the drone.
- Jamming will send out a powerful radio signal that can be used to triangulate the CUAS operator or jamming transmitter.

Directional antenna and radiation pattern

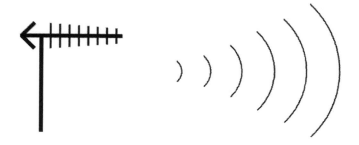

Omnidirectional antennas and radiation pattern

GPS jamming

GPS signal jammingis dangerous and can be counterproductive. Reckless jamming endeavors can affect friendly forces and civilians. Positioning devices, navigation aids, and cell phones can all experience severe disruption from GPS jamming. **FCC and other nations' regulations prohibit GPS jamming** due to its impact on not only businesses but emergency services as well. **Please note that jamming may interfere with critical navigation functions of manned aircraft and watercraft potentially leading to a major loss of life.**

GPS jamming[28] is not effective against a drone that is flying a pre-programmed path and navigating via dead reckoning. It is also not effective against a drone that is under manual control, although loss of the GPS signal can cause certain COTS models to self-abort or otherwise result in early flight termination. Possible effects are:

1. The pilot takes over manual control and flies the drone away.
2. The drone hovers in place.
3. The drone auto lands below wherever it is.
4. A runaway occurs.
5. It becomes unstable and maybe crashes.

Pro: nondestructive, likely to cause a mission abort, easier than GPS spoofing.

Con: active signal can be detected and triangulated, jamming may interfere with critical GPS-based services

Loss of GPS data, <u>absent any other programming</u>, will cause a drone to drift off-course or out of a hover. Inertial

---

[28] This section applies to all forms of GNSS, but GPS will be used for the predominately American audience and as most devices use GPS primarily.

sensors may indicate to the drone that it is moving but it will not know its location or have any precise reckoning of its movement without a good inertial navigation system (INS). A loss of GPS signal may also cause the drone to lose orientation and crash, however, if the control signal remains unjammed the operator may just fly it manually. Manual flying will result in lower precision, greater motor usage, and greater drag, all of which will lower the charge of the batteries faster than assisted flight. It is best to jam both GPS and control/video signals for maximum effect.

GPS frequencies

GPS L1 Band: 1575.42 MHz (civil)

GPS L2 Band: 1227.6 MHz (military)

GPS L5 Band: 1176.45 MHz (civil) transmitted from the satellites at 40-50 watts. Bandwidth is 11-15 MHz. At Earth's surface, the signal is very weak after descending 12,500 miles (20,000 km)—approximately -125dBm. By comparison, a Bluetooth Class 3 signal at 1m range is 0dBm or 1mW.

GPS jamming works by transmitting a noise signal on the GPS frequencies that is more powerful ("louder") than the legitimate signal. The receiver is unable to lock on to the coarse/acquisition (C/A) code. Narrowband signals work better than simple continuous wave (CW) signals. Note that each frequency (both for GPS and other GNSS) will have to be jammed separately, although the military signal is unlikely to be used by civilians or insurgent built airframes.

In a brute force attack, an overwhelming amount of power is used to block the receiver's ability to "see" the satellites. It does not provide false data but makes the receiver become ineffective as all it can receive is a powerful, non-GPS signal. This may display to the user as no satellites overhead or some sort of diagnostic error.

One way of jamming a drone's GPS reception would be to aim a Yagi antenna at it and transmit at an overpowering 10 watts (probably overkill) on those three frequencies. The directional nature of the Yagi would help reduce any unwanted "fratricide" jamming. An omnidirectional antenna could be used for wide-area protection, but this would render GPS useless in the affected area and for some distance beyond the protected zone.

The heart of common DIY GPS jammers consist of a phase-locked loop (PLL) frequency synthesizer chip, a noise generator, a radio frequency (RF) amplifier, a voltage regulator, and an antenna.

Proximity is important as many GPS receivers exhibit better resilience to low-power jamming so the closer, the better. Nearness is generally better than simply increasing the transmitter power. As one report stated, two watts covers "a few meters" and 20 watts would work for "terrorists at an airport." Off-the-shelf models can be purchased that, depending on the source, jam signals for several hundred yards/meters for as low as a few hundred dollars.

Cigarette lighter socket (12v auxiliary power outlet) devices are sold with the intent to block GPS reception of in-vehicle tracking devices. These are commonly used by commercial drivers to disrupt employer, insurance, or government mandated vehicle tracking devices. These devices ostensibly block signals in a 16 foot (5m) radius but due to zero regulatory oversight by the offshore manufacturers the actual radiated power, and the affected area, may be greater (10mW may affect up to a quarter-mile or 400m). One such device being used by a truck driver affected aircraft final approach navigation at a Philadelphia airport.

Spoofing

Spoofing is not jamming, except a spoofer uses a more powerful radio signal than the legitimate one to send the spurious commands, which by nature must overpower (thus jamming) the GPS or command signal. Spoofing is feeding false data to the UAV's receivers to either lead it to a predetermined point, such as a landing site for capture, or cause it to crash. Spoofing may cause one of the following effects:

    1. The pilot takes manual control and flies the drone away.
    2. The drone is deliberately crashed by the spoofer.
    3. The drone is deliberately landed by the spoofer.

Pro: can be non-destructive, allows for capture and exploitation of the drone

Con: active transmissions, can interfere with other GPS-based systems, requires good programming and electronics knowledge to DIY

There are two kinds of spoofing: *GPS spoofing* and *control signal spoofing* (a.k.a. hijacking or commandeering). GPS spoofing presents a false GPS signal, more powerful than the real signal, that convinces the GPS receiver that it is in a different location than it is. This differs from pure jamming because rather than pure noise overpowering the legitimate signal, the receiver is getting what it believes is a real signal.

GPS spoofing can blind an autonomous drone that does not use solely INS. It may cause any drone to self-abort as well. The spoofer is either providing malicious altitude or speed data to cause the drone to crash or false location data to maneuver the drone to wherever the CUAS spoofer wants the drone to go. GPS spoofing will not work if the aircraft does not use GPS or is being operated manually.

Control signal spoofing is hijacking control of the drone by sending malicious commands over its radio frequency. A successful control spoofing signal is indistinguishable from the real signal and the counterfeit transmitter uses higher power to overcome the legitimate commands. Control spoofing will allow the CUAS operator to control the enemy drone to varying degrees.

Control spoofing at the high end, can take command of the drone. At the low end, it may introduce confusing commands that causes the drone to self-abort or enter an unstable flight regime. Even if the actual pilot maintains control but chooses to abort the flight, this can be considered a mission success.

Sophisticated spoofing can literally hijack a drone. The drone can then be ordered to crash or even land for capture. In December of 2011, Iranian forces claimed to have crash-landed a previously top secret American RQ-170 stealth drone by jamming the satellite and landing control signals, then sending spurious GPS signals. Iran may have either made the drone fly into the ground by giving it data that, for instance, made it seem like it was flying higher and faster than it was. Or they may have caused a self-recovery mechanism to kick in and then tricking it to thinking it was landing at its home base.

Practical EW interference "downing"

Jamming and GPS spoofing are the two simplest methods that only require a radio transmitter and a directional antenna. Both methods do not require sophisticated knowledge to spoof GPS signals but uses strong radio signals to overpower the respective signal to force the drone into a failure mode. Black market devices can be bought that will do both and those with the electronics skills can also make them.

A combination of control frequency and GPS jamming is best; a loss of communication with the controller will put the drone in an autonomous mode and a loss of GPS will prevent it from navigating on its own. A blind and uncontrolled drone, depending on the circumstances and programming, may go out of control and crash. Alternatively, it could initiate an auto-land sequence wherever it is and land somewhere out of reach of its operator. Random landing sites are hazardous as it may allow the drone to be captured or lost if it attempts to land in accessible terrain or over water.

Blasting both the known/suspected telemetry frequencies (wideband jamming) and GPS signals will most probably effectively disable any COTS drone. Blinding the operator's video feed, jamming the control signals, and denying the drone its GPS location denies it all but internal navigation. The result of such a multifaceted attack would be either crash or a forced landing.

Anti-drone "disruptor" guns

Anti-drone electronic rifles, also known as "drone guns" or drone disruptors, work by emitting a powerful radio signal that interferes with the drone's radio receiver to either jam it or spoof the control signals. Rather than an omnidirectional antenna like a stationary wide-area jammer, drone guns use a directional antenna that can focus the radio signal in one direction, allowing the operator to target a specific drone or area. One system uses a steel can ("cantenna") as the waveguide for the emitter.

A jammer would involve the antenna assembly, a power supply, a frame for aiming and use, and radio transmitters. To jam most COTS drones, 2.4 GHz and 5 GHz transmitters would be needed. Any range of frequencies could be jammed if the transmitter and antenna are capable of transmitting within that band. Using the same principles, but with the intent to hijack the drone, a spoofing gun can be built as well, but needs a computer connection.

1st Squadron, 3rd Cavalry Regiment, operate the Drone Defender: photo credit US Army

Commercial guns are the most effective but are not legally available for sale to the public. Designs exist online for DIY builders and the knowledge on how to do so from scratch is not illegal. Sourcing the electronics (such as a RaspberryPi minicomputer) would be a logistical challenge in a domestic conflict where such items may be hard to find or embargoed. Coding a program to spoof control signals is the most difficult task.

It's important to note that the use of electronic guns to disrupt or jam drones may be illegal in some areas and can potentially interfere with other electronic devices and communication systems. Intentionally interfering with aircraft or radio signals is illegal.

Drone hijacking

Drone hijacking involves taking control of a UAV by intercepting its communication with its operator and sending fake control signals to the drone. A hijacker can then issue flight commands to the drone causing it to, for instance, crash or land for capture. Two things are needed; an antenna to communicate with the drone and a computer that can send the right signals.

The first step in hijacking a drone is to intercept the communication with its controller. This can be done using a radio frequency (RF) scanner or a software-defined radio (SDR) that can receive and analyze the drone's signal. Spectrum analyzer packages with associated software can do both when connected to a laptop.

For the best result, GPS spoofing is used in conjunction with spoofing the control signals to hijack the drone. This prevents any programming from overriding the hijacker's fake signals and using GPS to navigate the drone back to safety.

However, GPS spoofing is not always necessary to take

control of a drone. In some cases, the hijacker may be able to take control of the drone by simply sending spoofed commands directly. Knowledge of any encryption or command protocols is necessary to correctly fake the commands. This can allow the hijacker to control the drone's flightpath, altitude, and other settings. The hijacker's signal *must* be more powerful at the receiver than the legitimate signal.

DEW

Microwave directed energy weapons (DEW) generate high power radio waves that can overload and potentially damage circuitry by inducing electrical current through wiring and circuit boards. Microwave radiation is particularly dangerous as a weapon because it permanently damages the electronic components, even if the drone is off, and requires the entire electrical system to be hardened.

The microwaves jam communications and may cause some components to fail due to overloading the circuits. Sensors become inoperative or provide spurious data and malfunctioning electronics cause the drone to become erratic. A proper DEW weapon will instantly cause the drone to short out and fall from the sky.

The effectiveness of DEW weapons against a drone depends on several factors, including the range and power of the transmitter, the size and construction of the drone, and the type of material the drone is made of. Some drones are designed to be resistant to DEWs, such as those made of carbon fiber or other advanced low-conductivity materials that can withstand high temperatures.

On the pro side, there is instant stopping power and DEW "guns" can be aimed rather like conventional firearms on drones that are within range and LOS. The cons are they are very difficult to DIY, have a high cost, can cause potential collateral damage to other electronics, use a lot of electricity, and have limited range. It's unlikely all but the most skilled individuals or sophisticated groups will have access to such weapons.

Lasers

"What about a laser? You can blind a security camera with a laser." Forget about it. A security camera is usually fixed and cannot change its field of view to avoid the laser. Most readers probably don't even own an infrared aiming module for their rifle let alone a high-energy laser so let's be realistic here.

The high-energy lasers used against drones, aircraft, or for counter-RAM[29] work by heating up the body of the target until it materially fails, malfunctions, or explodes. It's a thermal kill, not a blinding one. Lasers with the ability to disable or destroy a drone will require a lot more power than can be supplied in a combat zone. Even with professional militaries, laser defenses are cutting edge technology or still in the research and development phase.

Access to powerful enough lasers, and the engineering knowledge, doesn't exist for the vast majority of the

---

[29] Rockets, artillery, and mortars

population. Reliable data is not readily available on what power level laser can cause damage to a drone's airframes or camera system. Amateur experiments have shown that DJI cameras can be shut down, and the video file corrupted, by a high-intensity laser pointer at fairly close range after approximately 10 seconds of dazzling.

Experimentation has shown that a laser pointer aimed at the gimbal camera:

1. Beam ruins the image, causing the pilot to shift the drone/camera position.
2. Visual impairment of the camera feed results in a mission abort.
3. The camera shuts down due to the intense light.
4. The intense light physically damages the camera sensor.
5. The intense light confuses landing/avoidance sensors and causes erratic flight

However, it does not appear from these experiments that the camera was permanently damaged. Infrared sensors may suffer interference from a laser, causing problems for an avoidance/landing system that uses optical IR sensors.

Unfortunately, these laser pointers are unlikely to do any physical damage and can be easily countered by continuous maneuvering. The laser would instantly make the position of the "firer" known to both the drone and anyone in the vicinity. That's worse than useless.

Could a high-power laser *pointer* cause issues for a drone? Probably not unless the drone uses LiDAR. Again, thermal damage is virtually impossible without a high-energy laser. The pilot's eyes will not be harmed by a laser shining on the camera the way it would if done to a manned aircraft. A display screen cannot grow so bright that it will damage the eyes.

A bright light, such as from a laser or a spotlight, could dazzle the camera enough to ruin the image, but this would be temporary. Lasers are highly directional, very narrow beams. All the pilot would have to do is maneuver the camera and drone out of the path of the beam. While a large number of persons or a very large spotlight would make aiming easier, constant unpredictable maneuvers make maintaining aim difficult.

Cheap high-powered handheld lasers make it hard for the camera to work. Perhaps very low quality cameras may fail, which would cause a mission abort and require the drone to be visually flown. Use of lasers to render the cameras ineffective for being unable to see anything but the light is plausible but would at worst result in an abort of the mission.

Protestors in Chile claim that a drone was brought down with the use of lasers. Video footage shows dozens of green lasers, that were also being used to dazzle the pilots of a police helicopter. As the lasers hit the airframe, the drone becomes unstable. It experiences several rapid fluctuations in vertical flight before eventually descending to the ground at a moderate rate.

It appears that the lasers' attribution as the cause of the downing are a case of correlation, not causation, as the video itself is inconclusive. Given the rapid vertical, versus lateral, movements it appears that the lasers *could* have interfered with an IR altitude measurement system. A pilot making evasive maneuvers likely would have evaded laterally and gained far more altitude. It is also possible that an unseen jammer may have been used to cause interference or well-thrown objects may have damaged the aircraft somehow.

Some drones *may* be equipped with LiDAR (Light Detection and Ranging) sensors, which use lasers to measure altitude, avoid objects, or map the drone's surroundings. A powerful laser beam could interfere with the LiDAR sensor's ability to accurately measure distances and could potentially cause the drone to crash. The laser light is essentially blinding the LiDAR sensor so any data the drone relies on from that sensor is invalid. LiDAR also add significant weight and cost to a drone so not all drones are equipped with it.

Countermeasures

Resilience can be improved by several means. The main way of overcoming jamming is to increase the transmitter power beyond that of the jammer, which may not be feasible on the drone itself, but possible for the control station. Other mitigation techniques include putting a terrain feature or structure between the aircraft and the jammer.

Another method for a UAV pilot is to use dual omnidirectional antennas to create a combined reception pattern that creates a zone of attenuated power in the direction of the jammer where the real signal can be received. This method may not work in a high-power brute force jamming scenario. Directional antennas aimed skyward have a better chance at avoiding jamming due to their orientation.

GPS cannot be encrypted or protected although control signals and drone telemetry can be encrypted (technically, not legally, speaking). Integrated inertial sensors, a magnetic compass, and barometric altimeter decrease reliance on GPS for stability and basic navigation but cannot replace precise positioning data. A radio altimeter or laser rangefinder could be used to indicate altitude especially in auto-landing situations.

Ch. 8 Drone Spotting and Air Guards

Seeing and hearing will likely be the main method of drone detection. Even with an electronic early warning network, visual confirmation is required to identify a drone, determine its threat and behavior, and develop critical intelligence. The Army considers visual identification and confirmation as very challenging.[30] The small size of drones, the visual clutter of a landscape or cityscape, and flight behavior all conspire against easy spotting.

Note that many smartphone apps that claim to detect drones no longer work or are of marginal value due to encrypted signals or poor detection range. Electronic detection does not replace visual observers no matter how sophisticated the gear is purported to be.

Organic observation and visual identification:

- Can be done by anyone without specialized equipment;
- Provides early warning without reliance on electronics or RF emissions;
- Is a source of intelligence about enemy operations and UAS capabilities; and,
- Is vital for avoiding aerial attack and mitigating what intelligence the enemy can learn.

Vertical surveillance is the key to UAV detection and survival. Ground-level 360° security isn't enough anymore and electronics are not a panacea; someone needs to be looking up at all times.

In environments where enemy and friendly UAVs are

---

[30] ATP 3-01.81 p. 1-5

active, target identification becomes critical to avoiding fratricide to one's own drones. In a self-defense situation, it becomes safer to shoot down an unidentified drone than wait to confirm its intentions.

How to spot a drone without technology

"Visual scanning" AKA looking is the primary observation method. Generally speaking, if a drone can be seen or heard, it is a Group 1 or 2 drone. The noise of the motors will probably be heard before the drone is sighted, due to their visual inconspicuousness and variable directions of approach.

Begin by assigning a sector of airspace to search. This could be divided up by persons or by an individual. Use fixed landmarks or other reference points to create the sectors.

Scanning 20° from ground level is the optimal height for drone observation at a distance. Obviously, this may not hold true depending on the height of the observer, the distance they are looking at, or the terrain, but for a person on the ground 20° is about the height a drone would be flying. Look at altitudes below 400 feet up to 1000 feet AGL; above these heights a small drone is not likely to be visible.

Scan the sky in a grid pattern. Actively move your head and your eyeballs over a section of the sky, looking left to right, moving up or down when you reach the end of the row. When you finish, reverse the pattern. Be sure to alter your scan pattern as you may have missed something. Take more time for more detailed background like a landscape/cityscape versus scanning the sky.

The FAA's recommend scanning technique is as follows:

"To scan effectively, pilots must look from right to left or left to right. They should begin scanning at the greatest distance an object can be perceived (top) and move inward toward the position of the aircraft (bottom). For each stop, an area approximately 30° wide should be scanned. The duration of each stop is based on the degree of detail that is required, but no stop should last longer than 2 to 3 seconds. When moving from one viewing point to the next, pilots should overlap the previous field of view by 10°."[31]

Though the described technique is intended for pilots, it can be used by observers as well. Once a suspected drone has been located, use binoculars to make more detailed observations. [see Figure 9-2]

A drone at a distance will appear to be a small black object that is either stationary or tends to move in linear directions without banking. Objects that bank and orbit may be helicopters, manned aircraft, or fixed-wing UAVs. Quadcopters don't bank and are frequently moving at right angles.

If at a loss for a location, look for areas of potential interest to a drone. This would include a firefight, a defensive position, an encampment, a convoy, or any

---

[31] *Remote Pilot – Small Unmanned Aircraft Systems Study Guide* (FAA-G-8082-22)

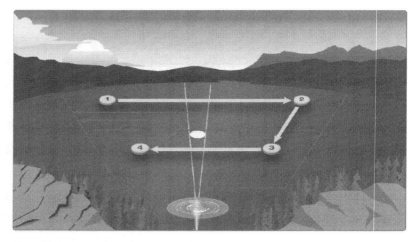

Figure 9-2. *Scanning techniques.*

formation of troops. Important buildings or strategic points should be scanned. The observer should put themselves into the mind of a drone pilot. What kind of activity or location would interest them? If someone else does have eyes on the drone, and you're sure it's the same or only one, have them give a fixed reference point that it is near.

Drone spotting at night

Spotting drones at night will obviously be more difficult because of darkness but also shadows and ground that is often darker than the sky. When available, use a spectrum analyzer and a directional antenna to intercept telemetry from the drone to localize it for visual acquisition. If you don't have any high tech, use your ears or move to where you believe the UAV will appear.

Sound will probably be how a drone is first noticed at

night. Simply turning around to hear the sound better can be a rough directional indicator. Cupping of the ears improves this effect. From there, a wide area sound amplification device such as a parabolic microphone moved in a grid pattern could pinpoint the location. A drone can easily move though, especially if the pilot sees what's going on, frustrating acoustic search efforts.

Acoustic detection devices for drone detection exist. These devices listen for the low frequency sound of drone rotors using an amplified microphone element. The key to the technology is isolating the sound of UAVs in particular from background noise. DIY devices are possible but will require electronics knowledge and creating a program that recognizes only UAVs.

Without the aid of NODs the distance a drone is visible at night will be much lower than during daylight. The nearer the drone is, the easier it will be to see. Get as close to it as you reasonably can. Ensure that your eyes are dark-adapted. This takes about 40 minutes in darkness. Do not use white light and use red light sparingly. Use large objective lens (50mm or greater) binoculars.

When possible, use passive image intensification night vision devices (NODs). If you don't have NODs, spotting will be a lot harder. However, NODs should only be used as an aid to observation. Limited depth perception, image distortion, and restricted field of view through a NOD can make it difficult to accurately judge positions and distances. Thermal imagers with good resolution over distance can be used to spot variations in temperature between an object and the background (sky). Night vision should only be used in combination with natural vision.

Walk towards the sound or suspected location of the drone. Move laterally and shift your viewing height (crouch if necessary) to attempt to shift perspective so the drone is silhouetted against a lighter background like the sky, moon, or a light building. Generally, it will be easier to spot a drone against an illuminated sky (moon or light pollution) or bright cloud cover.

A dark object will normally be lighter than the night sky, hence air forces have found that a dull gray color works better for night camouflage than flat black. In either case, a moving shadow in the sky, stars winking out and reappearing, or something moving against a background of lighter clouds or light pollution might be a drone.

COTS drones come with lights to aid maintaining visual contact and for navigational (avoidance) purposes. Typical aircraft navigational lighting colors are red (left side), green (right side), and white (anti-collision strobe). Not all drones adhere to this standard. FAA regulations require anti-collision lighting visible from up to 3 miles away for night flights.[32].

At night, one may see flashing lights nearby without hearing the sound of an engine. Do not rely on navigation or anti-collision lights, day or night, to spot UAVs. Many models also have status lights. These may be disabled, covered over, or not installed during hostile flights. Military

---

[32] FAR §107.29

drones may not have lighting at all.

At night, against a civilian or unsophisticated adversary, look for any navigation lights in the sky, which will probably be low on the horizon. These will be smaller, dimmer, and more irregular than manned aircraft. A drone will also hover and move irregularly, whereas airplanes will fly straight paths relatively slowly from a ground observer's perspective. Airplanes and helicopters will also probably be audible.

Consider using an infrared light detector. This doesn't have to be night vision but could be a camera with a filter. There are cheap camcorders and digital cameras that are capable of night photography that can be used to scan the sky for any infrared illumination being used by a drone. This may also reveal any IR lasers ground troops are using to designate targets for UAVs. The Taliban used this method to determine if American troops were operating at night.

Some online articles suggest using motion detectors. Traditional IR motion detectors cannot be used as they lack the resolution to distinguish small, distant targets and rely on changes in the thermal infrared (heat) background. Microwave motion detectors generally are intended for indoor use with a security system and are not well adapted to outdoor use. The sky is too large of a target but a purpose-made microwave detector with the range and resolution to be effective outdoors can be built/purchased.

Finding a concealed drone pilot through deduction

Assumptions

- You do not have any signal interception capabilities to triangulate the operator based on his control signals being sent to the drone. If you do, this makes your task easier.
- Group 1 drone, almost certainly a quadcopter.
- The UAV is not capable of BLOS flight (not using a satellite or airborne re-transmitter).
- The UAV is not flying a programmed flightpath autonomously (evident as the drone will hover and maneuver irregularly).

Know the general specifications and abilities of the particular UAV you are facing. The operator must be within a certain distance so he can control his drone. For example, high-end COTS drones have a 2.5-4.5 mile (4-8km) typical range while mid-level models can fly up to a mile and a half (3km). Based on the terrain and obstructions, you may be able to narrow that distance down and further localize the pilot based on the flight pattern.

Remember that quadcopters have a general maximum flight endurance of around 30 minutes so it may be easier to maintain visual contact and wait for the drone to land. This will reveal the launch/recovery point (LRP) if not the pilot himself.

Identify suspected operating positions and draw a circle for the practical range of the particular drone. Then, draw the same circle over your position or the drone's observed position. Prioritize positions that overlap with each other's circles. Most people are predictable and will fly in straight lines in the shortest distance between two points. Draw a line from the drone to the suspected operation location and start looking there.

Quadcopters need to be within line-of-sight, so topographical deductions can be made.

They will not be operating from a depressed area below where the drone is without some LOS to the aircraft. A pilot standing on a valley floor cannot fly up and over a ridge into the next valley as the signal will be lost approximately somewhere over the crest of the ridge.

Watch the flightpath where does it *not* fly, that is watch what terrain or buildings it avoids behind. An LOS drone will not be separated by terrain or structures from its pilot. An example is if a drone flies around the backside of a hill, you can be certain that the pilot is in a position where he can observe both the front and back slopes of the hill, as it appears to you.

If the pilot is using a remote antenna in a higher vantage point and taking cover elsewhere, look for the antenna the same as a pilot. Taking out the remote antenna is almost as good as taking out the operator (who will likely have to move to an exposed place to control the drone).

In areas of thick brush or other concealment, look for an antenna. UHF radio waves don't like impediments like vegetation between them and the receiver as propagation will suffer, so it will be in the UAS crew's best interest to have the antenna in the open. It may be camouflaged and placed remotely but will probably be no more than 30 feet (10m) from the pilot.

An omnidirectional monopole antenna may appear as

an unnatural vertical line in otherwise natural terrain. While antennas are usually black when unpainted, a camouflaged antenna could be other neutral toned colors. A directional antenna will either require a stand of some sort to hold it up (it may be attached to a tree) or a person aiming it.

Should you determine that the drone is being controlled remotely via retransmission, there should be three antennas. The first will be the one that communicates directly with the drone; this may be omnidirectional. The second will almost probably be a directional antenna that points towards the pilot's position and the third (also directional) antenna. Over shorter distances there may be a wire connection and if the wire is visible, follow it.

If you are on a coastline, the pilot may be in a watercraft as his view along the shore will be unobstructed and his line-of-sight extends into bays, inlets, gullies, between buildings, below cliffs, etc.

Altitude matters. The higher a transmitter (the drone controller) is, the further its radio horizon and the more likely the signal will not be affected by terrain or other obstructions. So as a general rule of thumb, if you are high, look down. If you are low, look up.

High vantage points will not simply be the crest of the highest point around nor the tallest building. A smart pilot will not do something obvious but will be on a subsidiary peak or concealed downhill from the crest. Likewise, in a city they will not necessarily be in the tallest building around, nor will they be on the roof or highest floor.

In a large city with tall buildings, like New York City, note the level that a drone will not descend below. This "floor" may indicate that the pilot is somewhere above that level. The exact flight profile will vary based on the cityscape and pilot's vantage point as he may be able to fly lower in urban canyons that run perpendicular to his position, so the LOS is maintained.

In a building, a pilot will likely be looking out a window in the direction of their UAV. A prudent pilot will keep visual contact with his LOS drone in the event of an emergency or for situational awareness. Standard techniques snipers use to stay safe behind windows or similar openings are likely to be used by pilots. Large buildings with intact, reflective windows make it difficult to see someone behind the glass under most conditions and create an ideal place for the pilot to fly from.

Roofs are the logical operating place for drone operations as roofs have a clear view of the surrounding terrain in often all directions, few obstructions to transmission, and an easy place to land/recover from. Depending on the sophistication of the model, your adversary, and the type of drone being used (military, homebuilt, COTS), carefully examine the building for a remote antenna transmitting from an ideal vantage point while the operator is elsewhere.

If a drone is flying through roughly level terrain or a cityscape at very low altitude, the pilot must be close. They will need to keep the drone within LOS of themselves. The best opportunity for estimating the location of the operator is to observe the drone traveling parallel to/above a long open space like a roadway and then check the areas back to the maximum flight range for the model and unobstructed terrain. The pilot may be out in the open walking a ways behind his drone or semi-concealed somewhere along this path. He also may be moving with any enemy troops either using them as protection or supporting them so look for enemy personnel as well.

UAVs are likely to be flown on one side of a large building in order to stay within range of the pilot. The building will otherwise block the antenna signal. Look for the pilot on the side of the building, including corners, where you see the drone. If you see the drone stop, hover for a while for no apparent reason, then begin moving around a corner, assume that the pilot was physically moving the vantage point across the building.

Air guard observers

Note: This role is different from a UAS crew observer. The latter is an assistant to the UAV pilot. The role discussed in this section refers to a sentry for drone threats.

THE AIR THREAT FROM UAS MUST BE TAKEN SERIOUSLY EVEN WHEN NO AIRCRAFT ARE EVIDENT IN THE SKY.

Most UAVs will probably be spotted visually, and given how not all units or organizations will have the resources to use electronic detection devices, an air guard must be maintained. Human senses are as important as radar and spectrum analyzers. Generally speaking, if a drone can be seen or heard, it is a Group 1 or 2 drone. The noise of the motors will probably be heard before the drone is sighted due to their visual inconspicuousness

Everyone is an air guard; some are dedicated to observation. Personnel can rotate air guard duty as long as they have been properly briefed and trained. Unlike UAS crews or operating CUAS electronics, observers do not need to be a special class of combatant or defender. LP/OP members should keep watch for UAS and may dedicate one person at a time to specifically be the air guard. Critical skills for an observer are good eyesight, good concentration, and the ability to read maps.

Training needs to cover:

- Drone types and characteristics.

- General flight profiles and UAS employment in flight and in support of ground operations.
  - Enemy drone inventory and their characteristics.
  - Specifics on expected enemy drone employment.
  - Friendly drone inventory and employment.
  - Passive and active air defense methods.
  - Observation techniques and observer responsibilities.
  - How to pass reports and keep notes.

Observers (air guard) must have optics, such as binoculars (minimum) to NODs, and have radio contact with their unit and/or command center. As an air guard is a 24/7 need, personal and equipment should accommodate both day/nighttime needs.

Equipment

- Briefing data on expected UAS threats.
- Binoculars and NODs.
- Maps of the area.
- A radio.
- Unit list (call signs) with radio frequencies.
- Sound amplification device (optional).

Observers and air guards need to be familiar with the basic characteristics of the class of drones they are likely to encounter, along with the specifics of the most common models in use in there are of operations. This is a more important skill where units are small and do not have an operations center or UAS SME to rely on. Knowing capabilities, specifications, and endurance can allow an observer to make basic predictions about a drone's flightpath or intent and hence its risk. Not being able to gauge the threat would be like being unable to tell which vehicle might hold more armed men, a panel van or a Corvette.

Briefings on expected UAS threats must include information on both friendly and enemy operations. Ground operations are important to know about so the observer can anticipate the threat. The observer is also probably watching more than just for drones as well so he will need to know what is going on. Also having information on what to expect from friendly UAV flights is important to avoid unnecessary alerts and warnings.

Dedicated observers (while on duty) cannot have any other duty besides watching, such as manning a checkpoint. Observers need to be free of distractions so they can keep their eyes on the sky. Observers need to refrain from listening to music, using smartphones, and engaging in any extraneous conversation. Headphones, except for sound-amplifying equipment, should not be used and one ear should be kept free of any radio earpiece.

Purpose

- Be the first line of defense, regardless of technology, to detect a potential drone threat.
- Alert friendly forces and commanders of UAS activity so appropriate tactical or force protection actions can be taken.
- Provide timely and accurate information regarding the location, behavior, and flight of the UAV.
- Identify the UAV if possible.
- Provide verbal direction to CUAS teams to acquire the drone *or* initiate CUAS defense (per local SOP).

175

Responsibilities

- Remain aware and alert at all times, free of distractions.
- Maintain awareness of the airspace and battlespace.
- Identify and report any UAS or other suspicious activity seen in the area in detail, including location, distance, and bearing.
- Issue emergency warnings of any hostile UAS surveillance or attack on friendly forces.
- Upon a sighting and making a report, remain on alert for further air or ground threats.
- Only quit observation duties when properly relieved or weather conditions deteriorate to where UAS operation is improbable, according to unit SOP.
- Does not initiate CUAS attacks unless he has been specifically tasked and trained to do so.

Observers can be slightly segregated into two roles: the *air guard* who watches over a unit and an *area observer* who is deployed to keep general surveillance over a fixed area. *Air guards* are more likely to be a part of paramilitary ground units whereas citizen defenders or property/base security will employ static *area observers* similarly to guards in a watchtower who will look for air and ground threats. Those manning an LP/OP would be in this second category. Though the exact duties will differ for the two roles, the procedures and responsibilities for UAS are the same.

While an air guard should be alert to UAS threats alone, he will need to monitor general activities and the rhythm of the battle, such as unit location. Knowing the general picture of what is happening tactically and where units are is important to differentiate between friend and foe as well as alerting specific units. Task saturation may occur if an air guard is asked to serve as a general sentry or is observing ground activity as well, so if the manpower exists it is desirable to add a second person for non-UAS related observation.

Procedures

Shifts should be limited to avoid mental fatigue, such as two, but not more than four, hours. Status checks should be conducted regularly via radio when EMCON is not a concern. Observers should not be afraid to call in unconfirmed but concerning observations.

A ground-level position will silhouette drones against the sky, making it easier to see them. An elevated position will offer a further view of the surrounding area but will make it harder to distinguish the drones against the background.

Observers need to visually scan the sky and landscape for drones. This involves actively moving one's eyes over their field of view, changing what they are looking at, to better focus on movement. The center of the eye (fovea) has about a 3° field of view so an observer can't just stare stupidly at the horizon waiting for motion to catch his eye.

An observer needs to be looking all around for suspicious movement. Focus should be directed to areas of friendly positions, friendly troop movements, or other activity that might be of interest for drone operations. Scanning should be done in a regular pattern such as a horizontal or vertical grid pattern. Looking up is difficult when wearing a helmet or other hat (cover). Remove any head coverings. A semi-reclined position (without falling asleep) is more comfortable than craning the neck and head.

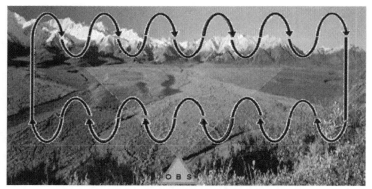

Figure 4-2. Observer (air guard) vertical scan technique

Figure 4-3. Observer (air guard) horizontal scan technique

Contact

Actual or suspected launches of an unknown nature *must* be investigated. An assumed friendly launch must be confirmed if you do not already *know* it is friendly. Once a drone is observed, it needs to be immediately reported to all affected parties (friendly personnel, command units, and civilians). It should be assumed hostile until proven otherwise. Types of contact include: ISR, targeting (for indirect fire or guided weapons), direct attack, friendly, curious civilian.

Civilian observation is quite possible due to the proliferation of drones and the lack of inhibitions regarding filming something "interesting." Wildfire aircraft operations are frequently halted because a careless sightseer launches his drone in an area where helicopters are flying. A lawless situation with intense combat may bring out those looking for something dramatic to film.

While mostly annoying, civilian drone flights should not be taken lightly. Every UAV observation made should be treated as potentially hostile until proven otherwise. An ostensible civilian may be gathering intelligence or propaganda material, or even if they have no real intent other than curiosity, they may pass on intelligence to an adversary intentionally or otherwise. So, while a "neutral" drone might not be automatically shot down, pains should be taken to control any intelligence it could collect.

How do you know it is a civilian drone? A drone that is merely watching unrest or a battle will behave much the way one conducting ISR will. Behavior will not be a final indicator. A civilian drone may be broadcasting its ID, or the pilot may be plainly visible somewhere, not attempting to hide. Contact should be made with the civilian to verify his identity, purpose, and ask him to voluntarily land his drone.

Friendly flights need to be coordinated across units and interested parties. Scheduled flights should be disseminated by leadership across an organization. In-person or radio announcements should be made when a friendly flight is made. This will reduce the likelihood of a blue-on-blue shootdown and may allow others access to UAS support in an emergency if they know one is operational.

Reporting

A general warning of drone activity is not helpful. Specifics about the threat have to be provided so that correct action can be taken to mitigate or eliminate the threat. Detection alone does no good if there is no warning passed along or it does not contain enough information to act upon.

Where the drone is, where it's going, and how fast it's flying allows the flightpath and potential destination to be calculated. Behavioral factors and airframe classification allow assumptions to be made about intent and threat. Even things like speed, altitude, and the flight profile for a simple camera drone can allow for the calculation of endurance and how long the threat may be present. Information allows for action; more information leads to better reactions.

A sensor may indicate the presence of a drone, but without sophisticated signal interception and decryption, only a human observer can provide certain, if not most, particulars of a UAV flight. Technology and eyesight have to work together making observers and air guards a vital component that electronics and gadgets can't replace.

Actual or suspected launches of an unknown nature

must be investigated. An assumed friendly launch must be confirmed if you do not already *know* it is friendly. Remember the **DOA cycle**: Detection > Observation > Attack. From the moment of drone detection, personnel must assume they have been detected, have been under observation for some time, and will be attacked. Timely air guard warnings are of critical importance.

Positioning

Observer positioning depends on your manpower. Yes, everyone is an observer, but the dedicated observation watches or air guards takes someone away from a task or other role. Ideally there are enough observers to scan the entire perimeter. Observers should be within a maximum distance of 500-1500 yards (500m-1.5km) of their units or positions. Visual contact between observers must be maintained at all times. The two forms of positioning for formations are *in-depth* and *linear*.

In-depth (perimeter):
- Generally, refers to full perimeter coverage.
- Ideal for convoys or formations.
- Redundancy in observation.
- Interlocking coverage.
- Needs assigned watch sectors (can coincide with fields of fire).

Linear:
- Suited to a static front line.
- Does not refer to a perimeter watch.

- Maximum observational area towards a threat.
- Should only be used when a threat is expected to come from one direction.

Figure 4-4. Observer positioning in-depth

ATP 3-01.81 1

Figure 4-5. Observer positioning linear

ATP 3-01.81 2

Additionally, observers can be stationed where they might do the most good, such as beyond your lines in a forward OP/LP that covers a blind spot that a command post observer can't see. Observers can go where there are gaps in sensor networks. You may wish to put observers on the four corners of a secured neighborhood perimeter. A single observer should be placed where he has a full view of the protected area and the avenues of approach. As long as the preceding is true, a single observer can be positioned in the center of a unit/area or nearest the most likely threat direction.

Spot report

Observers report **location**, **speed**, **behavior**, **weapon**, **type/class** of UAV, and **make/model** if it can be determined. Any additional information, such as the pilot's location or any enemy forces in proximity, should be passed on as well. Make UAV sighting reports on visual contact, rather than wait until an immediate threat develops to make emergency warnings. Report the sighting in detail, including location, distance, and bearing.

Bearing and distance are important for an air guard in relation to a formation or fixed position, rather than an observer for a wide area. While a general warning with the actual location will benefit multiple persons or units over a large area, an air guard should call out the bearing relative to his unit's position. On the other hand, a guard *not* integrated into a unit will want to provide general references.

An air guard of a ground unit will likely give his bearings as he sees the drone as his orientation will likely be the same as his unit. This is fine because the unit or formation will be close enough the bearing will be the same for all. An area observer informing parties over a wide area will need to give references to a fixed landmark/reference point as different parties will have varying orientations. Over a whole neighborhood, one person's 3 o'clock could be someone else's 5 o'clock.

Location reports should include a reference to known locations such as cross streets in an urban environment or a major terrain feature when possible. Different groups and unit compositions will have different needs. A small unit moving through wooded terrain might use the clock system and refer to easily visible trees or land features. A group of untrained civilians might use streets and refer to buildings. A military unit operating over wide terrain might use grid squares or latitude/longitude.

Examples: Unit observer—"Drone to your three o'clock, high! Area observer—"Drone, 300 yards west of the church steeple!"

Detailed report

- Cover the 5W1H: who, what, when, where, why, and how.
- Include your radio identifier (name, unit, call sign), your location, the drone's location, time (including if the UAV is airborne now or how long ago it was seen), flight speed and direction, its behavior, and any payload.
- Direction of flight (bearing), altitude, speed and location are the most important bits of information to get out.

- When did you see it? Include the actual time you first saw it or an estimate of how long ago you saw it. Also report an estimate of how long it might have been on station or how long you observed it flying to its current position.
- What is it doing? Loitering, orbiting, sector search, looking in a building, waiting to attack, etc. Flight characteristics and operational behavior can indicate the mission/intent of the drone or allow a commander to cross-reference your report with others.
- Provide the class of drone, armed/unarmed, make and model where possible, and a physical description that includes approximate size (wingspan/length), configuration or number of rotors (i.e., a quadcopter), and any identifying marks or distinguishing factors. What kind of payload is carrying; weapons or what kind of sensor/camera?
- How did you observe it? What brought your attention to it?

Line	Information Example	Example
1	Unit call sign and frequency	Red 1, FHXXX
2	Unit location	6 to 8 digit grid coordinate
3	Location of threat UAS	Grid or distance and direction from reporting unit location
4	Time threat UAS asset spotted/detected	DTG: 091024ZMAR16
5	Estimated time on site	Was threat UAS asset approach observed or was it spotted overhead? How long might it have been there?
6	Flight characteristics	Is threat UAS loitering in one spot (possibly already spotted reporting unit), is it flying straight (enroute to loitering location), what is the direction of flight, or is it flying randomly (searching)?
7	Estimated size, elevation, and physical description	Wingspan, height, color, tail configuration, other distinguish markings.
FH frequency hop DTG date, time, group UAS unmanned aircraft system		

Recommended US Army spot report format from ATP 3-01.81 (Figure 4-1).

USMC UAV REDEYE drill

A REDEYE drill is an immediate action drill when it is necessary to avoid *nighttime* IR (thermal) detection. It is applicable in daytime with appropriate modification.

- **Meaning:** UAV sighted, it may have not seen you.
- **Action:** Freeze in place and camouflage using ghillie blanket, poncho, or tarp to reduce the visual/IR thermal signature. If in the open, stop moving, drop and minimize shadow.
- Called by anyone making the sighting.
- **Example call:** "REDEYE, UAV twelve o'clock high behind City Hall!"

Brevity codes can be used locally, or military terminology can be used by citizen defenders. For example, the REDEYE drill above could be used during daylight with less emphasis on IR (thermal) concealment. For those civilian defense groups not using, or minimizing the use of, military terminology some simplified sample spot reports are provided below.

Unarmed drone: "Control, Observer 7. Drone, Main just east of the freeway, loitering in a left-hand orbit at 400 feet. Group 1, DJI Mavic." An observer reporting to a unit would give the bearing in relation to the party to be warned. "Patrol Alpha, it's at your twelve o'clock, high, 100 yards!" More specific information can follow the initial report, such as unique visual characteristics, a pinpoint location ("Behind the pine tree!"), etc.

Armed drone: Any spot report for an armed drone should be prefaced with a warning of weapons or explosives. A full flash spot report of a UCAV may be: "Attack drone! Mills and Main, northbound high speed just west of Mills over the parking lots. Weapon hand grenade.

Group 1, DJI Phantom 4."

Following a spot report, if so empowered, the observer may give orders or recommendations to the affected unit on how to react or survive. Unit commanders should give orders as necessary to react to the drill according to their own SOP, however, individual defenders or combatants should be trained and instructed on how best to react in given situations without further orders.

Summary

- Soldiers and citizen defenders *must* get into the habit of constantly looking up and scanning the sky, the same as scanning their sectors at ground level.
- Visual observation is a primary detection method and is not replaced by electronic detection.
- Where possible, integrate electronic sensors (radio signal detectors) with human observers. These work in parallel with each other to compliment hi-tech and no-tech. Observers both visually detect aircraft and confirm drone signal interception. The network members are responsible for passing on reports between members and friendly forces.
- Everyone is an observer; some are dedicated to observation. Dedicated observers (while on duty) cannot have any other duty besides watching, such as manning a checkpoint. Observers need to be free of distractions so they can keep their eyes on the sky.
- Actual or suspected launches of an unknown nature *must* be investigated. An assumed friendly launch must be confirmed if you do not already *know* it is friendly.
- Once a drone is observed, it needs to be immediately reported to all affected parties (friendly personnel, command units, civilians). It should be assumed hostile until proven otherwise.

- From the moment of drone detection, personnel must assume they have been detected, have been under observation for some time, and will be attacked.
- Reports must include specifics in order for others to locate the drone and contain enough information for interested parties to act on. Direction of flight (bearing), altitude, speed and location are the most important bits of information to get out. Armed drone sightings should take priority.
- After a UAV is spotted, remain on alert for further air or ground threats. The appearance of a drone may be the harbinger of an attack. Always assume if a UAV is sighted that you have been under observation for some time already.

Ch. 9 Kinetic Drone Defense: SHORAD

Net guns

Net guns are attractive options for CUAS due to the ability to crash a drone with misses causing no collateral damage. Besides causing a mission abort, a net might ensnare the drone, causing it to fly erratically, requiring an immediate landing to avoid a crash. In reality they don't work. Flying nets are impractical, obvious, and easy to avoid.

The problem with net guns, besides their complexity to construct, is that they are often very short range and are outclassed by firearms. Net projecting guns with any range are not DIY friendly and all of them will have a slow reload time. They only work against very low and slow flying targets. So, if you want to capture the local pervert's drone peeping in bedrooms, okay, but for a drone above the trees dropping grenades on you, no way.

Small arms CUAS, generally

Small arms fire here will mean long guns. Small drones can be disabled or destroyed by accurate rifle or shotgun fire. In CUAS operations, in 2015 Ukrainian soldiers claimed to have downed multiple Russian drones simply by shooting at them, likely with small arms including AK-series rifles. This is quite possible if a drone is hovering and moving slowly at low altitude and short range.

Hitting a flying or elevated target with a rifle requires

more skill than busting clay pigeons. As difficult as it may seem, drone shootdowns with commonly available firearms are not rare, though the conditions were optimal for the shooter. A distracted pilot who is watching a camera feed of a target rather than maintain defensive situational awareness may be unaware that someone is shooting at their stationary drone.

Machine guns, preferably of .50 caliber, are easily capable of destroying consumer-grade drones with a direct hit. A direct hit is dependent on the skill of the shooter and requires a high volume of fire. Since tracers will likely be required to spot the fall of the bullets, this makes it easier for the drone operator to evade.

Anti-aircraft artillery (AAA) guns typically have a caliber of 20mm or greater and utilize exploding cannon shells equipped with proximity fuses. These fill the air with shrapnel that can damage or destroy the drone without a direct hit. The nearest civilian analogue to this would be massed rifle fire or shotguns firing birdshot, neither of which have proximity fuses.

Shotgun drone shootdowns are not uncommon. Until the 2022 war in Ukraine, shootdowns have largely been on gun ranges, by an annoyed neighbor, or by an angry man who suspected the drone of peeping. Based on the limited information provided, these drones were close to the shooter and not seriously attempting to evade. Drones engaged in combat operations will try to remain as distant and undetected as possible and *should* evade upon initiation of a downing attempt, making a gun-based kill more difficult.

Group 1 and 2 UAVs are designed to be lightweight and thus quite fragile. They can be easily damaged by high velocity projectiles. Any impact may cause the drone to lose orientation and crash, the more violent the impact the better. Shotgun shells may be the best chance at shooting down a drone at low-level and a good skeet or trap shooter should be the one to make the attempt.

Range, altitude, and the drone's speed will all factor into the ability to hit it as much as the ability of the shooter, the gun, and the ammunition used. Wind, temperature, and altitude can affect range as well.

Small-arms fire

Nominal effective (high probability of a damaging hit) small arms range

Round	Velocity	Max height	Effective AA range
5.56	3,200 fps	2,650 ft	1,115 ft
7.62x51	2,756 fps	7,874 ft	1,115 ft

Heavier bullets or shot have more inertia and are therefore less affected by external forces such as air resistance, although they do not necessarily fly higher than lighter bullets or shot. The trajectory of a projectile is influenced by several factors, including its velocity, weight, shape, and aerodynamic properties. The most important factor affecting the trajectory of a projectile is its initial velocity. A faster projectile will typically travel farther and have a flatter trajectory than a slower one. While a heavier projectile may have a more stable trajectory, it does not necessarily mean that it will fly higher.

It is widely known that high-velocity, large bore rifles have ranges in excess of two miles. Early smokeless firearms often had sight gradations to one or two thousand yards and volley sights marked out to 4,000 yards. Though bullets can travel across a horizontal plane out to those distances, the laws of physics only dictate what is possible, not that accuracy at extreme range is probable.

Shooting vertically, the same problems occur. .30 caliber rounds have been known to fly as high as nearly two miles and strike commercial aircraft; this is mainly through chance, but it is possible, nonetheless. While innocent manned aircraft overflying a battle is unlikely, what is far more likely is all the missed shots resulting in bullets falling to earth long distances away. With massed fire, shooters must understand that persons can be in danger at distances *much* further than can be seen. This makes massed fire very hazardous in urban or residential areas. Knowing what lies beyond one's target is vital to avoiding collateral damage.

Dangers of kinetic kills
- Drone is damaged and cannot be repurposed if the wreckage is captured.
- Valuable intelligence may be destroyed.
- Collateral property damage.

- Injury or death to persons either by contact with the falling aircraft itself, parts, or stray shots.
- Legal violations.

Shotguns

Pro: cheap, low-tech, high proliferation

Con: shotguns have limited range/altitude, rifles require high volume of fire or great accuracy, falling projectiles can cause injury or death, gunshots give away the firer's position

Shotguns and individual shooters with the skill to shoot aerial targets by leading it, aiming so the bullet/shot intersects the target. The barrel of the gun will move and track the target. The difference with massed fire is in not leading the target but firing at a stationary point. When a high volume of fire is directed directly against the hovering drone, the aiming point must be *in front* of a moving drone and in its flightpath; it has to fly through the aiming point. In massed fire, the shooters don't track the aircraft the same way they would a duck.

Birdshot: No. 8 shot is reported to be effective, but at an unknown altitude and range.[33] Typical birdshot loads will have a maximum flight distance (not effective range, but how far away the shot will return to Earth) of 300-400 yards. Usually, shot fired upwards should not cause serious injury at this distance when it lands. Magnum shells and specialty loads may have additional capabilities however a balance

---

[33] Cyrus Farivar, "Kentucky man shoots down drone hovering over his backyard," *Ars Technica*, 7/29/2015.

will need to be struck between range/altitude and shot weight (effect on target).

An expert shooter can break clay pigeons at 100 yards, but ordinary range is 60-80 yards. Note that this is against a 4" target, so it may be easier to hit a much larger drone. Larger size shot should ballistically peak at 200 yards (horizontally from the shooter) fired at a 30° angle; this will result in an approximate maximum target altitude of 345 feet.

The longer the barrel of the shotgun, the greater the accuracy at further distances. Fowling barrels of 28-32" long would be ideal. The caveat is that at this length a choke may be needed to open up the pattern as longer barrels tend to tighten down the spread pattern.

Buckshot: Buckshot has a horizontal range of up to around 75 yards. The greater mass may cause more damage to a drone than birdshot. However, when fired vertically, due to the increased weight vs. birdshot, it will not fly as high, although the author has been unable to find any data on buckshot used against aerial targets.

Specialty shells: For example, 12 gauge Skynet Drone Defense ammunition, a three-pack retails for $20-25 as of this writing. The shell contains six weighted tethers in a star shape that is designed to entangle the rotors of the drone, causing it to crash via loss of control and lift. In the event of a miss, the expended projectile will fall safely to earth. Skynet shells in one test were fired at 70 feet (unknown if this is horizontal, diagonal, or vertical distance) and required 3-5 shots for a kill.[34]

These specialty snare shells may be handier than net guns but suffer the same drawbacks. Range is problematic as these are apparently not capable of any great distance or altitude. The drone also needs to either be stationary or flying in a slow, predictable path to have any reasonable chance of contact. Even so, these are likely a better choice than a netgun and could be viable in some circumstances.

Bottom line: The best shotgun defense is probably two or more shooters armed with semi-automatic shotguns firing heavy birdshot/turkey loads from 3" or 3-1/2" 12-gauge magnum shells. Barrel length can very but the longer, the better, and the tubular magazine should be extended to just behind the muzzle, if possible, for greater capacity.

A high volume of fire should be used to bring down the UAV. The shooters should be excellent trap/skeet shots—accuracy is the most important criteria. The shooters should have their shotguns concealed so as not to stand out as an obvious CUAS team until ready to engage. Shotgun specialists will be a high priority for attack.

Shooting falling munitions

"But what about the Russians who shot a falling munition out of the sky?"[35] In the footnoted video, this was a lucky shot, as all such instances are. Multiple muzzle flashes from what appear to be automatic weapons are visible from the trench beneath the UAV before weapon release. The

---

[34] https://www.youtube.com/watch?v=jlGdPrhRvBA
[35]   https://funker530.com/video/rifleman-shoots-drone-munition-out-of-the-sky/

munition was hit after the drone was already being fired upon, indicating that the munition itself was not the target.

Legends from WWI, and possibly other conflicts, claim that shotguns were used to shoot hand grenades thrown by German troops. Barring some lucky shots, this appears to be propaganda. While it is possible, it is difficult and probably not within the skillset of many shooters then or even today. Using nine-pellet buckshot would not spread out as much as birdshot and the patterning is not uniform.[36]

Machine guns

Prior to the advent of guided surface-to-air missiles (SAMs), anti-aircraft artillery was used to shoot down aircraft. Today, due to the higher attack altitudes and the standoff capabilities of modern combat planes bullets and cannon shells have taken a back seat to missiles. It is not easy to hit a very small, quickly moving, and easily maneuverable aerial target using visual estimation alone. A static-mounted machine gun or cannon does not traverse the same way a shotgun can lead a target. Anti-aircraft sights are uncommon on modern machine guns and to be useful require ample training.

Targets as small as mortar rounds can be hit by auto-cannon fire, though this requires radar guided systems like the Centurion C-RAM that use six-barreled 20mm Vulcan cannons. The small size of UAVs and the challenges of

---

[36] A video by Taofledermaus and C&Rsenal show the realities of this kind of shooting. https://www.youtube.com/watch?v=2t_RW1z7pUs

accurate fire from a large-caliber machine gun make employment difficult against smaller drones. A computerized detection, tracking, and traversing mechanism to automate a machine gun or assist the gunner would make this possible, but as of this writing there does not appear to be such a device, nor would small domestic groups be likely to have access to that technology.

Ukrainian forces report using, with unclear success, a .50 caliber DShK heavy machine gun on a vehicle mount with a spotlight for target illumination and identification at night. This may work well against larger drones or slow moving sUAVs (quadcopters) at very close range by trained gunners.

Other firearms

A .177 air rifle pellet took down a drone.[37] A felon shot down a police drone with a .22 rifle.[38] There is nothing that would rule out using an AR-15 or other type of weapon or cartridge over a drone. 5.56mm rounds will fly further, to a higher altitude, and do more damage when they arrive. However, rifle rounds of any caliber will pose a further danger on the ground when they ballistically return. It may also be difficult to spot and track the drone in the air. Also, aiming a rifle accurately at high angles to hit a target like a

---

[37] Haye Kesteloo, "Drone captures shooter before being shot down itself," DroneDJ, 11/20/2017.
[38] US Attorney's Office press release, "Lake County Convicted Felon Indicted For Illegal Firearm Possession And Destruction Of Aircraft," October 13, 2021.

quadcopter will not be in the skillset of most shooters.

Multiple shots of any kind may be required, and the drone may not be hovering, especially after the first hit. Test videos that are available show the drones at relatively low altitude and close distances. The combination of the two make shotgun shootdowns a last-minute thing which can be further complicated by an enemy who is ready to counter shootdown attempts. Also, a successful hit at close distance against an explosive bearing drone may result in death or injury to the shooter.

A skilled individual with a rifle or shotgun firing on a drone that is within range may well be capable of striking the aircraft with a single shot. Those who have the skills to take out a hovering or slow moving drone with a rifle know their ability. This is not necessarily going to be the case with most shooters and rapid, violence of action may dictate that volume fire is most appropriate. A proficient, but not expert, lone shooter would probably want to resort to the volume of fire technique in the case of a moving drone.

Gunfire should not be directed at UAVs above a friendly unit, personnel, or position as projectiles by others or debris may cause injury. Each unit should have the responsibility for downing threats above it so as not to injure others. All persons shooting need to be cognizant of where their shots will fall; most bullets and shot will miss even if the shootdown is successful. Depending on caliber, falling bullets can be lethal up to 1-2 miles and shot can cause injuries at over 100 yards.

Best practices

- When shooting down a drone, attempt to distract the pilot, who may see the shootdown attempt and take evasive action.
- Shootdown attempts should be undertaken at an angle and distance away from the distraction or the focus of the camera observation.
- Be prepared for follow-up shots/misses, multiple drones, evasion, and even returning drones.
- Anti-drone shooters should expect to be targeted by snipers, enemy forces, and even armed drones themselves.
- Ensure that fired bullets or shots that miss are unlikely to impact friendly forces or innocent parties.
- Combine jammers/spoofers to freeze a drone to make hitting it easier.
- Be aware that shootdown attempts will give away your position from the noise of the gunfire, the muzzle flashes, and any tracers.

Massed (volume) rifle fire

The US Army advises that that although small arms have a low probability of killing a UAV, the concentration of a high volume of fire has the potential to unsettle the pilot. Heavy small arms fire may disturb the pilot's concentration and either degrade their flying or targeting, result in evasive maneuvers ("breaking off") or aborting the mission. ATP 3-01.8 suggests massed fire using established small-arms aiming doctrine for manned aircraft is the best tactic for infantry anti-aircraft fire.

"Small arms" in this context refers to rifles, carbines, and machine guns. US Army doctrine assumes the use of the M16/M4 platform, M249, M240, and M2 machine guns. For civilians or irregular forces, this would include any semi-automatic rifle above 5.56mm in caliber. Pistols and .22LR rifles are suboptimal for volume fire as the former has too little range and the latter's bullet has too little effect on target.

Volume small arms fire suffers in lethality as the size of the projectile often is insufficient to cause damage to a manned aircraft that is frequently traveling at high speed and maneuvering aggressively. UAVs will be moving at comparatively much lower speeds (30 MPH/48 km/h) than an aircraft, but the small size makes them a harder target to hit. Maneuverability is another issue as drones don't have the same g-force limitations as a human pilot and it is much easier for them to change direction rapidly.

When shooting birds or clay pigeons, a shooter leads his target. Volume fire does the opposite of this. Volume fire and aim points refers to *moving* drones. The aim point is intended to maximize the chances of a hit by concentrating as many bullets as possible in that single space.

Football field technique

For small arms anti-aircraft fire, the US Army teaches the "Football Field Technique" which is a method of estimating lead distance to determine the aiming point. Lead is estimated in lengths of a football field (both kinds have approx. 100 yards/meters fields and pitches). Note that *lead* here refers to the distance necessary to select the actual stationary aim point.

The Army advises *against* leading drones. "Maintain the aim point, not the lead distance. The weapon should not move once the firing cycle starts."[39] What the Army is saying here is to saturate a section of airspace to create a "beaten zone" of bullets that the drone must fly through, relying on volume of fire to get a hit and kill.

The aim point can be established by a leader or other person with competent estimation skills. Tracer fire at the aim point can then be used to designate the general area, all though shots should not be concentrated on the exact aim point but an area surrounding it. "Accuracy in relation to target hits is not necessary. Accuracy in relation to the aim point is necessary. Coordinated high-volume of fire that the aircraft has to fly through will achieve the desired results."[40] Obviously, when employing shotguns, a marksman, or other projectiles individual aiming will differ.

Everyone aims at approximately the same point in space vs. constantly leading the aircraft. A scatter-plot effect is generated by individual variation in aim and location. This is considered a good thing as it disperses the bullets in space rather than concentrating them as greater accuracy would. The result is the creation of a zone, not a point, of hazard that the aircraft must pass through.

The anti-helicopter aiming technique is recommended for drones due to the lower speed and also the propensity that sUAVs will be quadcopters. Most commonly, the first instinct the pilot of a helicopter has to evade is to climb

---

[39] US Army ATP 3-01.81, p. A-3
[40] Ibid. p. A-4

which puts distance between the aircraft and the shooter(s). A drone pilot will almost certainly do the same thing, especially when hovering. Anecdotal review of downing incidents/attempts show that most drone pilots will climb before they maneuver laterally.

A designated marksman or the unit leader should use a magazine of all tracers to designate the aiming point. At night, a laser (visible, or infrared if the unit has NODs) may be used. Fire from a supported position when possible. The recommended rates of fire are 20-25 RPM (one shot every three seconds, approximately) for semi-automatic weapons and 50-100 RPM bursts at the aiming point.

	ATP 3-01.8 Table 4-1. Aiming Points.
COURSE	AIMING POINT
Crossing	(UAS Group 1) half a football field in front
Directly At You	Slightly above UAS body
Hovering	Slightly above UAS body

- Shoot around the area of the aim point to create a zone of fire.
- Always use cover for protection and shooting support when possible.
- A high/low knee shooting position can be used if there is adequate cover and concealment.
- If you are in a fighting position, remain in it and shoot from the supported position.
- If prone, roll onto your back and aim upwards.

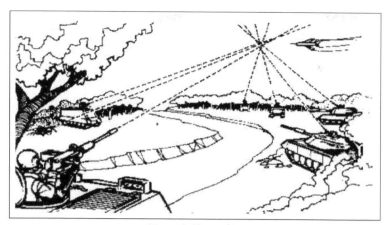

Figure 4-2. Volume fire.

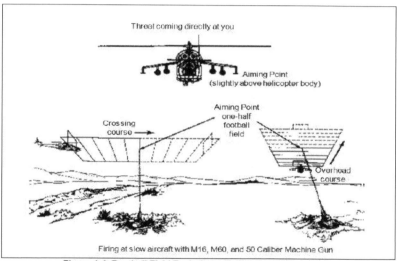

Figure 4-4. Football Field Technique: Helicopter aiming points.

ATP 3-01.8

Positioning

Positioning of CUAS is similar to that of an air guard but with more circumspection regarding sectors of fire and crossfire (very important when considering massed fire). *In-depth (perimeter)* positioning can often coincide with ground fields of fire to address omnidirectional attacks. In-depth coverage is a form of *balanced fires* where equal coverage and volume is given to each direction. This is the ideal form of coverage when the attack may come from any direction.

Linear positioning is better suited to a unidirectional threat. The air defense cousin to linear positioning is *weighted coverage*, where the bulk of the weapons are placed to address threats coming from the most likely air avenues of approach. For small units, this may be a risk if the attack comes from an unexpected direction, but multiple units over larger geographical area may stagger their coverage into different, mutually supporting weighted sectors.

It is very important that those behind a front line or in the middle of a formation or convoy who engage a drone do so with the utmost care to avoid fratricide or collateral damage. When outlining sectors of fire or briefing troops on the air threat, leaders must be careful to highlight potential danger areas and reinforce avoiding crossfire. Where the bullets fall also needs to be considered to avoid collateral damage.

For the volume fire technique, *mutual support* and *overlapping coverage* is necessary. Shooting into the air eliminates the issues of blind spots for targets high above the immediate surroundings, but lower to the horizon, the potential for crossfire makes supporting fire coordination along the lateral axis doubly important. When multiple units/formations are involved, leaders between them should harmonize each unit's sector of fire to prevent fratricide.

Defense in depth for small arms fire is hazardous because of the issue of fratricide and collateral damage. Bullets can remain deadly for thousands of feet. For instance, if a unit on the front line is weighted towards the "front," but a UCAV appears over the front unit, a rear unit, who is supposed to be watching the rear, could do a lot of damage if they begin firing in the direction of their sister unit.

For non-kinetic CUAS weapons, such as "drone guns" or jammers, positioning of individual CUAS elements should consider the broadest and most effective coverage. Since no bullets will be falling, the collateral damage/crossfire concerns are less, but CUAS teams need to consider where a downed drone will crash or land.

AMD Employment Tenets

MUTUAL SUPPORT

Weapons are positioned so that the fires of one weapon can engage targets within the dead zone of the adjacent weapon.

WEIGHTED COVERAGE

Weapons coverage is combined and concentrated toward the most likely threat air avenues of approach or directions of attack.

OVERLAPPING FIRES AND OVERLAPPING COVERAGE

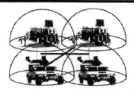

Weapons and sensors are positioned so that their engagement and detection envelopes overlap, eliminating seams in the defense.

EARLY ENGAGEMENT

Sensors and weapons are positioned so they engage the threat before ordnance release or detection of friendly forces.

BALANCED FIRES

Weapons positioned to deliver an equal volume of fires in all directions.

DEFENSE IN DEPTH

Sensors and weapons are positioned so that the threat is exposed to a continuously increasing volume of fire as it approaches the friendly protected asset or force.

Figure 1-2. AMD employment tenets

ATP 3-01.8

Placement

CUAS placement can be *static* (general support) to create an umbrella of protection over a given area, or *mobile* to protect individual units, formations, convoys, or a battle line as they maneuver. For static emplacement,

CUAS sectors should have overlapping fields of fire. Where total coverage of a perimeter or line cannot be accomplished, defenses should be concentrated in the most likely areas of approach, or interest, to UAVs.

A single mobile CUAS element should be placed towards the most likely direction of the threat but also centrally enough to offer protection for the whole unit. When there is no expected unidirectional attack vector, placement should be in the center. Larger units, formations, or convoys with more than one CUAS element should space them out so as to cover as much of the area as possible.

Multiple units will need to have areas of responsibility. When full coverage of a line or perimeter is possible, the elements will need to be given *sectors of fire* where they will have the primary duty to engage targets that appear. Each unit should be oriented in the general direction of the probable line of approach for that sector, the *primary target line*. The *secondary target lines* are for mutual support and overlapping fire. It is the responsibility of the unit commander or CUAS element leader to designate the sectors and lines based on his evaluation of the threat.

Consider the method being used for spacing. If you cannot defend an entire perimeter or area, consider denying the juiciest targets and the best routes of approach to the enemy. Place your defensive umbrella over your high-value targets or place your CUAS teams along the easiest avenues of approach. Force the enemy to contend with defenses if he wants to attack the target and force his movements into areas with obstructions, poor reception, or at the far end of his range.

Considerations

- What is the range of your omnidirectional jammers and detectors? Are there any radio blind spots?
- What is the range of any firearms or other projectile weapons?
- What is the range of any "drone guns"?
- Does one form of CUAS overlap another?
- Will there be electromagnetic interference caused by CUAS, detection sensors, or UAS control stations?

Warning conditions

Air defense warning conditions are issued to inform personnel of the current threat of air attack (risk) and how pressing that threat is or whether an attack is inbound. Both a color code and proword system are used by the Army[41].

Code Red/DYNAMITE: An air attack is imminent or is inbound and close.

Action: Take cover and engage immediately as appropriate.

Code Yellow/LOOKOUT: Attack is probable and/or an airborne threat is in the area. If inbound, reaction time is greater than above.

Action: Take cover, camouflage, and ready CUAS defenses as appropriate based on the ETA.

Code White/SNOWMAN: No air attack threat is in progress.

---

[41] FM 3-01.44 p. 1-7

Action: Stand down/normal alert posture.

Color codes are more of an assessment of probability, like a temperature gauge. Prowords may be more suitable for military veterans or formations when shouting or over the radio. For citizen defenders who may be unfamiliar with prowords, the color code is simple and the meanings pretty obvious even without explanation.

Rules of Engagement (ROE)

At all times the right to self-defense exists. Leaders and individuals have the ability and even the duty to take all reasonable actions to protect themselves against incurring losses or casualties. This does not mean that counter-attacks should *not* be done wisely and cautiously, but that no one should suffer death or injuries because they do not have authorization to fire. Some considerations on whether it is necessary to take self-defense action are:

- Is the aircraft capable of inflicting death or injury (bombing drone, loitering munition, UCAV)?
- Is the aircraft nearby or approaching directly?
- Is a threat imminent?
- If the aircraft is not capable of attack, is it supporting other forces that are capable of attack (artillery, assaulting troops) who will imminently attack?
- What if you do nothing?

Once a drone is observed, <u>it needs to be immediately reported to all affected parties</u> (friendly personnel, command units, civilians). It should be assumed hostile until proven otherwise. Once confirmed hostile, shootdown attempts can begin.

A hostile drone that has just been launched or in the process of launch should be targeted ASAP before it is able to gain altitude and begin maneuvering. Launching crews and pilots should be a priority for attack. Attacks might include areas weapon and indirect fire on the launching area or more precision attacks (sniper) on the pilot.

Hard Rules of Engagement (ROE) are generally not a concern for partisan or guerilla forces, nor domestic combatants. Political and legal considerations that legitimate government forces have been subordinate to success for civilians. Conventional forces do need to be concerned with the ROE due to the potential for escalation, target identification, and collateral damage.

Collateral damage is a concern of civilians and partisan forces especially as everything from jamming of GPS/communications to a falling drone or stray bullet from a missed shoot down attempt could cause a third-party harm. While legal repercussions in a domestic conflict would be minimal or non-existent, complications could arise from causing harm or death to innocent parties. Neighbors or friendly civilians may be antagonized by indiscriminate CUAS resulting in harm.

Modes of control

Varying levels of authority to engage exist beyond self-defense and would apply mostly to dedicated CUAS teams. A commander or leader may reserve all authority to target and engage to himself (*centralized or positive control*), ordering what will be targeted, how, and when. *Decentralized control* allows semi-autonomy to CUAS units to engage targets within a specific set of parameters given to them by their superior. A unit with delegated, decentralized authority would not need a separate command to engage if the engagement parameters are met.

The final mode of control is *autonomous*. A team that is not able to receive orders from a commander or has been given autonomy will choose what targets to engage, when to engage them, and with what methods, following established SOP. Citizen defense CUAS teams are likely to always be in an autonomous mode.

Where a command and control echelon exists, leaders should discuss with their subordinates what level of control will be exercised. Command elements may be coordinating other efforts with other CUAS teams or to other purposes, so to avoid conflicts, a level of control may be exerted. Otherwise, anything other than positive control should have the engagement parameters outlined so that a unit acting autonomously or semi-autonomously can effectively contribute to the defense without causing complications.

Weapons control status

Weapon control status is an order indicating when a CUAS team or a unit may engage. These are not the actual orders to fire, but an indicator of the level of delegated initiative. For an operational CUAS team, "weapons tight" will be the normal status as they have greater responsibility for that particular mission, giving them a larger degree of autonomy. A ground unit utilizing direct fire will likely operate under "weapons hold" unless a UAS threat develops.

Weapons hold: only fire in immediate self-defense or when ordered to.

Weapons tight: fire only on targets positively ID'd as hostile.

Weapons free: fire at will on any target not positively ID'd as friendly.

As always, barring explicit orders to the contrary, the normal right of self-defense against an imminent threat regardless of weapon control status or other ROE always applies. Note that volume fire, due to its greater inherent risk of collateral damage, should be limited in fire control authority except in immediate self-defense against an armed drone.

Fire control orders

Fire control orders are issued by a leader to indicate when to fire or not fire, such as in a *weapons hold* or *weapons tight* status, when a leader has a need to exert more direct control over CUAS efforts. These would also apply to a CUAS team leader or the team acting under the direction of a commander.

Engage: start firing on/jamming, etc. the target.

Hold fire: temporarily stop firing to prevent fratricide, collateral damage, or interfering with another CUAS attack.

Cease fire: stop firing, the engagement is over.

"Engage" for CUAS efforts is preferred because "fire" might be confused as an order for ground troops to start shooting at ground targets. Note that on a shooting range, the emergency command "cease fire" here is "hold fire." For citizen defenders, using only one variant to mean "stop shooting" may result in less confusion. *Stand down* may be a more appropriate command that the CUAS response is over, especially for volume fire.

Identification

Identify the target. Is it friendly, enemy, unknown, or neutral (curious citizen)? Once a drone is observed, it needs to be immediately reported to all affected parties (friendly personnel, command units, and civilians). It should be assumed hostile until proven otherwise; though the weapons control status may be either at *hold* or *tight* until positive ID. An unconfirmed contact cannot go ignored.

Confirmation of a hostile UAV prior to attempting a shootdown prevents unnecessary destruction of a friendly airframe. Identification is not as critical as it is with firing on a manned aircraft because drones are unmanned. No one dies if a drone is shot down unless it crashes on their head. More time and care can be taken to positively ID unarmed UAVs, but an armed drone that is or may be attacking should be shot down immediately if it is perceived to be an imminent threat.

Positive identification is actual, verifiable observation by eye or signals analysis that the object is a UAV and confirmation that it is hostile or not. Procedural identification is an educated assumption based on location, direction of travel, time, and activities. Assumptions get people killed. If you suspect it is friendly, eyeball it and verify with friendly pilots that the drone you are seeing is the one they are flying.

"CREW 1, COWBOY."
"GO FOR CREW 1."
"CREW 1, COWBOY HAS VISUAL ON A WHITE QUADCOPTER OVER 123 MAIN STREET."
"ROGER COWBOY, THAT'S US."

Due to the short reaction in urban areas for drones engaged in extremely low altitude (ELA) flight, CUAS teams must be ready to act immediately on their own initiative. Using the standard Manhattan block length of 900 feet (300m), if a drone flew half that length at an attack speed of 25 MPH that is a time-to-target of about 13 seconds.

Positive identification (POS-ID) of the drone must be made prior to engaging with counter-UAS active measures. This is to avoid downing a friendly drone, the shootdown attempt revealing your position, and to avoid unnecessary collateral damage/fratricide. POS-ID can include obvious hostile intent, such as an armed drone, when it is reasonably certain friendly forces are under-attack and the flight profile indicates it is *not* a friendly drone on an outbound mission. For this reason and others good communication/coordination with friendly UAS teams is vital.

Considerations

- Right of self-defense (legally and under what your enemies and neighbors may consider "fair").
- Positive ID of a hostile drone.
- Collateral damage/fratricide (from falling bullets and airframes).
- Engagement envelope.
- Will downing it give away your position?
- Threat posed if left alone?
- Will a counter-attack expose others (friendly forces, innocent civilians) to danger, such as from falling bullets or the drone crashing on people?
- Can you actually hit it?

An important criterion is that the drone is actually flying within a possible intercept envelope. Not only is it a pointless waste of ammunition or resources, but stray bullets may also cause collateral damage, or electronic device usage may give away your position or anti-drone capabilities. Small arms fire is a certain way to draw attention. The overall threat of revealing one's presence may be greater than the threat posed by the drone.

The simple appearance of a drone cannot automatically result in "weapons free." For instance, a distant enemy may have spotted you remotely on their drone but firing at it could give away your numbers or alert a nearer enemy that you weren't aware of. Consider that non-kinetic means can be detected through signals interception and also the loss of signal from a drone (or seeing a shootdown on the video feed) is a pretty obvious indicator of enemy action.

CUAS Teams

Establishing a counter-UAS Quick Reaction Force (QRF) is perhaps the best one-size-fits-all solution. This unit should include a detection element, an electronic "shootdown" element, a kinetic shootdown element, and a security force. In reality, small units will probably contain a few people who perform multiple duties. This CUAS QRF would perform missions from detection to electronic disablement of drones, as well as conventional shootdowns with shotguns/rifles to perhaps limited employment of snipers against enemy drone operators.

Detection/shootdown capabilities organic to small units builds redundancy for the force as a whole in addition to enhancing the individual unit capabilities. Area coverage and capabilities will overlap and provide defense in depth. Individual unit integration is ideal. This is similar to how a mortar with a weapons platoon gives a company organic access to (short-range) indirect fires without relying on an attached artillery unit.

To prevent counter-attack by ground forces, persons detailed to perimeter security will be necessary. Those in the security role can also form the "anti-aircraft artillery" element for massed fire with their personal weapons in adjunct to the dedicated CUAS weapons and devices.

CUAS allotment will be based on the availability of resources followed by need. A small neighborhood defense force that sends out a squad on the offensive may not have the equipment or manpower to send along an "anti-drone man." A squad member with some knowledge of electronics may be tasked with serving both as a patrolman and performing the CUAS role should the need arise. Alternatively, the group's CUAS expert may come along.

Larger forces, such as partisan/guerilla units or traditional militaries will probably integrate a specialist position into their field units. Where the members of a unit tasked with CUAS are permanent parts, this is an organic capability. Organic capability is more likely to be found with large, well-funded, and well-equipped groups. CUAS is either handled as a direct support mission to smaller units or as a general support mission. Independent missions are possible, such as being sent as a hunter-killer type unit, but we are focusing more on force protection here.

These relationships are *direct support*, *independent*, and *general support*. Direct support entails either a unit providing its own organic capabilities or specialists being attached to a unit that doesn't have CUAS or UAS capability. General support is providing capability for an entire force, area, or neighborhood, such as a dedicated air defense unit. Independent teams would be tasked with accomplishing a specific objective, like sending a drone to surveille a high-value target for mission planning.

Organic personnel are dual-role fighters and CUAS specialists that are integral parts of a unit. The unit provides its own security. One unit member may carry a CUAS device, and an infantryman might carry along a rocket launcher in case they encounter a tank. Larger units will probably have a small fire team of specialists.

Attached specialist are assigned from a large air defense unit or an at-large pool on temporary duty as operational needs dictate. Though they are not a regular part of a deployed unit, these visitors lend self-security to the unit. A unit operating under an existing umbrella of CUAS defense, but with no one specifically assigned to them, is receiving general support.

In the near future, modern militaries will almost certainly begin regularly fielding anti-drone equipment at the battalion or company level and below. Javelin and Stinger missiles are there now to deal with armor and aircraft threats, so it logically follows that as the UAS threat proliferates defenses will trickle down to small units. Partisans and guerillas without foreign support or deep financial backing will not have the resources to spread anti-drone tech so widely.

Neighborhood defenders will likely adopt a general support strategy where an umbrella of detection and jamming, as necessary, covers the area. A smaller direct attack team equipped with electronic "drone guns," suitable firearms, or other weapons can deploy for point defense or be attached as needed. Larger organizations with the financial/technological resources will probably employ both organic defense and general defense over a static area, with the latter using an umbrella and dedicated point defense teams.

Ch. 10 Camouflage and Infrared/Thermal Defense

Camouflage

Humans think of camouflage in a horizontal sense because that's how we've fought since time immemorial. We want to blend in with the brush, grasses, trees, and rocks as we see them. Camouflage from above, that is blending in with the ground as it looks to someone or something looking down, is new.

Sure, we've camouflaged things from airplanes for a hundred years but that was against relatively fast moving aircraft with low resolution cameras. Now drones with 48MP cameras can hover a hundred feet above the ground scanning and watching in ultra high definition, then zoom in! UAS's ability to loiter and inspect areas in relative leisure makes exposed or uncamouflaged troops far more obvious.

Camouflage is intended to prevent detection in the first place through hiding, blending, and disguising. Hiding is concealment from observation. Blending is looking like part of the natural background and most often what we think of when we think of camouflage. If this fails, camouflage then is a mitigation technique to disguise personnel, weapons, and equipment. Disguising, or decoying, is fooling the enemy's eyes or sensors into seeing something other than what they are seeing to conceal identity, purpose, or abilities.

To be effective, overhead camouflage has to render

the position as undetectable as possible to normal TV and IR cameras. No camouflage or signature reduction/mitigation techniques are perfect, but a half-assed effort will result in failure. It is not enough to make a target less distinguishable; then one is relying on luck, hoping a sensor operator does not spot the camouflaging. A drone pilot cannot suspect or experientially assume an unnatural anomaly is a fighting position. If it might contain enemy soldiers, why not hit it?

If this fails, there are mitigation techniques to disguise personnel, weapons, and equipment. Disguising is fooling the enemy's eyes or sensors into seeing something other than what they are seeing to conceal identity, purpose, or abilities. Decoys are outright fakes, such as a neighborhood guard shack that is totally unoccupied. These techniques take advantage of the human psychology of the operator.

The goal of camouflaging and signature management (SM) is to minimize the chance of detection as much as possible and limit what information an enemy can gain by observation. Both go beyond not being seen and blending in with the background. They also include:

- Appearance; not being seen, looking innocuous or like something else.
- Movement: movement attracts attention and can raise dust.
- Dispersion: smaller groups are less noticeable than larger ones.
- Light; self-explanatory.
- Heat; visible in thermal infrared vision.
- Noise; self-explanatory.
- Dust and debris; obvious indicator of human presence.

In a phrase, SM is being less obvious, which is more

behavioral than technological, and minimizes what info an adversary might gain if he does see you. Information minimization examples include:

- Deny the adversary intelligence gathering information, such as any identifying info.
- Lower one's threat profile: like an officer removing their rank insignia.
- If you are being observed, give away nothing by your signature or behavior that may indicate to an adversary that you, your property, or unit is worth watching or attacking.

Maintaining camouflage and signature reduction discipline is crucial for survival. These techniques may not be effective at remaining undetected, but it may deny valuable intelligence including manpower, the location of all positions/equipment, and the nature of the defenses.

Principals of camouflage

Shadow: Shadow can be divided into cast and contained types. *Cast shadows* are silhouettes of objects against their background—like a man's shadow against the ground—while *contained shadows* are dark pools below the shaded areas, such as the area beneath a pop-up canopy. Both are easily detectable. Shadows can be utilized to impede an enemy's detection efforts. Ideally, positions and obstacles should be placed under overhead cover, vegetation, or in any other dark areas of the terrain to minimize visibility.

Movement: Movement is readily apparent and moving at the wrong time can defeat even the best camouflage.

When in the open, it's important to minimize movement, even in darkness. Moving against a stationary background or uniform surface attracts attention, but slow and regular movement is less noticeable than fast and erratic movement. Preselect and improve concealed routes for defensive forces. Staying in the shadows, particularly when moving, can also mask objects.

Visual features: Color, texture, and tone are crucial factors to consider when it comes to positioning and camouflaging. It's essential to assess how a position or a person, including clothing and camouflaging, appears from an aerial perspective, not just a horizontal view. Utilizing a drone to survey your own position can be beneficial.

When selecting positions, it's important to avoid silhouetting which, from the aerial perspective, is contrasting badly with the color of the surrounding ground or vegetation. Up-facing surfaces should blend in with the surrounding ground or rooftop, avoiding the appearance of a dark shape moving on a light background. If the colors can't blend in, avoid stark color clashes.

Patterns: Like movement, the human eye is great at noticing patterns. Orderly stacks of equipment, rows of parked vehicles, or regularly spaced positions are unnatural and will garner attention from a long way off. This is especially noticeable from the air in UAV combat footage.

Shape: Familiar objects are a kind of pattern so not only are they recognizable, but they also often stand out from natural backgrounds. This is why camouflage, in addition, to blending colors tries to disrupt shapes. Break up the shape of instantly recognizable things, like helmets, wheels, firearms, vehicles, etc.

Shine: Light, emitted or reflected, can attract attention, so it's crucial to be aware of smooth or polished or shiny surfaces which may also reflect light (visible or IR). When vehicles are not in use, their headlights, taillights, and safety reflectors should be covered. Exposed skin can also reflect light and should be taken into account. Do not take off shirts when working as this makes the human figure easily perceptible.

Visual reflectance is how well something reflects visible light and how noticeable it is. Mirrors and shiny surfaces are obvious sources of visual reflectance, but it can also refer to the color of an object. At great distances, colors blend together and appear more uniform, becoming less significant and more difficult to distinguish. Color is also very difficult to distinguish in low-light.

Decoy: A decoy is something that you want to be seen, or, if it is seen, draws the enemy away from, or to a different conclusion, from whatever you're protecting. This could be a unit moving clumsily and obviously in a opposite direction from the covert unit or creating poorly hidden fighting positions when the real ones are better concealed.

Tactics, techniques, and procedures (TTP)

The difference between camouflaging against UAS and from the ground is the look-down overhead perspective. There is often little to no cover from above and vertical concealment can be rather transparent to a low-flying UAV. Use organic UAS, walk a distance away, or get above the position to check the efficacy of camouflaging. A position should be unobtrusive or undetectable from 100 feet (33m) up and away.

Vegetation

• Use cut vegetation to help break up shapes, hide outlines, add depth and/or realism. Cut vegetation from a wide area well away from the immediate vicinity of your position. Do not totally denude vegetation from a single location as this is a clear indicator of human activity. Vegetation should not be cut so much that it is conspicuously absent, or the signs of cutting are obvious.

• Cut vegetation is a temporary measure and it needs to be replaced often because it rapidly wilts and turns brown. Wilted, dead vegetation is a sure sign of a camouflaged position, and it will stand out. Note that vegetation is flammable, whether fresh or cut.

• Already dead plant matter, such as hay or straw, works well if it is expected in the environment, or if it is used as a base for texturing and blending. Dead vegetation can be used if the surrounding area is also full of dead plants, such as during a drought or in an abandoned field.

• When winter comes and deciduous trees drop their leaves, adjust your concealment and camouflage to compensate for the lack of a tree canopy. Your shaded, semi-hidden position in July needs to be moved or improved in October. Winter is a very vulnerable time for overhead attack by drones.

225

Cover trenches, foxholes, and other positions with camouflage netting at a minimum. Interior portions of any works should also be camouflaged (sandbags, wattle walls, etc.) including the bottom.

Camouflage nets can conceal vehicles, tents, shelters, and equipment. Closer targets have smaller shadows, making them less noticeable from the air. Properly draped nets can alter sharp-edged shadows of military targets, making them harder to detect. Nets can also help dissipate heat from artificial sources like fire.

Minimize movement; it draws attention and will raise dust, exhaust, increase the thermal signature, and can leave either visible footprints or vehicle tracks. Remaining static will make distinguishing a human versus the natural background more difficult. The camera may spot you, but the sensor operator's eye may not.

Avoid predictable patterns so an adversary does not know when to look for you and to limit what intelligence he can gather if he does detect you by pattern analysis.

Avoid using smoke whenever possible. Smoke is not something to prevent detection, it is to prevent observation. Smoke will draw attention and it can only conceal the nature of the movement, the direction of travel, and the identity of anyone moving. An enemy could always just fire on the smoke and stand a chance of hitting someone by luck.

You are not trying to hide from the sensor, but the sensor operator. Don't look like a human shape or do something stupid such as allowing your feet to stick out from beneath cover. Do not attempt to hide under an umbrella, even against ordinary photography; it will not work the way you think it will. An umbrella will make it hard for a drone to ID you (by face) but then all that the sensor operator or anyone on the ground has to do is track the person with an umbrella.

Pay attention to tire tracks, tread tracks, and obvious signs of mechanical excavation. Cover over machine-made marks in the earth with shovels or by marching through it until the highly identifiable vehicular signature is obscured.

HAWKEYE drill

The US military HAWKEYE drill is an order to camouflage a unit to near undetectable by a UAV at a kilometer's distance within 20 minutes. In this context, it is ordered based on the expectation of contact with enemy UAS. The procedure involves immediately transitioning to camouflaging duties by moving to defensive positions, dispersing first if necessary, and actively camouflaging. Once finished, everyone "stands to" or remains motionless and quiet, as if in anticipation of attack. HAWKEYE is an order to camouflage positions and take cover; it is not issued as an emergency warning.

Note that for civilian usage, use of code words should be minimized as those who need the warning may not understand the brevity codes being used. Camouflage drills, orders to take cover, or warnings of UAV approach/attack should be made in plain speech.

Infrared

There are two "kinds" of infrared light: near-infrared radiation (NIR) and thermal infrared radiation (TIR) or heat. All drones should be assumed to have low-light observation and navigation capabilities, either thermal or light-amplification "night vision." Even cheap camera sensors can employ limited digital light amplification. A UAV flying at night should be assumed to have either or both capabilities.

Near infrared (night vision)

The most common form of "night vision" takes advantage of near-infrared radiation (NIR). NIR is often used in night vision technology as it has longer wavelengths than visible light and can penetrate through some atmospheric conditions and objects such as clothing, allowing objects to be detected in low-light conditions. Most know this kind of night vision from the green cast footage of videos and movies.

Image intensification night vision is sensitive to near-infrared radiation as well as visible light and some portions of the ultraviolet spectrum. NIR light is just beyond the range of visible light and can be found in low-light conditions. Night observation devices (NODs) like "Starlight scopes" use this part of the light spectrum. Virtually all UAS image intensifiers amplify light using a digital process instead of the light sensitive tubes found in a NOD like the PVS-14. Many UAS camera systems employ NIR "night vision." As these devices are only amplifying existing light, they need ambient lighting like starlight or moonlight to work. Supplemental infrared lighting can be used, but this is uncommon in UAVs.

NIR works poorly in adverse weather the same way visibility is affected by precipitation, dust, cloud, fog, mist, or smoke. Clouds and mist are composed of tiny water droplets, or particles in the case of smoke, that scatter and absorb infrared radiation (and visible light). NIR does not penetrate cloudy conditions. What NIR sensors can see is similar to what full-color daylight cameras can, except the image lacks color and the resolution is poorer.

Thermal infrared

Thermal infrared (TIR) radiation is emitted by objects as a result of their temperature and is often used to detect and measure heat. TIR sensitive cameras create images based on the temperature differential of objects as they contrast with each other and their surroundings. These cameras may be referred to as FLIR, Forward Looking Infrared and a brand name.

TIR vision operates based on the fact that as an object's temperature increases, it emits more infrared radiation in a wavelength beyond the visible range of human sight. This additional radiation corresponds to an increase or decrease in the object's energy state. By detecting and measuring this infrared radiation, the thermal imaging system can differentiate temperature gradients and produce a visual representation. This variation in temperature is commonly referred to as thermal contrast.

Temperature reflectance refers to the thermal energy reflected by a target, with the exception of self-generated thermal energy. Vehicles and humans are the most common source of self-generated thermal energy. Absorbed, then radiated, heat from the environment could be considered similar to a self-generated source.

The visible image produced by the imager shows a range of colors or grayscale values (black hot/white hot) that correspond to the temperature of the objects in the scene. The temperature of the objects is determined by the amount of infrared radiation they emit, with hotter objects emitting more radiation than cooler objects.

Thermal imaging is degraded by precipitation, cloud, and smoke like with NIR, but for different reasons and to different degrees. This can make it difficult for thermal radiation to pass through these conditions and can also cause thermal radiation emitted from objects to scatter and become diffuse. As a result, the contrast and clarity of thermal images may be reduced in rainy, foggy, or misty conditions.

Thermal imaging can be useful for detecting objects and people in low visibility conditions such as fog, mist, and smoke. The effectiveness of thermal imaging in these conditions depends on the density the fog, precipitation, or smoke, as well as the sensitivity and resolution of the thermal imaging equipment used. TIR sensors may provide marginally better visibility in these conditions than NIR sensors.

Vegetation offers concealment from near-infrared sensors as it reflects light in that wavelength similarly to visible light. NIR radiation is reflected by the leaves of plants and does not penetrate very far into the vegetation. On the other hand, TIR radiation can penetrate vegetation better than NIR radiation because it is absorbed by the water content in plant tissues. The amount of TIR radiation that can penetrate vegetation depends on the density and structure of the vegetation, so a deep forest canopy may provide good concealment.

Target-to-background contrasts in thermal imaging are influenced by the thermal mass and surface properties, such as reflectivity, of natural and man-made materials. These contrasts can vary greatly over the course of a day. For instance, vehicles, generators, heated buildings, and soldiers are often warmer than their surroundings, and equipment exposed to sunlight can appear hotter than natural backgrounds due to absorbing solar radiation. During nighttime, equipment may appear cooler than its background due to faster heating and cooling rates.

Thermal crossover is a phenomenon that occurs twice a day, every morning and evening, when environmental background temperatures and an object equalize or blur. The natural environment—plants, the ground itself, objects manmade and natural—absorb solar radiation during the day, increasing their heat, and release it at night. Every object emits its own unique thermal radiation, however, when two objects with different temperatures are close together, their thermal radiation can mix and create a blurry, less accurate image.

This is because the thermal radiation emitted by each object can interfere with the detection of the other object's radiation, resulting in the crossover effect. At thermal crossover, a truck that sat out overnight, for instance, will have cooled off to a temperature relative to the environment. As thermal vision works by detecting and displaying the difference in temperature gradients, this low-contrast period can be exploited.

During thermal crossover, it can be difficult to distinguish between two closely spaced objects with similar temperatures. This can lead to errors in thermal imaging analysis and interpretation, so activity during periods of low temperature contrast decreases the chance of being seen. Human bodies and hot vehicles will be best camouflaged by the background thermal profile from midday to late afternoon when the ground and air is the hottest. Conversely, night and early morning will have the greatest temperature contrast.

Thermal camouflage principles

Exploiting thermal camo is very difficult while moving and most techniques apply to camouflaged static positions. For example, tempered safety glass in car windshields is basically totally thermally opaque, but not everyone can hide inside a car or, as the meme goes, walk around in a suit made of car windshields. With thermal camouflaging, it is easier to hide to avoid detection when the drone crew does not know when someone is out there. Detection during a dedicated search becomes more probable when anomalies are suspected and checked out.

Thermal hiding is getting behind or under something that blocks the source of the heat. For example, a person crawling into a bunker with a sandbagged roof or a truck parking beneath a bridge is hiding under thermal cover. In order of decreasing effectiveness, thermal cover includes earth overhead cover, earthen embankments (horizontal cover), thick vegetation (a tree canopy), camouflage nets, and smoke.

Getting below ground or underneath natural earthen cover is best as the Earth itself will block the sensor's view and help dissipate body heat. Horizontal cover blocks the straight line or oblique view of a sensor and helps, except when a UAV is directly overhead. Thick vegetation increases the ceiling of the drone, due to collision danger, and the foliage also helps disperse heat as well as offer concealment.

The construction of a survivability position can result in poor thermal discipline. Freshly-dug earth (spoil or excavations) can appear cooler than the surrounding earth. Plastic sandbags need to be covered with dirt, mud, or sod as they reflect light and can absorb heat and sunlight during the day to radiate heat at night. Disturbed vegetation may reduce natural concealment.

Thermal blending is attempting to blend the thermal signature in with its background the way camouflage attempts to blend objects or people with the environment.

Blending works by masking the heat signature. Cloth-like flexible materials that can be used to expeditiously cover a human or be used to construct a shelter work through blending and masking.

A *thermal barrier* is a material that can be used to block or attenuate the transfer of thermal energy from one side to the other. A thermal barrier can take various forms, such as a layer of insulation, a reflective surface, or a combination of both. The key characteristic of a thermal barrier is its ability to limit the heat transfer through conduction, convection, and radiation but all insulative layers will warm up with enough time.

A thermal barrier blanket blocks the thermal radiation and a layer of insulation (including an air gap) prevents the heat from warming the thermal barrier. These have to work in concert with each other. Note that the material may itself retain heat, such as from the sun, the environment, or from body heat beneath it. A hot barrier will standout and a canny sensor operator will recognize that a non-natural heat source is out-of-place. Seeing a uniformly black (cold) square in the middle of a forest will be a dead giveaway.

Many different ideas and materials provide some degree of protection from thermal imaging; some work better than others. There is no silver bullet and any intended solution should be tested for at least an hour. Videos show some common items working but these are short tests often using cheap sensors from a static, horizontal perspective; remember that drones can obtain views from multiple angles.

There are a lot of really terrible ideas out there on how to hide from thermal sensors. Glass, cooling mattresses, air and water-cooled "space suits", etc. What works is hiding below something thick enough to hide the heat signature, like in a dugout bunker, or by using material and vegetation to mask the heat signature to blend in with the environment. All other solutions are temporary and intended to camouflage, not render invisible, a human heat signature.

But what if I wear a wetsuit or something? I saw that on MythBusters. Wearing or attempting to move in thick clothing or other insulators will cause you to overheat, perhaps dangerously so, and your body heat will heat up the clothing. There is nothing you can wear for an extended period of time, especially while exerting yourself, that will hide you from thermal imagers.

Some thermal barrier materials use proprietary technology applied to burlap-like materials. The **Relv Eclipse** camouflage mesh drape appears to be very effective if either used for a short time as an expedient or used in combination with an airgap. It is multi-spectral and does reflect NIR. Vegetation reflects NIR light, giving it a ghostly or snowy look. NIR non-reflective camouflage may stand out from the plants around it.

- The thermal barrier stops the infrared radiation like a blanket over a flashlight, assuming the material has sufficiently thermally opaque properties.
- An air gap acts as insulation that also dissipates heat, preventing it from heating the barrier. All insulative materials

in contact with a heat source (body) will heat up eventually.

- There will always be some degree of thermal contrast of thermal camouflage with the background environment.
- Any "personal" thermal camo solutions are temporary; most of the item testing videos on YouTube do not show extended usage such as would be necessary during a persistent area search. Draping the body is intended for REDEYE drills to avoid being spotted by chance, not to evade a determined search.
- Some materials/items may offer limited, short-term protection that may be better than nothing, but should not be relied upon. All solutions should be tested over time and from multiple angles.

Infrared survival TTP

To hide from thermal imaging, minimize the difference in temperature between yourself and your surroundings. Totally hiding is impossible without getting out of the line-of-sight of the sensor by going underground, for example, but many techniques can reduce a thermal signature or confuse a sensor operator. To a good thermal sensor, an umbrella may block the body behind it, but the camera will still see an umbrella. Outsmart the pilot, not the sensor.

Thermal barrier

Do not place a thermal barrier directly against the body. Any signature reduction will be short as the body heat begins to bleed through the barrier, even if a Mylar blanket or thicker layer of insulation is used. Separate the barrier from any insulation or heat source with an air gap. A "woobie" poncho liner seems to be more effective than a wool blanket but less effective than purpose-made drapes.

Camo netting blocks light and a direct view through it, but it is not totally opaque. Layering multiple nets would increase the effect, but some light and heat would make it through. It's best to have an unbroken layer that is thermally opaque between any camouflaging outer layer and the thermal barrier. Combine the thermal barrier with insulation, an air gap, and natural concealment from vegetation.

Thermal blankets include mylar "space" blankets and thick (usually wool) blankets. Mylar blankets are a poor material because they are noisy, fragile, and very reflective and appear as the black square (above). Any "space blankets" need to have at least one side covered with a neutral colored cloth or non-shiny plastic material for durability and quiet, like heavy-duty survival blankets.

Mylar offers no insulation value, so an insulating layer will be needed. Try to use an air gap instead of an insulative material. Remember: silver side down. Survival blankets which are less noisy and more durable than space blankets often have shiny tarp plastic on one side that can violate the "shine" camo principal. One could use a ghillie blanket (like a ghillie suit but without the arms and legs) on top with a Mylar sheet beneath it.

Blend the thermal barrier in with the natural signature; do not create a "black hole" in the environment. Break up the shape of any thermal blanket so it is not taught and so the edges avoid straight lines. It should be uneven like a comforter tossed carelessly back on the bed. The uniformly texture-less surface of, say, a tarp will stand out from the texture of nature.

Break up any blanket or tarp by sewing a thermal blanket with added camo netting or burlap strips. Layer a thermal blanket with a camo net and place natural materials on the flat surface to give it texture and break up its outline. Cover with or attach sections of camouflage material, such as "cabbage patch" netting sections or ghillie suit strips to vary the texture. Use fresh-cut vegetation to help disrupt any shape or shine problems.

- Camouflage layer>thermal barrier>insulation/air gap>heat source (body)
- Do not expose any shiny Mylar or plastic. Cover these materials with a matte, natural or camouflaged cloth.
- Stay behind or under the thermal barrier without being in physical contact with it.
- Keep an air gap between the heat source (body), the thermal barrier, and the camouflage layer.
- Use tree canopies and vegetation to partially block your heat signature.
- Use camouflage netting to help dissipate heat and break up signatures.
- Do not use thermal barriers while moving; this will create a moving "black hole." If you must deploy the barrier on the move, stop, deploy it, and remain motionless until the threat passes.

Positions

The construction of a survivability position can result in poor thermal discipline. Freshly-dug earth (spoil or excavations) can appear cooler than the surrounding earth. Plastic sandbags need to be covered with dirt, mud, or sod as they reflect light and can absorb heat and sunlight during the day to radiate heat at night. Cover any "shiny" plastic with camo netting or mesh to reduce reflectivity.

Air-gaps between the edge of any thermal barrier or insulation will be obvious on a thermal sensor display, like the shadow beneath a camouflage net. Extend the outer layer of camouflaging or the thermal barrier over the insulation or cover. Camouflage netting over the top of a thermal barrier that reaches the ground will help minimize the air gap and break up any residual heat signature. Remember that drones will not always be directly overhead but can observe from oblique angles to see beneath coverings.

Construct shelters in shaded areas, both to help with hiding and also to keep the sunlight from heating up artificial materials. Rest under thick cover when possible; in dense undergrowth or below natural overhangs. Select sleeping (RON), resting (ROD)[42], or OP/LP sites under tall tree cover whenever possible. A high canopy helps obscure visual/infrared observation and prevents UAVs from getting too low for a better view.

Due to heat retention, blankets and tarps are only suitable for individual thermal protection during cold weather. During hot weather, heat exhaustion can occur rapidly. The discomfort from heat itself may lead to making deadly mistakes. Create a shelter that has plenty of airflow *beneath* the thermal barrier, such as sleeping in a "Ranger

---

[42] Remain Over Night and Remain Over Day, respectively.

grave" beneath a suspended wool blanket and camo net.

In urban areas, the variance in the visual pattern and thermal gradients from all the different surfaces, textures, and colors will interfere with visual, near-infrared, and thermal observation. Glare from windows or bright surfaces is problematic for thermal and NIR sensors as well. Move through, or setup positions in, areas with high thermal "clutter" like an area of thermal contrast with multiple heat sources.

Heat and light discipline

While red filters help preserve night vision, they cannot prevent near infrared from detecting light from long distances, and red light is extremely sensitive to detection by NIR sensors. To reduce the chances of detection, replace red filters with blue-green filters and practice strict light discipline. Any light of any color, infrared or not, should not be used outside of total cover.

Note that using NIR LED lights to try and "blind" a drone or mask something may obscure a face behind the light, but the light will make someone visible like waving a flashlight in the dark. Do not use infrared lights or lasers except in combat where the gunfire will give you away anyhow. Night vision supremacy is a thing in very poor countries overseas, like Afghanistan until very recently, not in the US. Expect sophisticated adversaries and government forces to have NIR sensors.

Clothing can reflect or absorb NIR light. Vegetation actually reflects it so there is a certain degree of value in having clothing that reflects limited amounts of NIR to blend in with foliage. In ambient lighting, this would give the effect of a person blending in, if their camouflage pattern is otherwise effective (color becomes largely irrelevant under IR). If a NIR light source is present, reflectivity is a bad thing. Infrared light sources (active night vision) are most likely to be used on the ground and not by UAS.

Camouflage doesn't work against night vision simply because it is camouflage. Some hunting clothing with camo patterns on them shine like a white shirt under a black light when an IR illuminator is shone on them. Avoid synthetic materials unless they have been treated to be IR compliant. Test all clothing against night vision using an IR illuminator. Modern US camouflage uniforms are IR reflection-resistant. Do not wash clothing being used for tactical purposes with any optical brightening detergent.

Heat discipline is just as important as light discipline, but heat discipline is more important at night than during the day due to the greater thermal contrast. To shield heat sources from thermal sensors, use natural materials to insulate or cover the heat source, and use terrain to block or obstruct the UAV's line-of-sight. Do not raise vehicle hoods because this exposes a hot spot for thermal detection.

Minimize the use of all heat emitting sources. No smoking, no fires, no heaters, no "hot hands," and turn vehicle engines off. It would pay to invest in a cheap thermal imager to check one's own thermal signature. Remember that heat builds up under coverings, so air movement (air gaps) is needed to dissipate it.

Any heat producing sources like cookstoves should either be used under deep cover (vegetation and underground) in shelters with good ventilation or in daytime. Any heating element at night will be obvious to any thermal-equipped UAV. Cooking fires should be kept low, using dry wood, with smoke minimized, preferably using the "Dakota hole" technique. Use camo netting to help disperse heat as it rises.

Movement

If you must move:

• Increase your distance from the sensor or adversary. Infrared radiation follows the inverse square law. In short, the further a heat emitter is from the source, the smaller its thermal signature is.

• Do not move unnecessarily. Remain static and under cover and concealment especially during the morning thermal crossover.

• Different objects absorb heat and release it at different rates, giving differing appearances on the display. Take advantage of this thermal variation "clutter" presents a sensor operator in distinguishing heat sources. Operate in a high thermal contrast area, such as an urban area among warm cars or around rocks that have been heated by the sun.

• Do not be in an area with a uniform temperature, such as an open field, unbroken ground, a road, or paved area. Although, one exception is in the late afternoon/evening thermal crossover is another time where heat-producing sources may blend with the ground.

• Moving in periods of high heat may work even against visual detection when the UAV is at a long distance and low altitude as heat distortion makes observations problematic.

- Operate during periods of heavy precipitation. Rain degrades the ability of the sensor to see further and washes out the temperatures. In winter or overcast weather, a high-altitude drone may not be able to see you, but sUAS can operate below very low cloud decks.
- Only use smoke to conceal the exact nature of movements, not that movements are occurring.

IR escape and evasion

- Put objects between you and the sensor.
- Hide in thermal clutter of areas with large temperature differentials such as a rock field.
- Blend, not cool. Do not attempt to cool yourself off. It will not work no matter how many ice packs you stuff in your pants and if you can afford to build a lightweight actively cooled suit then you can probably afford to bribe whoever is trying to kill you *not* to kill you.
- Do not attempt to hide in a stream or a body of water as the exposed parts of your body will be highly visible.
- If you are being chased, run into deep vegetation. Thick undergrowth or heavy tree canopies will make it very difficult to see through the foliage. Move under tree cover or in shadows whenever possible. Understand a smart adversary will expect this.
- Hiding under a recently driven vehicle with a still-hot engine is sub-optimal but is better than nothing.

Ch. 11 Surviving the UAS Threat on the Ground

Ground forces and civilians *cannot* continue business as usual upon sighting an unknown or enemy UAV. Forces must assume that they have been spotted and reconnoitered. One cannot assume that since the sighting was brief, and the UAV immediately departed the area that they were not seen.

The drone may have been surveilling undetected for some time and, if not, even a simple observation is enough to be devastating to a unit. Even the most ephemeral of sightings tells an enemy one's location. Video can also be replayed at leisure to map defensive positions, check for anything missed in real time, count personnel strength, and gather other intelligence.

A military unit would need to be wary at this point of a potential imminent artillery attack if UAS assets are integrated with long-range fires. In Ukraine, troops moving under cover have been seen by an unobserved drone only to be shelled minutes later. Furthermore, the limited appearance of one UAV may herald the coming of another for further intelligence collection. The more detailed follow-on flights may not be obvious, such as when a tactical unit's UAS report is used to task an undetectable high-altitude platform.

Upon spotting a drone, personnel *must* immediately execute the mitigation procedures and prepare for a defense. Defenses need to include counter-UAS against both ISR UAVs and UCAVs without forgetting that conventional attacks like infantry assaults or artillery fire are more likely than grenade drops. Citizen defenders should be alert for further ISR observation flights, armed drone attacks, or attacks by ground.

Not fighting openly

Not fighting openly is another consideration. Simply concealing one's arms, load bearing equipment, and not wearing a recognizable uniform will go a long way to not looking like a combatant. Combatants approaching an objective could appear to be workmen or refugees until the last moment, for example. Dozens of men standing around street corners in dark clothing could be seen by a UAV but not their concealed pistols or rifles stashed out-of-sight somewhere nearby.

The laws of war dictate that participants in an international conflict fight openly, in a uniform, or at least with some sort of recognizable symbol. Article 4 of the Third Geneva Convention (1949) requires that combatants wear a "fixed distinctive sign," carry arms openly, and conduct operations according to the laws of war. Otherwise, these *francs-tireurs*, "free shooters" or essentially guerillas, may be summarily executed.

In many western countries, such as the United States, an insurrectionist would need to be adjudicated prior to execution, either through the civil court system or by court martial. Such customs are not required by international law to be observed in domestic conflicts and may be totally ignored by a tyrannical regime. In many other countries and in actual "dirty" conflicts extrajudicial killings of partisans happen regardless of their conduct or reprisals on civilian populations.

Avoidance

Note: Always maintain an air guard detail 24/7 (separate chapter).

The **DOA cycle:** Detection > Observation > Attack. This is the process from which an attack evolves; consider it the "prey" side of the OODA loop. From the moment of drone detection, personnel must assume they have been detected, have been under observation for some time, and will be attacked. It is safer to assume that you are always under observation than to be complacent.

Camouflage any defensive positions and create decoy positions. Do not fall into patterns. Control light, radio, and sound emissions. Minimize the use of all light or heat emitting sources. Remember that if your adversary is sophisticated enough to have UAS, he probably can see infrared light sources and has thermal devices.

Radio signals can give you away to anyone capable of intercepting radio traffic or detecting telemetry-type signals. Even if adversarial units are remote from you, UAVs can be used to conduct RF surveillance. Sound is less of a concern with UAS since practically no platforms have microphones and if they did the motors will block out any environmental noise. Remember a UAV might be supporting scouts who *can* hear you.

Always be under overhead concealment, if not cover. Do not rest or take breaks in the open whenever possible. Inactive persons should be under camouflage or overhead cover. If you do not need to be exposed to the sky, get beneath something, i.e., camo netting, a tree canopy, inside a building, in a bunker, etc. Note that a smart enemy will expect you to move into treed/vegetated areas and search for you there.

Limit all unnecessary movement. Leaders need to keep subordinates in check to prevent them from moving around; this is especially important with civilians or irregular forces. When movement is necessary, move under overhead cover or behind terrain. Choose low ground or high-relief terrain to bivouac or move in. Use reverse slopes. Remain under tree cover whenever possible. Trees keep drones at a higher altitude and also offer protection from visual observation and thermal detection.

Travel at night or in inclement weather. Darkness will not work if the adversary has thermal imaging or night vision, but it will increase the probability of being overlooked. Darkness also has the advantage of helping to reduce whatever details might be more plainly seen in daytime, such as painted markings or recognizing faces. Move in the shadows early or very late in the day when the sun is low, and shadows are long. To avoid thermal sensors, traveling late in the afternoon during thermal crossover is a possibility.

If in an urban area, move between buildings inside or underground as much as possible. Note that uniforms in an environment or circumstance where they are unusual will attract attention. A line of ragged individuals walking through ruins may not draw attention from a UAV, but a group of men in Multicam with openly carried rifles will.

Disperse personnel, vehicles, and positions to reduce signature and complicate targeting. The smaller the element, the less chance it will be spotted. Imagine one ant versus a trail of ants. Smaller units or convoys also reveal less information about the strength of a group, ensure greater survivability of the group as a whole, and present less opportunity to give away information about intent, equipment, or identity.

Contact

Visual contact with a hostile or unknown UAV is a dangerous situation. The nature of the drone will likely be, at best, unknown. Once a drone closes to a distance where it can be visually identified, the danger has increased acutely as it can likely see you better than you can see it. Accordingly, your response must match the dramatically greater threat. You must assume that a drone has seen you before you have seen it, meaning that your adversary is already reacting to you.

Though in the past many UAVs had poor visibility that limited their view to directly forward, it was possible that an aircraft may appear and be seen before it saw ground forces. A very small window would exist for ground forces to conceal themselves or might go unnoticed purely out of luck. With today's improvements in technology, particularly with the use of multi-camera quadcopters, this can no longer be assumed.

Actual or suspected launches of an unknown nature *must* be investigated. An assumed friendly launch must be confirmed if you do not already *know* it is friendly. Vigilance and dissemination give yourself the earliest warning of a drone and pass that warning on to everyone else. Once a drone is observed, it needs to be immediately reported to all affected parties. It should be assumed hostile until proven otherwise but do not fire unless the weapon control status authorizes firing on an unidentified or hostile, but non-attacking UAV.

If UAVs are in operation in an area, one must assume that they are under observation at all times. The approach of an unknown UAV must be treated as an indicator of a potential imminent attack. All survivability and camouflage precautions should be taken until the all-clear is given.

REDEYE drill

A REDEYE drill is a military immediate action drill when it is necessary to avoid *nighttime* IR (thermal) detection. The REDEYE drill could be used during daylight with less emphasis on thermal concealment. If an unknown UAS signature is detected electronically in the vicinity, but not sighted, execute the REDEYE drill until it is confirmed not to be a threat or goes away.

- **Meaning:** UAV sighted, it may have not seen you. Act as though it has seen you.
- **Action:** freeze in place and camouflage using a ghillie blanket, poncho, or tarp to reduce the visual/IR

thermal signature. If in the open, drop and minimize shadow. Don't move unless absolutely necessary.

- **Example call:** "REDEYE, UAV twelve o'clock high behind City Hall!"

Actions to take before attack

- Camouflaged positions from above are necessary.
- Weapons and tactical gear may need to be concealed or disguised to allow defenders to appear like average civilians.
- Uniforms or camouflage clothing may give away a tactical unit and prioritize it for attack.
- Fixed defenses or locations, if not hardened, should have a hardened shelter constructed with sufficient overhead cover nearby.

Immediate action drill

- Callout and execute the REDEYE drill, modified to seek cover if it has seen you.
- Upon the approach of a drone, seek the nearest cover and freeze. Try to pick a place where you will be unseen by the drone and have adequate overhead and lateral protection from weapons fire.
- Groups should disperse and maintain five-meter separation.
- Non-combatants should take cover indoors under stout cover.
- Do not look up. Faces are instantly recognizable, especially when uncamouflaged, and facial recognition techniques could be applied to imagery by an adversary.
- Observe the drone. Determine its type and if it is carrying a payload (guns or bombs). Photograph it if possible.
- Wait until it leaves the area to resume normal operations, if possible.

- If it is within your capabilities and the drone is within range, you may attempt to shoot it down.
- Drone pilots may be regarded as snipers and handled accordingly.

Actions upon attack

Expect little to no warning of a UAV attack. Do not count on approaching motor noise to alert you. Upon attack/warning, personnel should take defensive positions with overhead cover and utilize mitigation techniques and CUAS active measures as ordered/appropriate.

Example: A drone spots you and appears to take no interest in you. No attack materializes. After some time, you return to base, thinking you are in the clear. Little do you know that another drone has been surveilling you, anticipating you unwittingly leading the enemy back to a juicer target. An attack on the more valuable target then occurs.

If you fall under attack, move, if in the open, to under cover. If cover cannot be found, find overhead concealment and remain still and execute the REDEYE drill. Do not run back to your concealed unit if the UAV does not appear aware of its location. Soldiers who flee from the kill zone can be hunted down by a maneuvering drone that has the ability to look behind and around obstacles. Before, forward observers were limited to static views and if an enemy went behind a hill or grove of trees, the observer could only assume the position of the enemy.

Static personnel units under UAV attack may deploy smoke to obscure their positions from above. It may not prevent an attack, but effective smoke concealment will complicate targeting. Note that smoke will be highly visible, so this tactic is only for use *imminently before or after* an attack has commenced.

If you are wounded, keep moving and get to cover if you are at all able to. Simply being wounded will not guarantee that you will not be hit by a second munition. Begin first aid under cover. If others are wounded, when practical, move the wounded to beneath cover and concealment before rendering aid. If the injuries are too critical to move them, stabilize the wounded and move them as soon as practicable.

Even when being attacked from direct fire or indirect fire, remain alert to the threat of UAS attack as the pilot may be working in concert with other forces. Do not assume that the first explosion will be the only explosion. Drones need to be treated like snipers; if a drone is or might be present, do not expose yourself to the sky if you don't have to the same as you wouldn't put yourself in the line of fire unnecessarily.

Cover and prepared positions

Any prepared position that is intended to offer protection from attack is a *survivability position*, which includes foxholes, blast shelters, bunkers, trenches, and other fighting positions. If armed drones are used in a conflict, these will be necessary to survive attacks. Open camps are not safe anywhere within UAS flying distance of the enemy. Bases and outposts need to be camouflaged and preferably setup in buildings with little to no external sign of military activity.

Choose positions where the land itself offers some protection from observation or allowing UAVs to get close. Use the natural terrain to your advantage. Why built camouflaged positions in the open when you can have half the work done by moving into the treeline? Certain natural features will inherently offer concealment:

- High-relief terrain (badlands, gullies, canyons, hilly, mountainsides, etc.)
- Low ground
- Under vegetation
- In shadows or low color contrast against both the ground itself (from the air) and any horizontal background.
- Inside buildings, avoiding any obvious silhouetting against the building's sides.
- Areas with lots of obstructions (like low wires).

When possible, use existing cover and concealment away from natural lines of drift (roads, paths, etc.).

Positions should be sited in deep shadow, beneath tall tree canopies, and deep in undergrowth. Whenever possible, do not site positions on the crest of elevated terrain; locate on reverse slopes, which is the "back" side away from the enemy. There should be no particular feature of interest around that may attract attention. Space positions and any objects in an unpredictable, irregular pattern. Vary the spacing, alignment, and coverage so obvious patterns are not created that may draw the eye.

Trenches are a thing of the past. They are way too obvious and are easily spotted from the air. Their size makes effective camouflage difficult. Likewise, fixed fighting positions are equally vulnerable, though probably safer than a trench network if the position is small, well concealed, and camouflaged properly.

Cover trenches, foxholes, and other positions with camouflage netting at a minimum. If hard cover (sandbags, earth) can't be used, use blankets or other suitable materials to create a thermal blanket beneath the visual camouflage layer. Use camouflage tarps with low-shine and cover them with either "cabbage patch" type netting or cut foliage.

Shelters need to be dugout for both camouflage (especially in winter) and overhead protection from air-dropped grenades and bombs whenever possible. Camouflage or hide both interior portions (sandbags, walls, etc.) of the sides and bottom of any trench, foxhole, or other excavation including the bottom. Shoring or wattle is distinctive and the color of the soil contrasts with the ground surface.

To be effective, overhead cover has to be able to withstand a warhead impacting directly. This means thick enough to absorb a blast, able to support the weight of the overburden, and strong enough to not collapse when there is an explosion. The standard should be for protection against mortars and grenades. US Army field manual FM 5-15 is obsolete but still offers good advice on how to build sturdy fighting positions.

The position has to be constructed in such a way that a munition detonated at the entrance can't penetrate into the shelter area. This will require covered entrances with at least one, if not two, 90° turns to deflect the shock wave and shrapnel. 90° turns in trenches, if utilized, are more important than ever. Cover trenches, foxholes, and other positions with camouflage netting at a minimum.

It's unlikely that a suburban neighborhood will have good locations for blast-resistant fighting positions, but everyone who is on guard duty or patrol should have somewhere to run to. Even a home will offer surprisingly good protection against a drone-dropped munition. Grenades don't have the force to seriously damage a house and larger munitions won't have the same velocity as if launched on a ballistic trajectory.

If using an earthen cover, carefully blend the dirt or replace the sod so the ground does not appear to be freshly disturbed. Plastic sandbags are known to shine in sunlight and need to be covered with earth or mud. Burlap sandbags should be used instead. Remove spoil from the area or disperse it thoroughly.

The best overhead concealment always has irregular 3D relief, like a camouflage net or ghillie blanket. A flat surface like a tarp, even if in an earthen color or camouflage pattern, is more recognizable. The top concealment layer should be irregular in color, shape, and depth like natural ground or vegetation. Place any thermal barrier *below* the concealment layer.

If using cut vegetation, ensure that it is replaced as soon as it begins to wilt or brown. Place it as naturally as possible as if it grew there but even tree boughs laid across a hole is better than nothing. Vegetation should not be cut so much that it is conspicuously absent, or the signs of cutting are obvious.

Ensure that any netting or tarps reach the ground and do not cast a shadow visible from the air. Nets and tarps should be tightly staked and guyed so that they do not blow in the wind, creating unnatural motion.

Netting to catch or deflect munitions can be used over protected areas, however, the nets have to be strong enough to bear the force of an up-to four-pound (2.2kg) object striking it and detonating after falling up to several hundred feet. If the warhead detonates, the height of the netting will be perfect to create a dangerous airburst effect. Protective netting should only be used to keep drones from flying into an area. Prisons use nets to prevent the delivery of contraband to inmates, not to stop explosions.

One thing that is immediately obvious in videos of drone attacks on Russian soldiers is that their fighting positions are very disorganized, messy, and surrounded by litter. Police the trash and keep the area neat. Blowing garbage scattered around the landscape is like a breadcrumb trail for UAVs to home in on and follow. Do not stack manmade objects in a natural area where they would be out of place. If you must use objects like tires in your shelter construction, cover them with dirt or other natural-appearing camouflage.

Grenade-bombing drones are accurate enough, owing mostly to their ability to precisely position themselves, to drop explosives down chimneys. Chimneys must not be open to the sky and if they are, should have some sort of grate to eliminate the possibility of anything being dropped in. Vertical openings to the sky are dangerous; horizontal ones to the ground less so, although an explosive detonated just outside the opening can send shrapnel inside.

In buildings, stay away from the windows. Remain deep in the interior shadows. Modern window glass will prevent thermal imagers from seeing through, but it is not impossible. Openings need to be covered with thermally opaque shields like blankets. Attempt to pick non-obvious positions, such as middle floors versus the top floor. Ensure that the building has multiple concealed access points.

In urban areas, the aerial view is visually cluttered from the air due to the artificial nature of the landscape. Use this clutter to your advantage by hiding in plain sight. The variance in the visual pattern and thermal gradients from all the different surfaces, textures, and colors will interfere with visual, near-infrared, and thermal observation.

Glare from windows or bright surfaces is problematic for thermal and optical sensors as well. In an urban setting, attempt to select positions or move through areas with lots of overhead obstructions like trees, buildings, or wires. At the bottom of narrow "urban canyons" with tall buildings on other sides will also help to limit UAS operations due to GPS and radio signals being obstructed.

Disperse personnel, vehicles, and positions to reduce signature and complicate targeting. The smaller the element, the less chance it will be spotted. Imagine one ant versus a trail of ants. Smaller units or convoys also reveal less information about the strength of a group, ensure greater survivability of the group as a whole, and present less opportunity to give away information about intent, equipment, or identity.

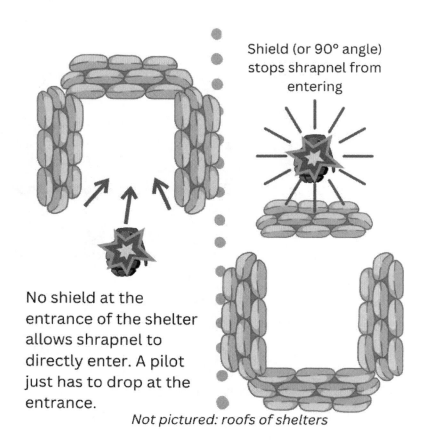

Shield (or 90° angle) stops shrapnel from entering

No shield at the entrance of the shelter allows shrapnel to directly enter. A pilot just has to drop at the entrance.

Not pictured: roofs of shelters

Evasion

If caught by a drone, do you evade? Based on the size of the drone, you can estimate how far the enemy is. A micro-drone puts them very close, probably well within rifle distance, certainly under a mile. A larger consumer grade drone (ex. DJI Phantom) would put the enemy within 1-5 miles, depending on terrain.

Custom-built or military drones operating low enough to be observed would probably indicate a 10-20 mile presence at max. However, just because a drone may be operating at its extreme range doesn't mean that it isn't supporting nearby ground forces that are maneuvering to your position.

Even indirect contact must be taken seriously. Assume that a hostile or unknown drone has observed you and act accordingly. If a drone is watching you, assume that it has been watching you for some time already. A UAV sighting should be warning that enemy contact may be imminent. Upon visually (or auditorily) observing a drone, take immediate action measures such as the immediate action drill.

- If you can see them, they can see you (applies to the drone and anyone being watched).
- Cameras can look in directions independent of the flight direction, i.e., tracking you while the drone is flying away or orbiting.
- On hearing or seeing a drone, move immediately to cover or concealment.
- Freeze if you can't take cover. Human eyes are drawn to motion and software can identify movement as well.
- Don't look up. Faces are easily recognizable to the human operator or AI and recorded images can be used for facial recognition matching if such databases and facilities exist.
- Cover exposed skin, especially faces. Light skin especially reflects sunlight and stands out against darker ground cover.

- If you are being chased, run into deep vegetation. Thick undergrowth or heavy tree canopies will make it very difficult to see through the foliage. Move under tree cover or in shadows whenever possible. Put objects between you and the sensor.

To run, or not to run?

Many Russian soldiers when attacked by a Ukrainian drone use the same self-protection procedures for any explosive attack; they go prone or find cover. This worsens the problem by fixing the target potentially in a point where a grenade blast is magnified, such as a foxhole. By contrast, running seems to have spared more than a few lives. Pilots must chase and re-aim anyone who runs, so it is easier for them not to follow and attack the slow or freezing soldiers.

There may be merit in running from a munition drop rather than going prone or into a fetal position. In many videos we see soldiers in a trench or lying in the open begin to react to a drone attack. Without cover, they are exposed to the full effect of the explosion.

The crux of this idea is that running takes advantage of the blast radius being relatively small and the "small bullet, big sky" theory. By increasing one's distance from the detonation, the chance of survival increases as the concussion is weaker and the shrapnel becomes less dense. Getting behind cover is the ultimate goal. While this is certainly not a guarantee of survival or a substitute for proper all-around cover, it is better than lying out in the open, totally defenseless.

Taking cover low to the ground, preferably in a

depression, is the traditional method to survive RAM attacks. This advice is predicated on a direct hit not happening and allowing the cover to protect from the blast and shrapnel. A drone-dropped warhead is different than a nearby RAM hit because an accurate drop is a direct hit; and most drops are quite accurate. Going prone will do little to protect you if you are at the same level and within the munition's blast radius when it detonates.

By contrast, running away has the ability to increase the probability of reaching lateral (not vertical) cover. If one can get behind safety, they will be offered better protection from the shrapnel than if they got low in the open nearer to the detonation. Video shows that most drone pilots can't reposition, accurately aim, and drop faster than a human can run so moving at the moment of drop may mitigate death/injuries. This mainly holds true if the detonation occurs in an open area with no cover or the munition will land in a fighting position. As the drone may have multiple warheads or there could be a second one out there, getting under vertical cover is vital to continued survival.

The actual fall of the munition from 100 feet would be approximately 2.5 seconds. It is not the time it takes for the weapon to reach ground that counts but when the UAV is making its final positioning maneuvers to "take aim." There will be a slight delay as the pilot completes his aiming maneuver, releases the weapon, and detonation occurs. In some of the videos, an alert soldier is able to take advantage of this time to get away.

For this to work, it requires above all luck; the casualty

radius of a typical hand grenade is 15-50 feet (5-15 meters), after all. The largest payoff will be to those alert soldiers who spot an incoming drone attack. Many of those killed in Ukraine by grenade drops were simply unaware of the drone's presence. Survival odds can be maximized by keeping an air guard, not remaining in the open except when absolutely necessary, and having vertical cover very close near by.

Drone behavior

- A drone that advances across a landscape or city blocks relatively slowly, but also seems to be examining areas to the front and sides of an avenue of approach may be performing recon for an advancing enemy.
- Just because the drone has flown by does not mean it didn't see you.
- A drone that is orbiting a particular area may be providing ISR or is on-station to provide targeting information or forward observation for indirect fire. One should assume that indirect fire or a UAV attack will follow.
- A drone orbiting your location may also be gathering detailed intelligence, including your response to UAS.
- A UAV landing or taking off indicates a potential LRP which means adversaries are nearby.

Tips

- Soldiers and citizen defenders *must* get into the habit of constantly looking up and scanning the sky, the same as scanning their sectors at ground level. **Everyone is an air guard**; some are dedicated to observation.
- Remain vigilant to UAV threats. Always post an air guard and use electronic detectors.

- Integrate EW (detection and jamming/spoofing) within small units. Make use of early warning networks and intelligence. Maintain good OPSEC.
- Think about what you look like from above and consider open sky as dangerous as having a direct line-of-sight to an enemy. In winter, when deciduous trees have lost their leaves, attempt to take cover beneath evergreen trees.
- Keep all positions neat, free of garbage, and as camouflaged from the air as possible. Your position should not look like a campsite. Police your trash; it's highly visible from the air and tends to expand your perimeter (and thus signature) as it gets blown or tossed around.
- Stay away from large collections of vehicles and military equipment. Do not stand around in large groups or queues. Crowds are more visible versus dispersed individuals.
- Do not park vehicles near your shelter whenever possible; keep them away at least 100 feet (33m).
- Travel in "dead space" or the ground below the crests of elevated terrain and on reverse slopes. Cross open terrain at night or in periods of inclement weather.
- If you see a drone, assume that it has seen you and has been observing you for some time. Do not assume that because the drone seemingly showed no interest in you that it did not see you.
- If a UAV flies over or orbits, do not look up. The US Army bluntly cautions: "One of the most obvious features on aerial photographs is the upturned faces of soldiers."[43]
- Gimbal cameras can point in any direction and the entire point of a fly-by may have been a deception to get you to think you were not detected/observed.
- Do not leave light objects with intelligence value, such as portable radios, outside where a drone can grab them.

---

[43] ATTP 3-34.39, *Camouflage, Concealment, and Decoys*, p. D-3

- Have dry chemical fire extinguishers on hand to put out fires. Water is not effective on some thermobaric or incendiary explosive components.
- Urinate and defecate under cover or at least quality concealment.

Ch. 12 Vehicles and Convoys Under UAS Threat

Not much can be done to reduce the signature of a moving vehicle or a convoy as most civilian vehicles are limited to hardtop or improved roads. Roadways are easily surveilled. Vehicular UAS defensive practices involve good route selection, good camouflage and siting when stopped, and skilled driving. All drivers in a hostile UAS environment should have undergone some kind of evasive driving education or course.

Camouflage

Whenever possible, vehicles should be in dull (matte) paint jobs versus reflective, glossy metallic paint. Glossy paint can be dulled by applying spray paint and completely painted over with other paints if necessary. Mud can be used as a temporary dulling agent. Vehicles that are already in earth tones (browns, light grays, and dull greens) are best. Black will probably standout against many light natural backgrounds than lighter colors.

If in an urban area, use a vehicle that blends in with the environment. A Humvee will standout anywhere but a war zone, a new, high-end Mercedes stands out in a poor neighborhood, and a large diesel pickup truck with armed dudes in the back stands out everywhere. Drive smartly, using tactics appropriate for the environment and the tempo of traffic. Don't drive in an aggressive manner that may be the best choice tactically but from the air looks like a police pursuit on TV news.

Cover the entire vehicle with camouflage netting when parking on the move. If possible, suspend the netting above the vehicle rather than just draping it over the body. Do not position the netting so it casts shadows of the area beneath it, like a shady area under an awning. The dark/light contrast is obvious in daylight.

Use poles, ropes, or wires to create an irregular shape that doesn't look like someone just threw a camo tarp over a car. Objects can be placed on the hood or in the bed of a truck to prop up netting to avoid the distinctive silhouette. Break up the shape of instantly recognizable things, like wheels, etc. Place disruptively painted cardboard pieces over the wheels/tires and cover with camo netting.

All vehicles should be carrying camouflage netting large enough to cover the entire vehicle down to the bottom of the tires. Pieces of cloth or blankets in neutral colors or large sections of cardboard should be carried to cover up window glass to limit reflections (shine). Since tires are highly recognizable and likely to be exposed, something similar to hide them and break up the distinctive shape should be carried. A section of brown cardboard behind camo netting or painted in a disruptive pattern may help.

Cover tracks over with dirt or sweep light tracks to minimize them but be careful that any replacement earth does not contrast with the torn-up earth. Pay special attention to points of hardtop roadways where vehicles enter/exit as these areas are likely to leave characteristic mud or dirt tracks.

EMCON

Practice EMCON, or emissions control. Radio transmissions should be limited to only that which is necessary, sent at the lowest power possible, and using a directional antenna, preferably sent a good distance away from the main body of any unit.

Light discipline including "shine" or sun reflection from glass or equipment needs to be considered. This includes blackout style headlights, face paint, covering windows of parked vehicles, using mud or other obscurants to dull shiny materials or easily recognizable equipment like sandbags, etc.

Minimize the use of lighting. Use passive night vision, when possible, infrared lighting for roadway illumination, if necessary (and the adversary does *not* use NODs), and if forced to use white lights use convoy lighting techniques by taping over the lenses.

Ground Route selection

Route selection is important to enhance the masking of the movements of a unit, convoy, or individual person or vehicle. Do not use obvious routes if you can avoid it. In some cases, using a backroad might be suspicious whereas blending in with normal traffic on the highway might arouse no concerns.

Utilize routes that have environmental vertical concealment. This could be beneath a dense tree canopy, roadways where trees shade the road, or taking underground passageways. Keeping terrain or buildings between a vehicle or unit and the direction of potential observation, such as traveling in a defile from the enemy, can also assist in remaining unseen. Remember that drones look down and at an angle, so sky-lining is not the only concern. Handrail blocking terrain features like a canyon wall, hedgerow, treeline, etc. on the reverse slope.

Travel in low ground when possible. sUAS cannot be used below the line-of-sight, so use routes with obstructed LOS to high ground/structures whenever possible to take advantage of any radio signal obstruction. Examples include dry riverbeds, taking a canyon or valley road instead of one on a hill, or remaining in an urban area.

Travel at night, in low light (twilight), or when weather conditions reduce visibility, such as periods of rain, fog, and snow. Precipitation will inhibit the operation of UAS and the distance that sensors, color and infrared, can see. Dense, low fog makes it hard to see both the target and to navigate the drone, which may result in a time when drones simply cannot fly. High winds may also prevent flight or reduce endurance as the drone fights the wind.

Avoid travel in periods of snowy weather as a picturesque white landscape provides an excellent thermal background and contrast for vehicles. If you must travel, use terrain masking to put hills and vegetation between you and any UAVs.

Traveling

Ambushes, surveillance, and reconnaissance of roads

usually focus on choke points. Narrow roads, high terrain, or barely passable routes are favored. Expect attack or observation at these points. Deploy reconnaissance before proceeding through, if possible. Travel through at the fastest safe speed.

Do not drive fast enough to raise a dust cloud; 15-20 MPH (24-32 km/h) should be the maximum on dirt roads in most conditions. Stop slowly. Panic maneuvers may cause accidents or raise dust. Stay on hard ground, when possible, as paved or hard-packed roads hide tracks, but be aware that mud, snow, and splashes will indicate disturbed areas where vehicles turned on/off the route. Consider making deceptive entries/exits from the road.

Consider the effect tires will have on the terrain; tire tracks in soft soil are *highly* visible from the air. It is difficult to conceal tire or tank tracks on any surface, especially snow and deep mud. To minimize detection, avoid sharp turns and follow existing tracks. Travel single-file so it is hard to count how many vehicles passed. In snow, follow wind-swept snowdrift lines in the shadows they cast.

Maintain at least three vehicle lengths from the other vehicles at all times. If stopping in traffic, stop so that the driver can still see the tires of the vehicle in front of him over the hood; this allows room to escape if a vehicle is disabled. Keep convoys as small as reasonably possible; six to 12 vehicles, at the most. Larger convoys should be broken up into smaller platoons of autos that keep, ideally, a mile's distance from each other (separation distance may vary).

Parking and long halts

When possible, select a stopping/camp site with multiple exits. Avoid spots with only one way in and out (in an emergency) because if your group must flee under attack there is a non-zero chance that one-way-out could be a fatal funnel where you are all ambushed. Pick a rally/rendezvous point and plan to disperse in any passable direction to reorganize later.

Do not park in any close, orderly pattern. All parking should be done in dispersed, semi-random arrangements, not linearly like in a parking lot. Patterns draw attention. Space vehicles at least 25 yards/meters apart to limit damage from attack.

When stopping for a long period of time or engaging in a camouflage drill (HAWKEYE), turn off the engine. To lower the heat and sound signature, do not run vehicle engines unnecessarily. Diesel engines are particularly distinctive.

Park under tree cover or inside buildings whenever possible. Cover vehicles with camo netting regardless of tree cover. Also be wary of the only concealment in open terrain as this may be an obvious place for an adversary to check first.

Use existing terrain to shield enemies from both ground level observation and oblique aerial view. In urban areas or where possible, park inside or under buildings. Avoid bridges as they only block the directly overhead view.

Once vehicles are hidden/camouflaged, individuals should either remain in the vehicle or under cover. Personnel should not be moving around in the open unnecessarily. Break up the shape of instantly recognizable things, like wheels or vehicle profiles. Mirrors windshields should be covered when not driving. When vehicles are not in use, their headlights, taillights, and safety reflectors should be covered since they not only reflect visible light but IR light.

Vehicles parked near any camouflaged shelters risk revealing the position. When possible, keep vehicles away from the bivouac area to reduce the signature, use the vehicles to draw attackers away, and keep tire tracks from leading to the camp. Persons traveling back and forth could also be easily tracked to reveal the hidden position.

Keep vehicles away from hidden positions by at least 100 feet (30m) to decrease the chance of discovery. Proximity to military vehicles in the open is extremely hazardous as the vehicles are easier to spot and will clue in the enemy.

Park early enough in the evening or before expected contact that the vehicles and engines can cool to reduce their thermal signature. Consider the effect of hot vehicles moving over the ground creating hot spots on the earth as well. Do not raise vehicle hoods because the hot engine will be exposed creating an IR hotspot. Armored vehicles must have their hatches closed at all times except when occupied and in such cases, there needs to be an air guard on watch. Open hatches make excellent attack points.

Stopping

- Disperse into the natural cover off the roadway.

271

- Perform an immediate area recon; recon the wider area for longer stops. Pre-mission planning or reconnaissance further back on the route should have been used to select stopping places.
  - Check for glare.
  - Camouflage and re-check for effectiveness.
- When leaving, restart engines at once to limit the duration of the sound, which may allow a rough estimate of the location of its source and lower the ability to count separate starts and thus approximate the number of vehicles.

Short stops

- For all but the briefest of stops (say more than two minutes), pull off the road. More than five minutes, disperse. Conceal the vehicles in natural screening terrain or vegetation. Deploy camouflage depending on the length of the stop.
- Disabled vehicles (from a convoy, not general abandoned vehicles) should be removed from the roadway and concealed. This will help hide the passage and route of the convoy, as well as deceive anyone who may expect the vehicle to still be in the convoy.

UAS threat

- If a UAV is sighted or an aerial attack commences; get off the roadway as soon as possible *then* disperse.
- If you cannot get off the road, attempt to find an area with overhead obstructions like tree cover, bridges, or wires. Exit the vehicles in a safe spot and flee for dense vegetation or a building.
- Assuming there are no obstructions or ambushes, only a UAS threat, accelerating to speeds above 50 MPH will outpace most UAVs. This should be done in consideration of the route, the roadway,

what other threats are out there, and the nature of the terrain. Speeding away in open terrain will still leave a vehicle/convoy visible for a long distance. In urban or densely treed terrain where sightlines can be obstructed, speeding away and engaging in evasive driving on a seemingly random path would be viable.

Part III: Offense

Ch. 13 ISTAR-Intelligence, Surveillance, Targeting, and Reconnaissance

Drones have radically transformed the understanding of the battlespace and will give both partisans and citizen defenders a major advantage during any unrest or conflict. Your purpose of UAS intelligence gathering is:

- Get a new or better perspective on your surroundings;
- To be aware of developing trends before they evolve into a threat;
- Warn of imminent threats; and,
- Gain tactical information to use to your advantage.

Information is raw data or knowledge. Information is of little value if you cannot contextualize it or apply it practically. *Intelligence* is information that has been analyzed and refined into a useable product. Taking video or observing things through the "eyes" of a drone but not passing that information on to someone who can make use of it invalidates the benefit of UAS.

Note: UAS augments traditional human visual observation and physical patrols. UAS is not a replacement and should only be used in lieu of the above when it is too unsafe, impractical, or there is no manpower. For many, the allure of UAS seeming to be a replacement for "getting out there" will be hard to resist. Do not allow your drone to be a crutch or send it up because you are too lazy or scared to walk the ground. Technology is a force multiplier, not something that we should become over-reliant upon.

ISR & ISTAR

ISR is an initialism for *intelligence, surveillance, and reconnaissance* used as shorthand to indicate using a drone's camera (and other sensors) to develop actionable information about the battlespace. Basically, it means a drone looking at something. ISTAR goes a bit further to include targeting: *intelligence, surveillance, target acquisition*, and *reconnaissance*. Since the reader is not expected to do much in the way of targeting, ISR is the focus and the term used most often.

Both surveillance and reconnaissance are done to gain info about an enemy. When reconnaissance develops a target of interest and more detailed information or continuous observation of it is required, then the mission transitions to surveillance. All types of UAS information gathering are contained under these terms; you're either scouting for something or staring at something.

Collected data alone isn't the product. It has to be analyzed to be useful. Intelligence is the final product of surveillance, reconnaissance, human intelligence (spies), and other sources analyzed from the raw data combined to present a product that leaders can use to make decisions on their own courses of action and about enemy intentions. A commander watching a video feed can issue orders based on what he sees the enemy and his troops doing; merely recording the "action" becomes essentially war porn.

Coordination of acquiring, analyzing, and distributing accurate, relevant, and timely intelligence is necessary for large organizations. A UAS team will be one part of an intelligence gathering apparatus. On the smaller scale, such as the neighborhood level, the UAS team might be a single person and working in close concert with the team of decisionmakers or the drone pilot might be all of the above. Whatever the circumstances, those who can benefit from the UAS "take" should have access to the intelligence developed.

By using ISTAR as a template we can see what tasks UAS can excel in. In short, some of these roles can be summarized as:

- Early warning;
- Situational awareness;
- Continuous surveillance;
- Locate the enemy and maintain visual contact;
- Report enemy activity and identify enemy vulnerabilities;
- Direct friendly forces to the enemy or defenders to optimal positions;
- Verify enemy actions to counteract deception attempts;
- Provide target coordinates or designation for another platform;
- Assess attack effectiveness/confirm target destruction;
- Guide friendly forces to targets or around danger; and,
- Provide a real-time battle picture to assist with command and control.

What ISR can do for you

Reconnaissance

Purpose: early warning; intelligence; learn about an area.

Reconnaissance is the process of making observations of one's surroundings to gain situational awareness about the terrain, the presence of the enemy, or the nature of potential threats. Field manuals define reconnaissance as the search for answers to a specific military question. It is a process of finding out what you need to know or *don't* know that you need to know. The information it returns is analyzed to create intelligence.

Recon often is a preparation activity before an engagement or on arrival in a new area of operations. It is a process of discovery that will lead to more specific activities. Reconnaissance can be done at any time, before, during, or after an engagement or for static defensive positions. Regular reconnaissance dovetails with a UAS security mission.

Applied reconnaissance can be really broad in practice ("What kind of Coke do you want? We've got Diet, Sprite, Dr Pepper..."). At the simplest level, UAS reconnaissance is sending out a drone to see what the terrain over the next hill looks like or find the enemy. Any time one needs to send a UAV to "find out what's going on" or "go learn this information" it can be considered reconnaissance.

Tactical recon goes beyond awareness. A drone acting as a scout provides a commander or a unit real-time information to maneuver through the most suitable route to engage the enemy at the most effective time and place. Armed recon drones can attack targets of opportunity that they find. Small units with a drone may achieve better success and sustain fewer casualties through aerial recon immediately before assaulting an objective.

Broad and focused reconnaissance

Broad reconnaissance

In *broad reconnaissance*, you don't know what's out there or what's going on and the geographical area is broad, like a city or valley. Strategic intelligence would fall into this category. A zone of interest is a large area, such as a city, district, or section of the countryside such as a certain valley. Where these areas are defined by borders, this is known as *zone reconnaissance* by military manuals. For instance, a military unit that is going to occupy an area will perform zone recon before moving in, so it has a rough idea what to expect. An "area study" would be zone reconnaissance.

Example: A partisan unit intends to cross a ridgeline and make entry to a valley with a village at the center. Their UAV would be deployed to investigate the entire area, create a map as detailed as possible, locate salient terrain features, locate positions of the enemy, obstructed and ideal routes, etc. A zone recon in this instance is the "first look" at an area off a map to understand what is actually being faced.

A neighborhood defender might want to know the current conditions of enemy and friendly activity, or perhaps weather conditions, in his immediate part of the city/county. On the other hand, trying to find out the current situation in a regional area of operations would be of more actionable interest than creating a collection of facts on the area. The complexity of the recon is dependent on the level of detail required. Expanding on vague information about an unfamiliar area will be more time consuming than in a familiar area.

Example: A city descends into chaos and a neighborhood defense force doesn't know what's going on around it. A UAV deployed in a systematic survey of the city (as far out as it can go) to identify conditions and possible threats. *This would provide intelligence about the general "zone" security situation and early warning.*

While most small UAVs will have limited capabilities to cover large areas of terrain, a COTS drone might be launched to look over a hill or examine a section of a city. A drone that doesn't have the ability to fly long distances is going to be limited in how much terrain it can survey. That's why drones should be used in concert with other intelligence collection methods, such as open-source or

HUMINT, to prioritize locations.

A police command post during major riots will do this based on helicopter observation and radio reports. Citizens can use online sources, TV news, or scanner/radio reports to identify items of interest for investigation, such as checking local malls for evidence of looting. A drone conducting a broad tactical recon can look for hotspots for later investigations or return when recharged for a deeper look.

Focused reconnaissance

In *focused reconnaissance*, you know what you're looking at or for, you need more information or evidence, and the geographic area is small and confined. Tactical intelligence would fall into this category. In military parlance, this is known as *area reconnaissance*. For instance, a military unit that is going to occupy an area will perform zone recon before moving in, so it has a rough idea of what to expect.

Another way of describing it could be *point* or *area of interest* recon. The area is any geographic space or place that detailed information on is needed. A point of interest may be a certain road pass, a piece of property, a neighborhood, or a hilltop. Area recon is what many drones will be doing on reconnaissance missions especially in urban areas. Drones are well-suited to covering a specific objective from multiple angles often more closely than a human could do safely.

In an area/focused recon, the target is generally known, and the mission tailored to that, whereas a zone recon may identify precise targets for later, more detailed flights. Area recon may be used, for example, to get video of the layout of a target. These missions will include discovering the position of the enemy and his strengths. Area recons are often conducted by a unit that is already in proximity to the target. When constant contact with an objective or person/unit of interest is maintained, the mission transitions to surveillance.

Example: Gunshots and screams are heard coming from a neighboring farm. A drone is dispatched to look and see what is going on.

Example: A drone is sent to find the exact location of enemy troops below a specific ridgeline.

Example: A cartel is rumored to have taken over a warehouse in the industrial district of the city. The drone is sent out to obtain information on the level of activity in that district and attempt to locate the cartel's warehouse.

Armed reconnaissance

Reconnaissance in force, also *recon by fire*, involves intentionally making contact with the enemy and engaging him in combat. The limited ability of many sUAVs to carry large payloads will limit how many targets they can attack, so an attack mission, once the weapons are empty, may transition to reconnaissance or provide targeting to other more capable platforms.

The intent of recon by fire is to see how the enemy fights, what strength he has, and where the weak spots are. This is largely a human factor to see what the enemy does under the pressure of battle. It is hard for a drone to do this because they cannot replicate the effects of a ground unit waging a gunfight. Dropping hand grenades is not the same thing as recon in force by an infantry unit engaging an enemy ground unit.

Due to the incredible details a drone can gather, many details that can infer a unit's fighting ability can be made by an astute analysis. Accurate counts of the enemy can be made. Observations about the state of weapon readiness, ammo stockpiles, defensive positions, depth of defenses, and the behavior of the enemy might provide clues to how an enemy may fight when attacked. Indicators of poor readiness and discipline may lead to a conclusion that an enemy is unprepared and will show poor resolve when attacked.

Drones can conduct recon by drawing fire, that is, forcing the enemy to reveal is location. A low, slow flying drone will rapidly become a bullet magnet once troops become accustomed to what they can do. This will be especially prevalent among low-discipline groups such as street gangs. A pilot may enhance the survivability of his UAV by using cover, concealment, altitude, and rapid maneuvers, however, drones will be vulnerable when drawing fire.

It must be cautioned that nothing a drone can do is a substitute for an actual recon in force. Observations can be faulty or what is surmised may not reflect the adversary's actual state of mind.

Armed reconnaissance by a UAV is basically synonymous with an attack mission. An armed UAV is dispatched to find the enemy and attack him when found; hunting. To differentiate between a pure attack mission and armed recon, the former already has the target objective in mind and the purpose is to inflict damage on the enemy. The latter may not know the location of the enemy and has a dual-role of information gathering but is free to attack targets of opportunity.

Example: A drone is sent to find the exact location of enemy troops below a ridgeline. The drone is armed and upon finding the men in the trees, drops grenades on them. The coordinates can then be fed to an artillery unit for a fire mission, or an infantry squad is guided in for an attack. *This is more of an attack but illustrates what an armed drone can do to targets of opportunity when conducting reconnaissance.*

Example: Information regarding the enemy's strength and discipline is needed but it is considered too risky to unnecessarily send men to recon by fire. However, the drone is able to get close enough to find that men on watch are sleeping, weapons are dirty, and the fighting positions are poorly prepared, indicating that the enemy may be surprised and fight poorly.

Special reconnaissance

Special reconnaissance is a clandestine or less-obvious attempt to gather information. For UAS, this would cover largely visual observation of a known objective (person or location) to gather information without the target becoming aware they are being observed. This happens in hostile, denied, or sensitive areas where the consequences of being discovered are greater. For civilian defenders or insurgents, typically this would be legal consequences. In a post-SHTF or wartime environment, discovery may compromise interest in a target or damage relations with another group.

For the civilian/insurgent, this might include a "peacetime" flight in a denied area, such as a National Park, to conduct a zone reconnaissance in advance of an operation or for SHTF background intelligence. A military example would be the U-2 overflights of the Soviet Union; they were quite informative until Gary Powers was shot down and the public disclosure of the flights harmed US/Soviet relations and arms control talks.

While the techniques of special recon are not different, greater care and deniability is used in order to lower the probability of collateral damage should the UAV be detected. UAVs are well-suited to special recon because no human is put in harm's way and a properly sanitized drone will yield little information about the operator if it is downed.

- If conducting special reconnaissance where deniability is needed, consider creating some sort of cover activity to appear innocuous or disguise your true intentions.

Example: You are a rag-tag team of deputies, soldiers, and volunteers after an EMP happens. You need to rescue a dozen women from a cartel camp and need to gather intelligence about the camp and its operations without discovery. The drone flies in a fog, making observations while concealing itself in the low visibility of the clouds.

Example: You need to overfly a cartel compound and get video of something. However, the cartel has great aim and can shoot down your drone. They also have connections with China to trace the serial number of the drone to see who it was registered to. You use a drone anonymously purchased for Bitcoin from someone halfway across the country so any leads couldn't possibly be traced back to you.

Scouting

Scouting is a form of reconnaissance but to a UAS team it will be more of a dynamic search that blends elements of recon, surveillance, and tracking. "Spotting" might be another good term as the drone is being used as "eyes in the sky." Scouting covers a variety of activities:

- Gain and maintain enemy contact (assuming you already know of his presence and general location).
- Guide friendly forces around obstacles, threats, and deviations using the vertical perspective (facilitate movement).

- Tracking someone or attempting to locate signs (spoor) of their presence.
- Investigate suspicious activity or other items of interest.
- Combat search and rescue observational support.

The potential tasks are endless and go beyond "getting a look" at something.

If a human would be sent out to perform an activity on foot, why not a drone? A machine, no matter the cost, is "cheaper" than a human life, so for high-risk investigations, UAS may be preferable. Consider what advantages a drone could provide given its rapid response ability and the aerial view.

Example: Suspicious radio transmission are picked up nearby. A drone is launched to look for signs of enemy activity. In a clearing a mile away, several vehicles are parked and armed men are resting in the shade.

Example: Riots and looting are occurring nearby. It is rumored that an angry mob is moving towards your neighborhood. UAS is used to confirm this, and once the mob is spotted, maintain visual contact with them.

Example: Someone goes missing from your property. You have limited people who can search for the person, but the drone can rapidly cover the most probable routes taken to hopefully indicate what area should be searched first.

Example: A patrol is sent to intercept a theft ring

walking through your area. The UAV is used to locate the ring and then provide directions to the patrol. The UAV also keeps tabs on both groups, safely guiding the patrol around potential traps and ambushes to attack the gang from the rear.

Example: An attack occurs on your farm. Rather than send men beyond the defensive perimeter, where they could more easily be isolated and attacked, the drone goes out to find the intruders.

Target spotting

Note: We are differentiating "targeting" from attack and scouting as the role here is providing targeting data and guidance to another weapon or platform.

Forward observers and tactical air control are vital assets for artillery and air/ground support. UAS can augment traditional human "shot callers" on the ground. In austere environments where skilled individuals may be limited or absent, a drone could perform these tasks. A second observational platform may also be necessary or helpful for "suicide" drones/loitering munitions.

Drones make great targeting support platforms because they are already out scouting around and simply need to pass on the target information to the attack platform. Usually, this is some kind of ground-based long-range fire or aircraft. Domestic groups may send out a ground force to attack the target, have limited long-range fires, or send armed drones. More sophisticated groups or militaries may use drones to laser designate a target for precision strike by another platform.

The targeting mission is an evolution of reconnaissance and surveillance. An organization with the capability of UCAVs and long-range fires can take advantage of this to avoid having to send in men to neutralize the target. Many small groups and neighborhood defense teams will not have access to precision guided weaponry like laser guided missiles or attack drones, but the concepts here will carryover except in the execution.

In practice, this looks like a reconnaissance mission that finds something of interest. The pilot, a commander, or analyst determines if that item of interest is a target. An assessment is performed to identify any downsides to attacking it, i.e., collateral damage, civilians, something you'd rather capture instead, etc.

UAS teams and those working with the intelligence they collect should be familiar with the OODA loop—Observe, Orient, Decide, Act. It is not so much a decision making strategy as it is an explanation of how decision making works. First the observation is made, its implications are processed (the analysis phase), a decision is made, and then the chosen course of action is implemented. The *kill chain* is a related concept.

Kill Chain

To vastly oversimplify, the kill chain is: "I found a target, this is what it is; here it is, come kill it." It consists of target acquisition and identification, directing attack forces to the target, the actual attack, and analysis of the attack or confirmation of target destruction. The kill chain is also known as the *F2T2EA* model: Find, Fix, Track, Target, Engage, Assess; formerly "Four Fs" (find, fix, fight, finish).

- Find - Where is the enemy?
- Fix - Exactly where is the enemy?
- Track - Monitor enemy behavior and movements
- Target - Direct the weapon to the target
- Engage - Fire the weapon on the target
- Assess - Determine the effect of the attack (BDA, Battle Damage Assessment)

A target is identified by friendly forces, or through surveillance or reconnaissance. The target is then precisely located for friendly forces to attack, such as a grid square, latitude/longitude, address, etc. The UAV then monitors the target, relaying information to decisionmakers who may order an attack. If an attack is ordered, the drone maintains contact with the target to continue feeding updates on the target's location and behavior. The attack is ordered. Direct-fire weapons such as artillery cannot be recalled, but a UAV may stay on-scene to guide in ground troops or UCAVs. In some cases, UAVs may "paint" the target with a laser designator to guide incoming ordnance.

One problem that will be faced is accurate "fixing" of the target. Civilian drones almost universally will not have lasers for target designation or range finding This will complicate precision fixes on point targets, though "good enough" geolocation is no challenge. Models that groups may have access to should come equipped with GPS at least.

It should be assumed that all drones can provide fairly accurate location data, either by conventional geographic recognition or providing latitude and longitude (GPS). Civilian GPS is accurate to within about 10 feet (3 meters) which is sufficiently accurate for long-range fires like mortars or artillery. At night, terrain reference is difficult so often UAS targeting is done by directly overflying the target to obtain the coordinates. A drone overflight should be considered targeting and appropriate precautions taken.

COTS drones may not be able to compute the target location from the camera image. The drone should overfly the location when possible to obtain the precise coordinates, or, estimate the range from the drone's location as precisely as possible and extrapolate the correct target coordinates. Exact coordinates should not be expected of a UAV, but determinations can be made through the use of maps or mapping software in combination with the drone's position and imagery.

At the neighborhood level, the UAS team should be capable of describing the location in terms of addresses or cross-streets. As gathering address numbers from the air is difficult, house/building descriptions or counts (third house from the NE corner, east side of the street) is best. This should be acceptable because neighborhood security groups probably won't be using armed drones. Precision or long-range fires for military units will need to be fed proper coordinates (MGRS or lat/long).

BDA

BDA, or Battle Damage Assessment, is the analysis of the results of an attack or combat. A UAS crew will perform it by visually surveying the battle or impact area. This goes beyond marveling at the damage to tanks and buildings or how big craters are. BDA takes into consideration functional factors (can the enemy still fight and how well?) beyond simple material damage. The intent is to gauge the impact to the enemy (or your own defenses, if turned inward) and the need to continue the attack or re-attack.

UAVs make excellent BDA platforms and will be the only aerial platform for many small units and organizations. Drones allow assessment of long-range fires or ground attack without having to send men in on foot or within visual range. UAS can also monitor particularly the impact of long-range fires in real time with comparative safety.

The best results come in in real time so parts of BDA can spill into the command and control role. Usually drones on targeting missions to support long-range fires do BDA as a secondary task, but they can be sent to fly over after a battle as well. Traditionally BDA has been after-the-fact given how live television transmission from military aircraft is a relatively new technology. Elements of a BDA mission include:

- Watch the impact of munitions from a safe location.
- Order adjustments of long-range fires as necessary.
- Return after the impact to inspect the damage and impact on the enemy.
- Return after a ground engagement or other battle to gather overhead imagery for assessment.

Surveillance

Surveillance comes from the French to literally "watch over" which is apt considering the aerial perspective of UAS. Surveillance differs from reconnaissance in that whereas recon is more of a process of discovery, surveillance is more deliberate, prolonged, and persistent involving continuous observation. Almost always surveillance missions will begin with a specific objective in mind. The objective will usually be a fixed and static point, person, or group of interest. Some examples are:

- Continuous surveillance on a specific person or place (target).
- Flying observation post or flying security camera.
- Outer picket/screen.
- Watching avenues of approach or areas of interest.

If recon is about answering questions on the unknown, surveillance is narrowed down to knowing what someone is doing or what is going on at a specific location. Using the Bid Laden analogy from the Army, reconnaissance on his Pakistan hideout allowed the CIA and SEALs to map the layout and understand what the conditions on the ground were like.

Surveillance came in as drones watched to identify the tall, robed man that came out on to his balcony, tracked the courier, and gathered information on the patterns of life around the compound. Another example is a police officer patrolling for drug deals is conducting reconnaissance, but when he stops to watch who comes in and out of a drug house, that's now surveillance.

Surveillance has a narrow focus not just on the objective

but what it's looking for. It is

monitoring things like behavior and communications. Drones may be used to get information on enemy activities that could indicate intent or strength. Men unloading artillery from trucks could indicate an upcoming offensive. Large numbers of people of a certain demographic or dressed a certain way might indicate a gang house. Watching an enemy position for days might enable planners to discover potential weaknesses when/where to attack.

Screening provides early warning through detection of the enemy and using UAS allows small groups to maintain better defensive situational awareness. The UAV is looking to make direct sightings of the enemy and signs of his presence. UAS is well suited to searching areas beyond the view of OP/LP, often on the flanks and covering denied or inaccessible terrain.

A moving flank screen is an area where UAS can excel as it is more difficult for ground troops as they have to move outward away from the protected area (route) and also move in parallel down the route. A drone can do this much more easily due to perspective and speed of travel. If the area between the enemy and the perimeter/unit is otherwise observed/protected by friendlies, the drone can recon further forward to maximum range.

Using UAS conserves manpower that may be needed on a defensive line versus making a patrol. It also reduces time that patrols may spend investigating by pre-identifying areas of interest versus "clear" areas. It is important to note that surveillance does not replace, but augments ground patrols, watchmen, guards, and ground surveillance (OP/LP).

Example: A high-value gang leader that has been terrorizing your neighborhood needs to be apprehended. Your defensive team sends a drone to fly high above his house to gather intelligence on his actions, security measures, and routine.

Example: A drone looking for insurgent activity sees what appears to be rockets being carried into a barn. The drone shifts from reconnaissance to surveillance as it keeps a constant watch on the barn to see if any of the suspected rockets are brought out.

Example: An angry mob is loitering around the entrance to your complex. UAS is used to look for weapons, identify any potential leaders, gauge the tone of the crowd, signs of incitement, etc.

Example: You expect that an infiltration attempt will occur through a certain avenue of approach. A drone is sent to watch that area at the time the attempt is expected.

Security operations

Surveillance is a form of security operation. Security

operations are those missions that provide early warning of attack in order to offer a more effective defense. The Army states that "the ultimate goal of security operations is to protect the force from surprise and reduce the unknowns in any situation."[44] Keeping watch should be a no-brainer; it gives reaction time and the chance to stop an attack at a distance, which UAS makes easier as physical human movements beyond one's perimeter are reduced.

A drone also has the advantage of the look-down view that altitude provides and the ability to get sightlines a stationary observer cannot. UAS aids security operations through:

- Providing early warning of enemy approach.
- Continuous (or intermittent) surveillance on avenues of approach.
- Reporting and investigating enemy activity in/around the protected area.
- Gaining and maintaining contact with an approaching enemy.
- Guiding reaction forces to contact and assisting them with enemy interdiction attempts.

The frequency of surveillance can be increased through the use of UAS as little preparation or recovery time is needed versus the time to mount a patrol.

UAS is integrated with other continuous forms of observation and information like OP/LPs, watchtowers, security cameras, patrols, and warnings from the community. Visual contact with the enemy must be maintained when detected in order to pass the most

---

[44] ADRP 3-90, p. 5-3

accurate information along. Contact doesn't have to be maintained by UAS alone, but mere detection that doesn't seek to gain an advantage by monitoring the enemy's activities is next to worthless.

UAVs can patrol the perimeter of one's property, neighborhood, or position to conduct *area security* and also move further out into the surrounding area for *local security*. Area security would involve area recon as outlined above but local security would be limited to the areas immediately adjacent, or within, the protected perimeter.

Security operations share elements of surveillance and reconnaissance but focus on the entity or place to be protected, rather than "finding" the enemy. It is not a mission to find the enemy to engage him, but to determine if the enemy is near in order to better prepare a defense. Preventing a surprise attack and not being caught unprepared is the goal. In this context, surveillance and reconnaissance for early warning would be part of a security *screen* where the drone is watching between a potential threat vector and the protected area.

Example: An intrusion attempt occurs on your perimeter. Rather than send men "outside the wire" you send a drone to confirm that the suspects have fled the area but are lying in ambush for any pursuing squad.

Example: A drone is launched daily to fly around the perimeter and other areas to look for signs of enemy activity. The footage can be run back at high speed and compared day-to-day to look for any changes, such as a camouflaged sniper's hide or OP.

Example: You would like to have an OP located in a high place, but you have none and the ground is flat. At intervals, the drone is launched high above your property or neighborhood to pan around and scan for threats.

Example: The looting/riot mob is moving away from the mall towards your neighborhood which contains the home of a policeman who was involved in a high-profile shooting. The drone is used to fly to the mob, then maintain visual contact with it, relaying information about its behavior and location. Once in contact, the drone can begin surveillance of the mob or certain individuals in it.

Example: The morning UAV flight is launched to see if anyone infiltrated the neighborhood overnight. Several blocks away, smoke is seen coming from the yard of an abandoned home. A large group of refugees are seen camping out there.

Convoys and patrols

UAS has a very useful place for movement of ground elements. Two of the most obvious uses are scouting ahead of convoys and patrols to both look for obstacles/ambushes and help the unit navigate. Imagine the level of warning that a convoy might have if a drone is flying a mile ahead of the vehicles and can detect a barricade and ambush before the vehicles arrive.

Route reconnaissance gathers information on a specific route, including terrain, obstructions, the presence of the enemy, and any other factors that could affect travel along that route. Not all information about the geography of an area can be learned by maps, nor will a paper map display real time conditions or threat information. Sending someone out ahead of the main body of a unit/convoy is one method but use of a UAV will be safer and more expedient.

Route recon can be divided into *informational* and *mobile*. Informational recon seeks to learn more about the route for general intelligence purposes. The unit conducting the recon is likely static or defensive and either expects to move along the route or encounter the enemy along it at some point in the future. Checking avenues of approach to one's AO to detect signs of an impending threat would fall into this category.

Mobile route recon (also a *moving screen*) would be a UAV supporting a vehicle or convoy moving down a road or in support of a unit on foot. The purpose is to scan ahead, to the flanks, or behind for obstructions, ambushes, enemy/civilian presence, other traffic, and to understand the nature and condition of the road and its surrounding terrain. Mobile recon can be done while the unit is moving or in sections while at halt. The UAS capability doesn't have to be organic to the mobile unit, but aerial recon support can be provided by an external UAS team if the aircraft has the range.

Example: A convoy is approaching a bridge that may be an ambush site. A drone is launched to inspect the bridge and the terrain around it for signs of boobytraps, barricades, or enemies lying in wait.

Example: A patrol leaves a compound. A drone is launched from the compound to follow along with the patrol, watching for suspicious activities, IEDs, ambushes, or for anyone to attempt to approach the patrol unseen.

Example: A patrol or convoy expects to be attacked from a certain direction on its flank. A drone is used to fly along that flank to try and spot any enemies approaching or lying in wait.

Command and control

Drones above all are great situational awareness expansion tools. A commander can use them to facilitate command and control because he can see what his troops and the enemy are doing so he can issue orders in real time. The Army calls this "positive control of movements." He doesn't have to be physically present, and he can also cover much more ground with a better picture than in person.

The map-like, look-down perspective of UAS and the ability to dynamically move around a battlefield gives a commander his great situational awareness. A commander doesn't have to put together an entirely mental picture of the battlefield or piece together a 2D map from scattered reports. He doesn't have to rely on scouts, intelligence analysts, or subordinates radioing in to make observations or get information. A drone can do all that and allow the commander to see it vicariously first-hand.

Example: A commander watches his troops cross the front line. He is able to make sure that all units move in sync with each other to offer support and so that one section doesn't overextend itself. He is able to identify an enemy strongpoint and order it to be attacked before it can decimate his forces.

UAS ISR tips

- Make decisions based on the tactical situation and observations insofar as orders and SOP permit. Take advantage of situations when possible, such as calling for fire or even attacking if the drone is armed.
- Maximize the use of UAS to spare human lives and provide the most intelligence as far as endurance/performance will allow. Tools are only helpful if used.
- Coordinate UAS with other units or organizations especially when operating near friendly troops. Coordination includes providing timely intelligence to interested parties but also avoiding fratricide by knowing who is on the ground and that the UAV is friendly.
- Notify interested parties (commanders, analysists, or even members of a radio net depending on UAS intelligence) of the UAV's status. Announce when infiltrating, on/off target, and exfiltrating.
- Pass all information, including that which may seem unimportant, to decisionmakers as soon as possible. Live viewing of video or other sensor feeds by analysts or

commanders is preferred. Don't withhold intel from those who can use it.

• Consider whether or not the drone should attempt to remain undetected. An observed enemy may change his behavior which could be potentially advantageous or disadvantageous.

• Share intelligence beyond commanders and intelligence groups. Provide real time information to ground units, sentries, etc. to help them accomplish their objectives.

Ch. 14 Observational Flight Tradecraft

UAS doctrine, at least from unclassified and publicly available information, revolves around mainly administrative tasks and offensive ISR use, not actual tactics. The one area that has been explored in-depth has been mainly camouflaging and signature management for ground troops which is largely a carryover from manned aircraft. As one soldier opined, "Few if any Army ground force commanders have encountered enemy UAVs, and Army doctrine and informational literature do not seriously consider enemy [intelligence collection] assets."[45]

Pilot's visibility

Situational awareness is an issue for the drone pilot. He cannot feel the aircraft move, his visibility is restricted to what the cameras show him, and his gauges are a datalink. His senses are not his own.

UAVs suffer from visibility issues. Unlike in a manned aircraft, a pilot does not have the same ability to turn his head to see what's around him. Overall situational awareness is poor as the pilot is usually concentrating on the forward view and concurrently keeping the gimbal camera on task. If the gimbal camera is not monitoring a target or actively reconnoitering, using it to scan can cause the pilot to suffer from task saturation. The gimbal camera is also

[45] CPT Jeremy M. Phillips, "Training for the Enemy UAV Threat", *Infantry*, May-June 2013, p. 47

mounted below the fuselage making it difficult if not impossible to look upward.

- When not in use otherwise, use the gimbal camera to scan for threats continuously.
- Have a sensor/camera operator so the pilot can concentrate solely on flying.
- Operate the drone in visual range whenever possible.
- Use a visual observer to scan for aerial and ground threats when in VLOS.
- Use a secondary "cover" drone to scan for threats.

Reports from ground forces, other drones, and other intelligence assets need to be coordinated and provided to the drone pilot to augment his awareness of the tactical picture.

Sensor/camera

Do not use cinematic aerial videography techniques; what looks "cool" on YouTube may risk the mission or the airframe. Use the camera zoom to get more detailed shots. Flying in closer increases vulnerability and the probability of detection.

Gimbal subject-locking may be used to keep the camera oriented on the target as long as the firmware doesn't override the intended flightpath. Do not be reliant on automatic subject tracking modes.

Note that for drones without dual cameras (cinematic and forward-flight/FPV), if the camera is tracking a target, it cannot be used to see the route or obstructions ahead. When the camera is watching a target, ensure that the flight area is clear of obstructions and navigation can be done visually from the ground or a second drone that is providing overwatch. Obstacle avoidance is not a replacement for visual awareness.

Begin recording *before* you enter a target area in order to capture details that may not be obvious at first. This also ensures that the recording is started before the sensor operator may be too distracted by events on the ground. Anywhere from 15 seconds to a minute is appropriate, although it may be worth it to run the camera and record the flight in to later analyze for additional details.

Zooming in improves the ability to distinguish infrared camouflaged targets. Do not attempt to fly under tree canopies at night for a better view; let the camera do the work for you. Tree canopies especially in darkness will dramatically increase the probability of a collision. Attempt to see beneath vegetation by using oblique angles.

Shot flight maneuver types

Linear: The drone flies in a straight line and the camera is fixed in any orientation; may include ascents and descents. The typical camera orientation is straight ahead. Used when recording the ingress/egress or reconnoitering a route. This has value in showing others what the flightpath or route looks like as one travels it.

Panning linear: The drone flies in a straight line and the camera pans or tracks freely. This is probably the most common type of shot in forward flight. When the drone overtakes a target that the camera continues to track as it passes overhead, this is known as an *overlook* shot.

Sideways/sideward: The camera is fixed perpendicular to the direction of travel. Used when performing a fly-by to a target that parallels the flightpath. Often used to look "over the shoulder" of sensitive areas or to conceal the interest in a particular target as it appears to an observer that the UAV is simply flying by. Panning/tracking may be incorporated.

Dynamic: Both flight maneuvers and zoom are used to keep the subject in frame, to track targets, and get the best imagery. This includes free flights and tracking a moving target, such as a vehicle. Overhead shots will often be of the dynamic type.

Orbit: The drone flies in a circle around a fixed point, usually a point of interest. The camera may be slaved to track a specific target or can be maneuvered freely. Orbiting is less energy intensive than a hover and the orbit can be adjusted for moving targets. A variation of the circular orbit would be a figure "8" maneuver.

Hover: The drone remains stationary, and the camera moves freely as desired, often from directly overhead (*lookdown*). Adjustments to altitude may occur as needed.

Orbits and hovering

Orbiting manually around a fixed point can be a challenging skill. Pilots should be well-versed in orbital flight and not reliant on autopilot modes. Orbits will be the only way that a fixed-wing UAV can maintain continuous surveillance of a target as they cannot hover. Orbiting (flying in circles) at a slow speed will increase endurance as hovering more rapidly depletes the battery due to higher constant motor speed across all units. The difference is usually slight but may make a difference when minutes count.

Select an altitude that is free of obstructions, out of shotgun range, and high enough to minimize the sound signature heard on the ground but still allows the best quality image. Maintain a level altitude and track the target with the camera. Instead of hovering, orbit the target to keep the drone constantly moving, although an unpredictable path is best.

Orbit on the observed side of buildings or terrain features to keep the target in sight at all times. This allows the camera to slew constantly during the circle to remain pointed at the target. To limit visibility of the UAV, orbit towards the backside of the target but note that this will cause a period of loss-of-sight of the target as well.

Consider that orbits make it obvious something is being watched. The target area can be identified by the circle of the orbit and seeing where the camera is pointed. For example, think of the attention a circling police helicopter attracts. Tight orbits will give away the target; looser orbits will increase the margin of ambiguity.

Avoid giving away your target by slowly and casually overflying it in a straight line. Let the camera do the looking around while the drone passes by, seemingly on its way to somewhere else. For reconnaissance of a fixed target, instead of a circular orbit around the perimeter of the target, consider flying by each "side" at different times. Deceive your adversary by taking lots of time to obviously survey random locations. This may convince an adversary that the drone is conducting a grid search, rather than looking at a specific objective.

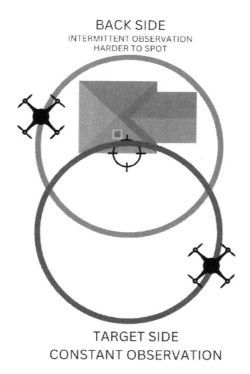

BACK SIDE
INTERMITTENT OBSERVATION
HARDER TO SPOT

TARGET SIDE
CONSTANT OBSERVATION

Hovering directly overhead, high enough that the motors can't be heard on the ground, and slewing the camera straight down is an astonishingly effective mode of remaining undetected. People usually don't look straight up. If the target is not moving, hover with the sun directly in the line-of-sight of between the target and the drone.

When possible, hover behind trees or other concealment and point the camera through an opening. Stay above tree canopies to avoid collisions and to let the foliage both conceal and diffuse/absorb sound. Looking out through a gap often provides a better field of view while obscuring the observer (UAV).

Endurance

Orbiting (flying in circles) at a slow speed will increase endurance as hovering more rapidly depletes the battery due to higher constant motor speed across all units. Hovering requires more power as each motor runs at a higher constant speed. Normal flight gives more power to the "rear" motors and less to the "front" to enable directional flight, so overall consumption is less than in a hover. Ordinarily the difference is relatively slight, but it may make a difference at extreme ranges or in tense situations.

Fluctuations in individual motor power levels to remain stable in wind also decreases battery life, depending on the wind speed. Downwind flight is less strenuous than flying upwind as the wind imputes additional energy to the UAV and the motors have to work less. Conversely, flying upwind requires more power and will increase power consumption.

The higher the wind speed, the greater the effect in either direction.

A pilot should be experienced enough to plan for the effect of wind when plotting their route or estimating their time on station, especially when operating at the extremes of range and endurance. Low speed in low-wind conditions is the most efficient mode of flight. Manufacturers often specify different values for flight vs. hover endurance. Note the manufacturer's specified hover endurance and plan range/loiter time accordingly.

Extensive evasive maneuvers or long deceptive flightpaths may drain the battery and reduce the overall mission time or time on-station. Deceptive or evasive return paths should be considered in calculating endurance.

- *Maximum* range is a one-way flight until the batteries are drained or fuel is exhausted.
- Combat *radius* is half the maximum distance range under a given payload. Combat *range* includes the time to arrive on target, complete the mission or deliver the payload, and return.
- Loiter time: How long can the drone stay above a target or how long can its reconnaissance missions be?

Specific mission TTP

ISR

- Locate the enemy and maintain contact as long as the information is needed, or observations can be made. Recon transitions to surveillance if it persists long enough on a single objective. Handoff observation to other UAVs or assets as conditions or endurance dictate.

- Keep the aircraft/sensors focused on the objective such as by hovering or orbiting in the safest position where the best view can be maintained. Balance the need to get video or etc. with survivability.
- Maintain visual contact from the maximum altitude and standoff distance from objects to safely maneuver, while maintaining an optimal observational position. Balance surprise, survivability, and quality of observation.
- Conduct recon/surveillance at all operational stages to provide real time information for defense, exploitation, awareness, etc. Continuous observation should be maintained as much as possible considering crew fatigue, maintenance, and the risk to the aircraft.
- Using more than one UAV in an orbit or search pattern increases the observation time and decreases the time between passes. Pilots will need to remain alert and keep visual contact to avoid mid-air collisions.
- Sub-249 gram micro drones are ideal for patrols as they can be man-packed. They are smaller, lighter, and faster to deploy than larger models. Heavier drones being transported will slow a patrol down, will take longer to launch and recover, and will hinder mobility if attacked. A very small drone can be easily carried along and used to augment the patrol where a larger drone (such as a DJI Phantom) providing overwatch is not available or to clear or recon areas in lieu of sending in a man.

Recon

Some areas deserve more scrutiny than others during reconnaissance missions. These include good vantage points for adversarial UAV pilots. Rooflines should be so obvious that they shouldn't bear mention. Others more applicable to supporting fighters on the ground are:
- Buildings or promontories that dominate large areas.
- Ideal firing positions for mortars or missiles.

- Positions that offer good cover and concealment along with good views or could be used to apply suppressive fire on the area below.[46]

In a building "search and clear":

- Examine rooftops, loopholes, and windows.
- Drop weapons to "flush out" any enemies.
- Clear yards and adjacent areas.
- Watch rear areas for "runners."
- Use the UAV as a distraction while troops make entry.

Screening

- Drone flies between the protected area and the threat, while maintaining contact with the screening ground force or the friendly perimeter, but carefully so as not to overextend.
- Report the presence of the enemy, any signs of his presence, and any observed activity. Attempt to determine the enemy's strength-in-depth (second echelon/follow-on forces).
- Identify the enemy's avenue of approach, judge their speed, and identify any potential points of attack beneficial to the defenders or estimate where the enemy may make contact with the protected area/friendly forces.
- Maintain continuous surveillance until ground observers can take over; if there is only one UAV, replace the batteries and re-deploy as soon as possible. If continuous surveillance of a unit is not possible due to the size of the attacking force, concentrate observations on critical avenues of approach.
- Guide ground troops to the target. Once ground units are engaged, UAS should provide supporting surveillance or move to cover another threat. Provide targeting for long-range fires if available.
- Harass and impede the enemy when and where

---

[46] Paraphrased from USMC MOUT manual, p. 3-16

possible, while considering the impact of the loss of the UAV or if the UAV should remain undetected. Drones can be used to herd persons wary of surveillance to, or away, from an area.

Supporting ground forces

- Screening forward of a unit or its flanks to provide security.
- Check choke points (potential ambush sites) or other locations of interest, including scouting routes.
- Scout for good defensive positions, good observation positions, and fields of fire *for both sides*.
- Look for signs of potential traps or ambushes.
- Determine alternate objectives, routes, or targets.
- An armed drone can attack targets of opportunity or eliminate strong points (such as a machine gun nest).
- Serving as a form of precision strike.
- Use UAS to scout alternate routes or screen flanks and dead zones when manpower is low and a separate party cannot be sent to do recon.

Residential security operations

- UAS performs recon & surveillance of sensitive areas/places, routes, convoys, critical points, such as the perimeter of a neighborhood or property.
- UAS looks for approaching threats, detects intruders and investigates suspicious activity.
- An armed drone can attack intruders and delay/stop the intrusion.
- A drone can precede the QRF response and support its deployment.
- A UAV can be deployed to monitor a security event, such as a riot or looting, near the protected area to gather more information.
- Drones can supplement security patrols, but not replace humans on the ground.

- For long surveillance of, say, a group on a street corner, attempt to hide near the roofline of distant buildings and zoom in. Keep the drone above the subject's natural line-of-sight for that distance.

Tracking tips

- Note that tree canopies and deep undergrowth make good hiding places and interfere with infrared/thermal sensors. Look for other signs and spoor of enemy personnel in the area or use other tactics to attempt to flush adversaries into the open. Flying beneath a tree canopy may be hazardous.
- Persons who are aware of the threat that UAS poses will take cover on its approach. Look for them beneath tree canopies, in deep vegetation, or other areas with natural cover and concealment. Experienced "quarry" will often freeze until the UAS threat has abated. Consider using the drone to pin subjects in place while ground units maneuver in.
- If someone you are pursuing "goes to ground" search the area you last saw them in thoroughly or begin backtracking. Do not assume they took another route or continued in the direction they last headed. Most people who are untrained, if they do keep moving, will take the path of least resistance, such as downhill, following roads or open ground, or "handrailing" terrain features.
- If a subject is hiding in a known location, to flush him out, spend a few minutes flying around "searching." When this mock search is complete, fly the drone out of the subject's visual and audio range. Continue watching their hiding spot for them to emerge.
- Remember any camouflage or other deceptive techniques are being used to try and fool you, the pilot/sensor operator. Sus out where a suspected enemy might be hiding. Use critical thinking skills to assess anything that appears suspicious.

- Investigate any usual thermal signatures that appear out of place especially at night; these are likely concealed persons or positions. If you suspect it is an individual under hasty thermal camouflage, attempt to wait them out by seeing if they grow uncomfortable or their body heat warms up the thermal barrier.
- Expect an adversary to dash from cover-to-cover and use concealed routes. Look behind reverse slopes, along low ground, or in high-relief terrain. In urban areas, check out uncommon potential routes, like storm drains and utility rights-of-way (watch for power lines). Do not focus only on open areas.

Ch. 15 Standard Operating Procedures for UAS Pilots

All manufacturer's cautions, warnings, and instructions should be heeded insofar as it is operationally possible. Homemade models should reference a manual of a substantially similar COTS airframe. Failure to adhere to these guidelines may result in the loss of the aircraft, mission failure, injury, or death.

Readers should have basic familiarity with Part 107 (14 CFR 107) Unmanned Aircraft Systems guidelines and review FAA materials including the *Remote Pilot – Small Unmanned Aircraft Systems Study Guide* (FAA-G-8082-22) before attempting to operate a UAV. While in terms of domestic conflicts and use in without rule of law (WROL) scenarios legalities can be dispensed with, for peacetime, hobby, and training flights, as well as general familiarization with the principals of flight, a basic study of airman's materials is appropriate and recommended.

This chapter and this book is not a guide for basic operations of individual airframes, nor does it contain exhaustive, liability-driven warnings like "Beware of propellers—they may cut your fingers," "A drone falling from a high altitude can hit someone's head and kill them," or "Modifying a drone to drop grenades on people is a felony." You are responsible for your own legal, aircraft operation, and flight basics education.

Safety

The most common causes of accidents are people who are untrained, inexperienced, or are reckless. Failure to observe basic safety procedures will result in an accident if given enough time. UAVs are not toys; they are valuable assets that may be difficult or impossible to replace. Loss of a UAV due to carelessness or incompetence may result in a mission failure and have repercussions larger than the loss of the aircraft.

Operate in the safest manner practicable given the mission parameters. Stealth reconnaissance, combat support, or attack missions may require risks to the airframe and persons that peacetime flying will not. These risks must be calculated, have a reasonable chance of success, and the harm incurred must not adversely affect friendly forces beyond the loss of an airframe. Whatever the mission requirements are, a pilot should never take any avoidable risks.

Unmanned aircraft should always be flown in a manner that will allow the mission to be completed without unnecessary risk to the aircraft. In the event of mishap, the pilot's duties are to limit damage to the airframe and to mitigate the hazards from a crash. The primary safety and security concerns are:

- Avoiding a collision with terrain, vegetation, utility lines/poles, structures, and other aircraft (see and avoid).
- Protecting friendly forces, civilians, and property from harm in the event of a crash.
- Evading CUAS fire, other intentional interference, or capture of the airframe.
- Limiting what counter-intelligence can be gained by analyzing the drone's behavior, flightpath, or payload.

Situational awareness is the first step to avoiding a collision or other loss of the airframe. If you can see it, you can avoid it. No collisions means that the drone can only fall if shot down or due to mechanical failure. A pilot who is conscious of who/what he's flying the aircraft over will also minimize the chances someone is injured or property is damaged should his drone fall out of the air. Attentiveness, good planning, and tactical skill can mitigate what information an enemy observer can glean about your UAS operations by watching a drone in flight.

Safe operation depends on skilled, alert, and observant operators. Pilots should not be more than trivially ill, exhausted, or suffering from a distracting level of emotional or psychological problems. These conditions all may impair judgement, fine motor control coordination, alertness, observational skills, and memory. Intoxicated persons or those under the influence of medication or drugs that alter the cognitive state should not operate UAS.

Flight rules

Weather

Do not fly in severe weather conditions, defined as:

- Heavy precipitation (rain, hail, snow, sleet).
- Especially avoid icy conditions such as freezing rain.
- Cloud ceilings of less than 300 feet.
- Thick fog, smoke, or snow where visibility prevents visual contact with the drone at all times. If operationally required to fly, minimum horizontal visibility distance should be at least 300 feet (100m).
- Do not fly during thunderstorms including dry lightning storms.

Most consumer multicopters should not fly at windspeeds above 22 MPH (35 km/h—10 m/s). Note that as altitude above ground level increases, so will the windspeed, making it necessary to plan for sudden gusts, increased deviation, and keeping greater distance from obstructions. Alternatively, fixed-wing UAVs should be launched *into* light wind to gain additional lift. Blowing sand and dust may cause damage (abrasion) to the aircraft or clog/jam important components.

Terrain and buildings affect windspeed and movement. Wind blowing around a building or mountain peak may cause turbulence on the leeward side, causing the aircraft to become unstable. Wind shear in wind-exposed altitudes near the building/feature may exceed the margins for an airframe but likely be safe below it in the lee. Crosswind is a concern with fixed-wing UAVs as the configuration of the launch area may discourage a launch directly into the wind.

Urban terrain will pose challenges due to microenvironmental factors such as updrafts and downdrafts. Wind conditions may be extremely variable depending on the wind speed, direction, and building position. Shifting breezes or gusts focused by urban canyons into artificial wind tunnels may cause unexpected forces on a UAV. Expect winds parallel to blocks to be stronger while wind blowing diagonally or perpendicular to be calmer in the lee near the ground.

Note that downdrafts tend to force aircraft down and into terrain whereas updrafts tend to carry aircraft up. Rising heat off a surface may also cause an aircraft to rise. This effect may be most noticeable in urban areas or deserts on hot days over surfaces like asphalt that absorb a lot of solar radiation. Updrafts may also be caused by uneven heating of paved surfaces (heat island effect).

Air temperature (very hot and cold) affect battery life which may reduce flight time. Air density and temperature decreases as altitude increases. Cold temperatures drain batteries and lower air densities reduce lift. Air density is affected by several factors: altitude, temperature, and humidity.

At higher altitudes the air is less dense, so the rotors will not generate the same amount of lift as they would in denser air of lower altitudes. At lower altitudes the weight of the atmosphere literally makes the air column heavier. Maximum altitude will be dictated by the individual airframe specifications and local conditions. DJI recommends caution flying its drones above 19,685 feet (6,000m).

Air density will decrease with altitude and air density change is inversely proportional to temperature. The changes are not necessarily uniform as air currents, terrain, humidity, and other weather factors can cause variations. Humid air is less dense than dry air because water vapor is lighter than air. Thus, a high relative humidity reading will tend to indicate lower density air and drier air will be comparatively denser. Cold air will hold less water vapor than warm air. However, with the light weights of sUAVs at most commonly inhabited altitudes air density does not matter enough to seriously affect performance outside of extreme conditions.

Minimum altitude varies in context; absolute minimum is that altitude above ground level or any obstruction where a flight can be conducted safely. Under combat-type conditions, a drone should stay at least 12 feet above ground level to avoid being easily grabbed or knocked down by enemy troops.

Flying in dense, low clouds like fog for any kind of aircraft navigating under visual flight rules (VFR), which applies to virtually all drones, makes safe navigation very difficult. One might know via GPS their drone's altitude, speed, orientation, and location but they cannot know what obstructions are lurking in the fog. Helicopters rarely operate in zero visibility conditions mainly because descents without being able to see any potential obstacles is very dangerous. At low altitude and zero visibility, it may be impossible to see things like power lines or tree limbs until it is too late.

Altitude under a low cloud deck should be no higher than the base of the clouds. The drone should remain visible at all times unless the clouds are being used as tactical cover. In that case, the drone should only be flown high enough into the overcast to hide it from view. Once the drone is no longer visible, its climb should be halted after an additional 10 feet. A small distance above the clear air to descend until visibility returns allows for a greater safety margin.

Flying in precipitation should be avoided whenever possible. The water resistance of a given airframe is determined by the manufacturer's specs. Many models do not have basic waterproofing while others may be able to safely operate in heavy fog or drizzle. Advanced, specialty, or military-grade models may be able to fly in heavy rain.

Water ingress can cause electrical components in circuit boards, wiring, and motors to short out. Motors may become disabled, the drone may become unresponsive, or batteries may fail. Replacement of damaged components is a matter of maintenance but should a serious failure in flight develop the airframe could be lost. Drones should not be used in conditions that exceed what the manufacturer recommends.

A light rain (drizzle) or heavy mist is mainly a hazard to non-waterproofed drones and visibility. Flying in light rain or snow is similar to flying in a light fog as the water in the air makes it harder to see further and there is less light to see by. Heavy rain may add resistance to lift and horizontal flight, reducing speed and range. Precipitation in very cold temperatures may cause icing which will decrease lift and may freeze control surfaces.

Water droplets collecting on camera lenses can impact both navigation and imagery collection. If you've ever seen helicopter or webcam shots on rainy days, you know that raindrops on a camera lens can totally obscure all detail of an image. Unlike cars, water will not necessarily bead off a camera lens and increasing speed to "blow" the water away increases the risk of collision with something you can't see.

For image collection, a downward facing lens may be less prone to droplet blur but even if a pilot is able to get good images, he must balance the mission with the safety of the airframe. Rain may degrade obstacle avoidance sensors' effectiveness or negate them entirely. Being blind and lacking any automated collision avoidance, it should be needless to say, is not good.

At the higher frequencies that GPS and drones operate at (gigahertz) moisture attenuates the radio signal. A low power levels, this can be enough to degrade reception/transmission so as to reduce the ability to receive video and control the drone. A poor GPS signal will create errors in positioning, altitude, and speed which may prevent the drone from operating correctly. Optical object avoidance sensors may become confused by precipitation, inhibiting features such as auto-land or cause it to become unstable in flight.

Terrain and obstructions

Be aware of terrain blocking GPS signals which may prevent pre-planned flight plans from being followed or return-to-home (RTH) features from functioning. Narrow, deep terrain may block the controller signal and GPS. A line-of-sight should always be maintained with the UAV whenever there is a chance that a clear view of the sky is obstructed or vise versa.

Nap-of-the-Earth flying in defiles, natural and urban, may create reception problems. Terrain may interfere with the reception and transmission of radio signals. Canyons, tall hills, mountains, dense forests, or large buildings are just some examples of features that can block or severely attenuate reception of GPS or telemetry signals. A loss of signal may cause a drone to become uncontrollable or crash.

When flying low-level, terrain or structure masked flights, the operator has to be very careful to keep the drone within line-of-sight of the controller transmitter. Autonomous flights made via a GPS flight plan need to be routed so as to keep the drone out of areas that will cause loss of the satellite navigation signal. Large ferrous (iron/steel) structures such as buildings and ships can cause inaccurate compass readings.

Keep away from rooftops, terrain, or other objects by at least 30 feet (10m). Do not fly closer to an object or obstruction any closer than necessary. Avoid power lines, transmission towers, or radio transmitters due to the risk of collision or electromagnetic distortion. Tall radio towers in particular may have guy lines extending from the sides that could be practically invisible during periods of limited visibility.

Whenever possible, fly above the rooflines of buildings. In operations where you must violate stand off distances to ensure mission success or survivability of the aircraft, make a safety assessment of the risk and do not operate so close it will create an undue hazard. Be aware that near obstructions, particularly trees and utility lines, wind gusts may move the cables or branches; not just the drone around (hence the safety margin).

Night navigation will be more difficult outside of developed areas due to the lower incidence of artificial landmarks. Lighting conditions in natural terrain will be generally uniform due to the lack of artificial illumination, but widely variable in urban areas. Night flights need to have an established minimum safe altitude. This can be ascertained in daylight through flying at a visually safe distance, recording that altitude, and estimating the difference in height of the tallest obstructions below. At night, ground observations or reference data can be used for planning if daytime data collection isn't available.

To calculate the height of an object, we need to know the distance from the observer to the object and the angle of the observer to the top of the object (an expedient way to obtain the angle is by using a plumb bob and a protractor). Line-of-sight is the direct line from the observer to the top of the object, or the hypotenuse of a right triangle.

Angle of elevation is taken from where the line-of-sight/hypotenuse meet the line parallel to the ground level at the observer's eye level. The angle of elevation is also called the tangent (tan) in trigonometry. The angle is multiplied by the distance from the observer to the object. This will give the height of the object. The formula is height = tan x distance.

Launch and recovery

Launch areas for operational missions should be done in areas where the chance of enemy observation and interference is minimal. Open fields or lots that do not have much public visibility make for a safe, but semi-private, launch and recovery point (LRP). LRPs should be shielded from direct enemy fire and from enemy or public view as much as possible. Be sure to consider distant tall buildings or terrain features where an observer may be located. Try and place a building, hill, or trees between the LRP and any possible observers.

Select launch/recovery areas that do not have large obstructions within 100-300 feet (30-100m), no terrain/structural obstructions that will block radio signals to/from the operator and have a clear view of the sky for GPS reception. A minimum of 10 feet (3m) on each side of the drone is necessary for a safe launch and recovery. Attempt to select a site where loose debris, vegetation, or dust will not be stirred up by the rotors. In addition to a FOD hazard, this may create a dangerous launch/landing signature.

In addition to obstacle clearance concerns, areas with communications equipment, antennas, and power lines should be avoided due to the possibility of electromagnetic interference with the UAV or the controller. Due to the potential of the control signal being triangulated by EW specialists, the LRP should *not* be located near any high-value target. If the enemy has long-range fires, launching a drone that they may shoot at when it starts up next to a command post or fuel storage area is a bad idea.

For fixed-wing aircraft that are hand launched, such as the RQ-11 Raven, the launch point should be elevated above the surrounding terrain when possible, such as a hillside, the edge of a cliff, or the top of a building. While these craft can be launched at ground level, this assumes they will be launched into the wind, have the assistance of a catapult, or from a moving vehicle. Elevation with a drop off, like a roof top, allows the aircraft to safely fall or "settle" until it generates enough lift and speed to fly. In any case, fixed-wing aircraft will require much longer launch areas than multicopters; exact takeoff needs will depend on manufacturer specifications and the wind.

LRPs should be marked to assist the pilot and for safety of personnel on the ground. Landing zones at night should be illuminated when possible and include the use of beacons, including, infrared lights as necessary. If there are no indicators of windspeed present, such as trees, use of an anemometer or windsock may be prudent, especially if the pilot is not present or cannot observe the LRP directly.

If not using the launch point as the recovery point, program in a safe return to home location prior to flight in the event the controller connection is lost. Alternate or emergency landing zones can be marked to facilitate rapid landings in exigent situations without reference to maps. The UAS flight crew should identify emergency landing sites along the flightpath during mission planning and identify others while the flight progresses.

Launch with a full battery and, if operationally possible, return to the landing site upon the first low battering warning. Do not operate with partially charged batteries or beyond recovery margins unless operationally necessary where lives are at stake.

Always manually scan, with cameras and with the eye, the landing area prior to touchdown even if in autonomous mode. The safety observer should be present in the LRP as well.

Best practices

- Do not use in high wind, in reduced visibility, or during precipitation.
- Avoid flight near sheer terrain or tall buildings which may obstruct controller or GPS reception.
- Do not fly near large metal structures such as high-tension power lines, their towers, or radio transmitters (antennas) where electromagnetic interference may affect communications, the compass, or GPS.
- Avoid flying near airports and manned aircraft.

- Be aware of the effects of payload, windspeed, flight speed, temperature, and altitude on battery life/endurance.

Perform operations an appropriate distance from persons not directly participating in UAS operations. Keep a greater distance from civilians or enemy forces as they would not be in communication with you or under your control. Select training areas that are sparsely populated.

Check the weather before flight to ensure that the flight will take place within acceptable visibility and wind margins. Take a live wind measurement (sustained and gusts) before flight, including at the ground launch site and from the roof of a building (if possible).

Do not launch a drone or otherwise attempt operations when the wind exceeds 13-18 MPH (20-28 km/h, 11-16 knots). This corresponds to a Beaufort scale number of 4, which can be determined by blowing dust, light debris, and small tree branches in motion. Some drones may have higher or lower wind ratings. Contingency operations may take place with higher wind gusts (vs. sustained winds) within the manufacturer's ratings or by conducting launches/recoveries from a wind sheltered location.

Do not fly in low visibility conditions unless necessary to save lives. Low visibility dramatically increases the chances of a collision and reduces camera effectiveness. If mission necessity dictates, try to fly over known areas free of obstructions and keep the drone at an altitude above the highest known local obstruction. The secondary camera should be used in addition to the navigational camera to pan and scan for greater visibility.

Launch with a full battery and, if operationally possible, return to the landing site upon the first low battering warning. Do not operate with partially charged batteries or beyond recovery margins unless operationally necessary where lives are at stake. Remember that range usually can be expressed multiple ways, as in maximum range—a one-way trip—or radius, which includes the flight back.

Keep the aircraft within the pilot's (or observer's) line-of-sight and under control. Note that first-person view (FPV) goggles reduce the pilot's own situational awareness. The view in the goggles may contribute to a false sense of security due to immersion while a threat out-of-view goes unnoticed. FPV operation must be accompanied by a safety observer at a minimum.

Account for terrain during planning and flight so that structures or terrain will not interrupt the telemetry and video feed to the operator. If the operator's situational or spatial awareness is lost, climb the drone to a safe altitude, follow collision avoidance guidance, and reorient. Worst-case, put the drone into auto-recovery mode.

Why are margins important?

Flying during emergency situations may require low approaches, orbits, and hovering close to terrain, structures, and obstructions; risks that wouldn't ordinarily be taken by a hobbyist. With survivability being paramount, these hazardous flight profiles may be essential to remain undetected. Proximity to obstructions becomes a balancing act against mission success.

Safety margins are a necessity for the survivability of the drone in a non-peacetime environment. A shootdown attempt may make rapid evasive maneuvers necessary. There may be little to no time to scan for obstructions. Based on the orientation of the threat, the movement required to evade may be sudden and in the direction of the obstruction. When feasible, a safety margin will allow a buffer space to maneuver in without risking airframe loss.

Safety margins include:

- Altitude; stay away from obstacles.
- Distance; provided a buffer for wind gusts or inattention.
- Time; consider daylight and flight distance.
- Range; a radius is only half the maximum range.
- Standoff distance; remain out of CUAS range.

Autonomous flight

The FAA considers autonomous flight "an operation in which the remote pilot inputs a flight plan into the [control station], which sends it to the autopilot onboard the small UA. During automated flight, flight control inputs are made by components onboard the aircraft, not from a [control station]."[47] In the context of this work, autonomous flight will refer to a wholly pre-programmed flightpath where the drone does not, or may not be able to, receive pilot control inputs.

Semi-autonomous (SA) flight would refer to where a

---

47 AC 107-2 p. 5-2

pilot may augment the programmed flightpath or where computer and sensor assistance may provide automatic input, such as collision avoidance modes. SA modes are an adjunct to the pilot's own skills. They are not perfect and should be considered a failsafe rather than true autonomy. SA camera tracking is for photography, not defensive applications. An operator needs to be manually controlling the camera during ISR missions.

Through the use of onboard sensors, processors, and algorithms, some UAS can operate without a pilot's live input. Autonomous flight involves a sequence of operations, including takeoff, navigation, and landing, that are performed by the drone based on pre-programmed instructions or real-time decision-making using sensor data.

In autonomous flight, the drone's flight plan is defined, including the route it will take and the altitude it will fly. The drone uses its onboard sensors, such as GPS, IMU, cameras, and ultrasonic or laser obstacle avoidance sensors (which all coordinate to form the INS), to navigate along the planned route. The drone continuously adjusts its flightpath to avoid obstacles and stay on course. The flight computer adjusts the drone's speed, direction, and altitude to maintain its flightpath and land safely or impact a pre-programmed location.

Autonomous flight is ideal when the drone needs to restrict its RF emissions, such as on a stealthy special reconnaissance flight. Autonomous flight using INS and/or GPS would enable a drone to fly a predetermined flightpath. Without a command link there would be no way to alter course or manually control the camera. It would be good only for preprogrammed reconnaissance flights, deliveries, or attacks.

In autonomous flight at low-level, obstacle detection becomes critical as the precision of the flightpath may vary, straying near obstructions. Detectors can be optical or radar but should be capable of distinguishing something as small as a power line wire. To defeat jamming, a drone should be fully autonomously-capable and have use INS in combination with of all forms of GNSS.

Obstacle detection systems may have trouble sensing small obstructions like power lines. A pilot using semi-autonomous flight needs to watch for obstacles the software cannot see. Reflective surfaces like water or glass, snow, or unusually bright or dark situations may confuse the sensors. Ultrasonic sensors have difficulty measuring distances in certain condition such as flying at high speeds, sound reflective surfaces, and sound absorbent surfaces (vegetation).

If not using the launch point as the recovery point, program in a safe return to home location prior to flight in the event the controller connection is lost. Program a failsafe altitude that is above the highest obstruction in the operating area in the event that the controller connection is lost, and any obstacle sensing systems fail. Autonomous flights made via a GPS flight plan need to be routed so as to keep the drone out of areas that will cause loss of the satellite navigation signal.

Etiquette

- Minimize any inadvertent intrusion of privacy.
- Limit activities or behavior that may engender mistrust or outrage.
- Limit incursion of overflights of private property.

Hovering: Minimize hovering over specific properties or persons when unnecessary for intelligence collection or operational support, even if the camera is pointed in another direction. Hover over public spaces whenever possible.

Orbiting: Avoid tight orbits that could lead a specific person to conclude (or assume) that you are surveilling them or their property.

Windows: Avoid flying outside, near, or looking into windows to prevent accusations of invasion of privacy.

Altitude: Fly well above rooftops, ideally 50-100 feet and at least 30 feet over open private property or persons. Altitude above potentially hostile persons should be increased to 50 feet due to concerns over objects that may be thrown at their drone.

Frequency: Frequent flights over particular routes or locations should be minimized both from an operational security standpoint but also to limit public annoyance.

Time: Flight operations should only be conducted during hours of daylight or early night (before 10 PM) except when necessary for operational purposes. Night or early morning flights can be conducted well away from homes or campsites.

Safety: Do not engage in unsafe maneuvers or persons, vehicles, animals, or near buildings.

Animals: Fly well above and away from pets or livestock. Avoid spooking animals.

Noise: Minimize the impact of noise of the aircraft by flying at 100 feet minimum altitude above structures and persons, fly only during daylight, use other environmental noise to mask the rotors' sound, fly downwind, keep the drone moving, and use camera zoom to avoid flying closer than necessary.

Locations: Do not overfly or fly near sensitive locations, which may include military bases, defensive positions, troop formations, police activity, law enforcement stations, detention centers, utility substations, airports, etc.

- When feasible, notify the public that you will be operating a drone in the area including who you are and for what purpose. A defensive or protective purpose that is adequately explained may turn potential complainants into at least neutral parties.

- Notify potentially impacted parties about your operations to assure them that they are not targets of your operations. Be willing to answer any reasonable questions they have.
- Show the camera feed (or recordings) to concerned parties to assuage their fears.
- Record and retain a chart of the flightpath and profile.
- Attempt to make a personal benefit to reluctant or uncongenial parties such as offering a free recording of their home or property for curiosity or security purposes as they may find it interesting or helpful. Everyone likes getting something for free.
- Turn cameras away from sensitive scenes.
- Delete any especially personal or sensitive images captured inadvertently, such as: through windows, persons sunbathing, children, relating to personal security, etc.

High risk

Risk of injury, property damage, or damage to the aircraft will always exist. Combat or lifesaving operations may require that some risks be accepted to complete the mission. Constant risk assessment and good judgement are vital in the operation of drones. A balancing act will always have to occur; some risks may be inherent to flight while others are more universal. Rules that apply in civilian flight may be bent or totally disregarded in wartime applications.

Informed acceptance of risk requires understanding the factors involved. This includes having thorough knowledge of the mission, the consequences of success/failure, the drone's capabilities, and the enemies CUAS resources. The following are some risk factors that can result in airframe loss:

- Launching with a known malfunction or other problem;
- Continuing flight despite malfunctions or warnings;
- Bypassing flight safety mechanisms or deviation from standard flight and control principles;
- Unstable landing approach;
- GPS signal loss;
- Loss of navigation camera;
- No line-of-sight to the aircraft; and,
- Adverse weather conditions.

The choice to continue depends upon the mission priority. How critical is the intelligence or support of the UAS to operational success? Can the mission proceed at a later time or date? If not, best practices need to be implemented to mitigate risks.

Flight crew/drone team

While a UAS operations team will typically be one or two people, a larger team could consist of the following roles. None of these beyond the pilot are strictly necessary but a two-man crew that includes an observer is probably the most likely combination.

The pilot and observer must work as a team who communicate freely and who are comfortable working with each other. A top-down hierarchy is not conducive to safe and effective UAS operations. Questions, concerns, information, and advice should be freely shared between pilot and observer. Neither should be afraid to ask for clarification or respectfully express their concerns. Sterile flight communication rules must be observed; no extraneous conversation unrelated to the mission itself should be exchanged.

Pilot-operator: The drone pilot who is responsible for flying the drone via its control device and operating the sensors (camera) to obtain intelligence. The pilot is the commander of the UAS team.

Visual (safety) observer: In a two-man crew, the safety observer assumes all the roles except actual piloting of the drone. They are responsible for the physical launch and recovery process, ensuring the that the LRP is safe to launch from, and maintaining a security watch over the area (ground and sky). In a two-man crew the observer should not be operating the sensors/cameras as well. Safety observer responsibilities:
- Serves as the spotter, and handles the physical launch/recovery, when operating as a pair with the pilot.
- Maintain awareness of the airspace and battlespace.
- Responsible for monitoring the physical security situation when in a pair without a security element.
- Ensure the pilot is aware of hazards and potential collisions including terrain, structures, weather, other aircraft/UAVs, and shootdown attempts.
- Communicating with other elements.

Sensor (camera) operator: If the drone supports separate flight and sensor operations, the sensor operator is responsible for the intelligence collection and any real time communications with other units or upper echelons. Many larger military drones have a pilot and a systems operator.

Launch/recovery person: Someone who can run from a concealed position to deploy or recover the drone, including changing batteries or swapping camera/payload packages. They share the role of safety observer with the spotter (or may serve as both).

Spotter: Physically monitors the drone visually with their naked eyes or binoculars, etc. to watch its progress, warn of any shootdown attempts, or keep a directional antenna pointed at it for longer range operations. The spotter shares the role of safety observer with the launch/recovery person (or may serve as both).

Security element: An overlooked but important part of any team would be the security element who protects the operator and other team members. A pilot will be preoccupied with being head-down with their drone controls and the camera feeds, not monitoring their own immediate surroundings. Enemies might sneak up on a distracted pilot and kill or capture him if he is detected. Therefore, if working from any non-fortified area, a security team will be responsible for area defense. A security element is not required if the UAS crew is closely integrated with a ground combat unit that is already providing defense.

Team member responsibilities

A pilot's main goal is to safely operate the UAV in a manner that successfully completes the objectives of the drone's deployment. The operator behind the controls is the pilot-in-command and is directly responsible for the actual flight and control of the UAV. The pilot has final say regarding the aircraft's operation. No one shall interfere with the pilot, the controls, or the aircraft. Pilots have full authority to reject, terminate, or abort a flight to prevent injury or protect the airframe within local parameters.

Ideally the operator/pilot should have Part 107 certification from the FAA and extensive UAV flight hours prior to operating in any conflict type situation. A licensed (manned) pilot is not required but their experience and knowledge would make them an invaluable resource. At a minimum, the drone pilot should have extensive experience operating and maintaining at least consumer-level UAVs.

Pilot duties

- Pilots shall make human safety and survivability of the airframe as their top priorities except for allowances made based on the nature of the mission.
- Pilots shall maintain full alertness and situational awareness while flying a UAV.
- Pilots shall practice see-and-avoid techniques and maintain proper principles of flight to ensure safety of the airframe and mission success.
- Pilots shall respond to their flight observer and any remote observations if the drone is beyond the line-of-sight in order to safely accomplish the mission.
- Pilots shall communicate any necessary information to decision makers regarding their observations, flight or

aircraft conditions, and any other concerns that arise which are not otherwise immediately obvious to all.

Visual (safety) observer (VO)

- An observer's primary duty is to aid in the safe operation of the drone by watching its flight to help avoid collision and shootdowns.
- The observer should visually check that the launch/recovery site is free of debris, obstructions, and persons prior to takeoff or landing.
- Observers shall maintain a line-of-sight view of the airframe at all times except when mission contingencies or planning takes the drone out of sight.
- If observers are not in speaking distance of the pilot, they shall maintain direct radio contact with the pilot.
- Observers shall promptly report any factors that may affect the aircraft or the mission without bidding, including:
  o The aircraft location, attitude, altitude, and direction of flight; and,
  o The position of other aircraft or hazards.
- When deployed alone with a pilot, observers should also maintain awareness of their physical surroundings to ensure their physical safety from attack.
- Observers may handle communications between the UAS team and others.

Ch. 16 UAS Mission Planning for Pilots

Note: Although it is expected that most will dispense with formal orders and planning forms, military format planning can be found in Appendix A of *Army Unmanned Aircraft* FM 3-04.155.

Requests for UAS Support

UAS has the advantage of short turnaround time for launch and recovery, giving it the ability to respond rapidly to requests for aerial support. For a well-prepared UAS team, the main complicating factor will not be in deployment but in mission planning/briefing. The more time that is available to plan, the greater the probability of a successful mission. However, not every needed deployment will be known about in advance.

Scheduled: The UAS need is known well in advance and the mission can be scheduled and planned at leisure.

Immediate: The UAS is needed on short notice for an unanticipated mission and planning is done immediately before flight. Planning may be abbreviated due to exigency.

Emergency: The UAV is diverted from other activity or launched from standby. Planning may be abbreviated or may not occur at all. Briefing and requirements may be passed on while the drone is airborne. Such instances may include:

- Urgent air support from UCAVs.
- Urgent reconnaissance request from a commander.
- Real time observational support for in-contact ground units.
- Combat search and rescue.

Extended: An element without dedicated UAS is detailed an unallocated, or otherwise allocated, UAV for assigned use over an extended period of time.

Mission planning considerations

- Consider the current tactical situation and weather.
- Will the weather help or hinder flight/sensors?
- Will UAS operation seem unusual (pattern of activity)?
- What is the task and purpose of the flight?
- What capabilities will be needed (sensors/payload)?
- What is the identity of the target or the geographic area the drone will operate in?
- Consider the range/flight time in terms of endurance (battery/fuel) and radio signals.
- Maximum range (one-way flight); radius (half max. range) combat range (to, from, on-station, with payload), and loiter time.
- Evaluate the terrain and threats for all phases; ingress, egress, and while on station (route and threat analysis).
- Do terrain and buildings pose a hindrance to launch, recovery, or flight operations?
- Is there cover/concealment on the ingress/egress?
- Does the terrain canalize the avenues of approach?
- What CUAS will you face, if any?
- Will additional support be required?
- Who is the beneficiary of the information gathered or activities conducted?
- If any ground units are to be contacted/supported, what is the means of communication with them?

- What is the alternate plan, and what are the consequences, if the flight does not succeed?
- Is there a secondary mission or objective that can/needs to be accomplished?
- What level of detail in information gathering or support offered is needed?

Preflight

- Be up-to-date on the overall tactical picture and the weather. Review the latest information on the CUAS environment. Consider the physical, operational, and human risks from the flight. Flight assessments should include the mechanical condition of the drone (known malfunctions, battery performance, telemetry issues, etc.).
- Ensure that the mission requirements are clearly stated, the objectives/target are clearly identified, and any waypoints/routes have been accurately located. Understand the objective clearly and have proper information to positively locate and ID the target. If the end-user of the information is not present, be sure they provided detailed instructions on what exactly they want collected.
- Perform a map reconnaissance by reviewing maps (street, topographic, military) and satellite/aerial photos. Oblique imagery from a prior manned aircraft or UAV flight can provide better estimates of obstructions and terrain/structure height. The map recon will allow route planning and identification of objectives/areas of interest, as well as potential hazards.
- Note the call signs, frequencies, and any contact procedures (SOI[48]) for any units that the UAS team will be communicating with during the flight. Notify all interested parties (especially CUAS elements) of the flight.
- Brief all interested parties, as far as OPSEC will allow, on relevant mission routes, waypoints, and range/endurance/loiter time.

---

[48] Signals and operating instructions

- Have any necessary support ready to go *before* the flight begins, including alternate recovery points identified and staffed as necessary, replacement munitions or batteries pre-staged, and alternate or relief UAVs ready to go.
- Perform all pre-flight inspections and procedures according to the model's manual. Integrate the manufacturer's checklist into your pre-flight procedures and use that to ready the UAV for flight. Test all sensors and other payload mechanisms prior to deploying or arming.
- As appropriate, ensure any automatic RTH location is either updated or disabled as needed, sanitize any storage media or the drone itself as appropriate, and disable or deactivate any RID (if using in a WROL environment).

Post Flight

- Any stored imagery should be downloaded, edited as appropriate, and disseminated for exploitation as soon as possible.
- Electronic flight logs should be downloaded and preserved along with all imagery. Details of the flight including conditions encountered should be recorded. After-action reports should be prepared and include any pertinent observations or information the chain of command or other UAS team members should be aware of. Some things that are learned during a flight may not be readily apparent in a review of photos or video alone.
- Carefully inspect the aircraft to determine if it sustained any damage. Note any damage and repair/replace the damaged components as soon as practical. Damage or wear should be remedied as soon as possible to maintain the drone in a flight-ready state. Perform all post-flight inspections and procedures according to the model's manual.
- Ready the drone for flight as soon as possible, even if no mission is expected in the immediate future. One never knows when an emergency mission might be necessary.

- In any case, but more so during a hasty departure, a repacking checklist should be followed when packing up the UAS equipment to ensure nothing is left behind.

Data security

- Whenever the drone is not in use, disable Wi-Fi and cellular connectivity and power it down to limit any data downloads by a third party who may be using software backdoors. When possible, do not operate a drone with any Internet or cellular network connections.
- Remove any removable storage such as a SD card during any firmware updates to prevent third parties or the manufacturer from accessing imagery. Sanitize any storage media after a flight and ensure it has been cleared prior *to* flight in order to deny access to old data/imagery in the event of capture.
- Any controllers that require a cellphone or tablet to be used for flight control or imagery viewing should be placed in "airplane mode" or have their Wi-Fi and cellular connectivity disabled to the extent permissible by the drone manufacturer. When possible, unlocked devices without service should be used (no SIM cards).

Weather and environmental factors

Since many UAS missions will be short-lived, weather forecasting in many cases only needs to consider the next half-hour to hour. Longer, preplanned missions will need to take into account longer range weather predictions.

- **Air conditions:** Consider the affects of extremely hot or cold air, humidity, and altitude.
- **Visibility:** Will visibility improve or deteriorate during the mission? If it does not improve or gets worse, can the mission be completed, or will the drone be able to safely RTH? Does the enemy employ some kind of obscuration like smoke?

- **High winds:** High winds will degrade drone performance and weapons accuracy, as well as tax endurance. Long range missions are not suited for windy conditions. Also consider the effect of wind outside of sheltered locations that the drone may fly into.
- **Precipitation and storms:** Summer thunderstorms can be unpredictable and volatile, creating rapidly changing weather conditions that can become violent. Is a storm approaching? Will threatening rain arrive before the mission is complete? UAS sensors and signals in the high UHF/SHF range can be degraded by rain and snow.
- **Lighting:** Will the pilot/observer be staring into the sun to maintain visual contact? Will sun glare blind the camera? Consider the time of sunset and nautical twilight if the aircraft doesn't have night vision/IR capabilities. Fighter pilots like to attack coming out of the sun; can you approach from up-sun to inhibit visual sightings?
- **Noise:** Consider the ambient noise level. Is it quiet enough that your drone will be heard on its approach or will background/battle noise mask the audio signature?

Route planning

Effective route planning requires examination of the mission's needs, against the enemy's CUAS abilities, while considering the advantage and disadvantages that the terrain presents. Limitations of UAS and the aircraft in question also cannot be overlooked.

Terrain analysis for flightpaths

Terrain analysis is particularly important for UAS flightpath planning because their flight at low altitudes will present challenges from vertical obstructions like trees, wires, utility poles, antennas, buildings, and narrow defiles.

These and the LOS requirements all affect the ability of UAS to approach, acquire, and observe a target. In normal ground terrain analysis, *observation and fields of fire* directly correlates to the LOS of the pilot to the drone.

Terrain masking must be balanced with maintaining a LOS to the control station at all lines. Utilizing terrain to hide a UAV from visual or electronic detection is known as *masking*. Masking enhances survivability and maximizes surprise.

Concealment such as vegetation or a visually noisy urban background, if it does not completely hide a drone, makes it more difficult to spot. Backdrops should match the color of the aircraft where possible, though a dull, dark gray color airframe may be the best compromise for all environments. Ground clutter also presents a problem for radar detection of drones.

Contour flying maximizes the use of terrain masking by flying very low behind buildings or landscape features, going around or between features whenever possible instead of over them. Contour flying can be used on the approach and egress. Be aware that during contour flying the terrain may canalize the flightpath to a point where enemy observation or defenses are concentrated. Any advantageous or stealthy flight plan you identify can also be reverse engineered by the adversary, so consider his point of view.

KOCOA

Note: This discussion can be used for mission/route planning and also evaluating weaknesses in defenses.

KOCOA describes military terrain analysis.

- Key terrain
- Obstacles
- Cover and concealment
- Observation and fields of fire
- Avenues of approach

Key terrain for UAS is any terrain feature or artificial structure that benefits UAS operations or CUAS at the expense of the other side. High ground is usually always the key terrain, and it is more so for UAS. High terrain or buildings allow a pilot to maintain LOS with his drone. Denying it to the enemy, depending on the topography, can limit the range and freedom of movement for an adversary's UAS. Other key terrain includes any features that restrict flightpaths or complicate UAV operation in those areas.

Obstacles are terrain features that block reception of radio waves, most importantly between the pilot and the UAV. This may be a ridge or building between the pilot his UAV or the target or an area with no clear view of the sky (no GPS). Obstacles differ from *obstructions* semantically in that obstructions are collision hazards while obstacles complicate or prevent free flight. Some examples of obstacles are anything that:

- Prevent or restrict contour flying.
- Canalize a flightpath into an area of concentrated observation or CUAS defense.
- Forces a UAV to fly into an area of poor signal, forces movement from cover/concealment, or flight at an undesired altitude.
- Restrict evasive action or escape.

- Force flights into areas where they may be more easily detected.

Finally, CUAS itself can be considered a form of obstacle.

Cover and concealment can enhance survivability and maximizes surprise; alternatively, they can hide the approach of a hostile UAV and provide protection from CUAS efforts. Cover is usually a structure or a vertical ground feature that is sufficient to <u>block radio waves</u>, laser beams, and kinetic projectiles. Concealment is anything that will keep a drone visually hidden from an observer, such as vegetation.

Note that cover for UAVs must block radio waves. A jammer or spoofer can still attack a drone through radio transparent concealment. Concealment, such as vegetation or poor cover may deflect or degrade RF waves but not defeat them totally. Signals a drone broadcasts may find pathways over or through some types of cover, depending on the band. Concealment might be a total visual obstruction or simply hamper easy observation. Vegetation or a visually noisy urban background, if it does not completely hide a drone, makes it more difficult to spot.

Observation and fields of fire applies to visual and electronic detection and UAS defenses. LOS observation and direct fire are only one aspect; radio waves have to be considered as well. Sensors may have different ranges, sensitivities, and properties than human observers. Overlap of human and electronic means should be considered. A drone can be detected by its radio emissions at far greater distances than a human can see/hear it. One form of CUAS may have greater range than another.

Consider how sensors, observers, and CUAS elements are deployed. Does the terrain or a particular approach favor the way the enemy has deployed? On the other hand, a drone on the offensive will benefit from having the best view or an unrestricted field of fire. Locations should be considered from both enemy and friendly perspectives on what advantages/disadvantages they present to either side.

Avenues of approach

Human nature being such as it is, it is quite probable that in an urban area a pilot will follow existing roadways and other obvious features to assist with navigation. Ideal avenues include valleys, canyons, gullies, or streets. Avenues do not need to be direct routes, and probably shouldn't be, as long as LOS is maintained with the controller. Note that avenues will not always coincide with ground routes or take advantage of terrain masking the whole way.

The maneuverability of a UAV allows many of the restrictions of avenues of approach to be overcome simply through altitude. Altitude, however, can present its own problems which may make low-level flight attractive. A drone can always escape a canalized avenue of approach by climbing, but this may give away the drone and expose it to CUAS.

Avenues should permit escapes other than simply "up", so flightpaths should be plotted to have escape routes like side streets or the ability to dash behind concealment. Avenues also need to maintain a line-of-sight to the controller and avoid loss of GPS signals where applicable.

Because of the endurance and LOS limitations of a typical COTS drone (quadcopter), the most likely avenues of approach will be based on range. As direct an approach as possible will give the most time on station, so for ISR missions, one can assume that the avenue will be relatively direct. If the launch point is known, but the target is unknown, one can assume the avenues of approach will radiate out from the point of origin like the spokes of a wheel. Avenues have a launch point, a target, and a recovery point (except for "suicide" drones).

Objectives can include providing real time surveillance support to maneuvering enemy ground units, so while an enemy unit isn't a "target" per se, that unit's presence gives a drone a reason to be there.

- Identify the point of origin by determining probable LRPs for the enemy
- Identify controller positions for pilots (high terrain, tall buildings).
- Locate probable targets in your AO and work out ideal avenues of approach backwards, mapping probable LRPs and control positions along those routes.
- Recognize infiltration, exfiltration, and alternative routes; one route may be better suited to travel in one direction than another.
- Does the avenue:
o Assist with navigation?
o Is it a relatively direct path between point of origin and the target?

o Make terrain masking possible, and if so, what parts of the route?
o Provide access to multiple targets?
• What is the relationship of the avenue to potential CUAS or drone detection sensor coverage?
• If a drone is in a standoff orbit, what are the access points to and from targets from that orbit?

Avenues of approach need to be considered from the foot perspective as well. How long will it take the enemy to reach you? By foot, by vehicle? Accurate distances aids accurate estimation and traveling the distance in a simulated approach allows commanders and observers both to gauge the time from drone observation to attack. This walking of the ground from the enemy's perspective, whether on the ground or via friendly drone, helps your side visualize what the enemy sees and what obstacles or obstructions he has to navigate.

What are your targets?

Target identification goes beyond offensive action. One must assume the role of the enemy to critically assess their defenses and facilities to know their vulnerabilities. Defenses have to be prioritized by every side, so knowing where efforts are likely to be concentrated helps offensive UAS planners to avoid these areas or mitigate risk when penetrating them. Defensively, commanders and CUAS leaders will know what needs to be protected most of all and, by anticipating what the enemy might be interested in, foreseeing the avenues of approach and tactics of enemy UAS.

Once one has identified both friendly and enemy points of interest, the CARVER matrix us used to calculate the value of a target through assessing the potential impact of attack. The matrix is an assessment tool that assigns a numerical value to various potential targets to determine their risk or vulnerability. CARVER is an initialism which stands for Criticality, Accessibility, Recuperability (or Recoverability), Vulnerability, Effect and Recognizability[49].

CARVER seeks to provide an objective, quantifiable to offensive or defensive planners to prioritize their efforts. Offensively, planners use it to determine high-value targets that should be attacked first to inflict maximum damage and disarray to the enemy and defensively to identify what should receive the most protection. The results of your analysis and calculation are then used to classify both your own vulnerabilities and potential enemy weaknesses.

Aircraft threat profile

UAS proliferation on the battlefield

- What is the enemy UAS inventory and the kind (type, make & model)?
- How widely does the enemy use UAS?
- Consider the friendly, neutral, and enemy pattern of UAS activity.

---

[49] How to use the matrix and assign values is outlined in Army FM 34-36, Appendix D

Low proliferation

Strategic: area reconnaissance

Operational: battle reconnaissance and limited surveillance.

High proliferation

Tactical: target identification, targeting for long-range fires, support to ground maneuvering units, attack/strike. Harassing attacks.

Total proliferation

Sub-tactical: use by small ground units (company/platoon level). Widespread anti-personnel strike or use of "suicide" drones in lieu of precision strokes from other platforms.

If the enemy doesn't have a lot of drones, they will ration their usage carefully to avoid losses. This limits their utility on the battlefield and as a result UAS will not be employed widely. The fear of loss can be exploited by using CUAS tactics to foster overcautiousness.

Enemy UAS threat assessment

Planning for the efficacy of your UAS operations also bears assessment of the threat of UAS operations against you. Understand what the enemy has, what he can do with his UAS, and how well he can use it. This is your threat assessment, and it allows you to plan a defense or exploit weaknesses offensively. It is not only about knowing what your enemy has but how it positively or negatively affects your operations.

This goes beyond "what" the enemy has. It is not a list but involves a thought exercise. How does he use what he has? As you do your threat assessment on your enemy, do the same thing from his perspective. What does he know about your UAS capabilities? How could he exploit it against you? Remember to consider both what your enemy knows and doesn't know.

Logistics

- Class and type of drone in their inventory.
- Flight and endurance profiles for each different model.
- Payload or sensor capabilities.
- Use of these drones? i.e., ISR, grenade drops, "suicide" strikes, etc.
- Number of airframes in their inventory.

Strategy

- What are the enemy's objectives (strategic, operational, and tactical)?
- How does UAS help him achieve these objectives?
- How would a UAS attack or ISR hurt your side?
- Does the enemy's doctrine/practice leverage UAS to aid conventional forces, to replace conventional forces, or in place of precision guided weapons?
- Tactically speaking, in any engagement or potential engagement, what is the enemy's threat objective?
- How does enemy UAS support other areas of engagement?

Control and employment

- Does the enemy have strategic control over drones with assignments or attacks being ordered or coordinated centrally?
- Is upper echelon command approval necessary to employ UAS?
- Are sUASs (quadcopters) used at the small-unit level (company/platoon)?
- Do individual UAS teams have authority to independently "hunt" like mobile snipers?
- Are they able to coordinate ground and UAS attacks? Are they able to "swarm" UCAVs?
- Do they have long-range or remote control systems?

Operational

- Examine in what roles the enemy employ his UAS.
- Do you have CUAS capabilities to counter how the enemy uses his drones?
- Are drones only used for ISTAR or are they capable of attack?
  o Small domestic groups and cells will probably have few UAVs, of the COTS type, which can only conduct daylight and limited nighttime ISR.
- Do you or the enemy have long-range fires (RAM— rockets, artillery, mortars)?
  o Militaries and well-equipped insurgencies may have access to long-range fires (RAM) and could use their UAVs to provide targeting for long-range fires.
- Do the UAVs carry munitions?
  o Any multicopter capable of carrying small munitions can hunt individuals and small units in small-scale bombing raids.
- Do you or the enemy have fixed-wing ""kamikaze" drones" or is there ample supply to expend a modified drone in a suicide attack?
- Is there a time preference?

o For example, Ukraine's specialist drone unit, *Aerorozvidka*, locates targets by day and returns to go "tank busting" at night as the darkness conceals the approach.

Competency

- Do you or the enemy follow the same flight routes or fall into patterns? Are the pilots proficient at terrain masking or do they not use it?
- How does your side and the enemy respond to CUAS?
- What is the resiliency to jamming/spoofing?
- Is your enemy sophisticated enough to understand techniques like electronic detecting, jamming, and spoofing?
- Resiliency: if a drone is sent to orbit a position, are there enough UAVs to have one arrive on station to relieve the departing one? Or will there be a gap in coverage while the batteries are changed, etc.?
- Are the people watching the video feed competent enough to understand what they are seeing to derive intelligence value?
- Can the UAS crews think creatively and independently to solve problems and overcome unique challenges on the fly?

Range, endurance, and performance

Establish range and endurance profiles for individual types/models of UAVs.

- Maximum range, combat radius, combat range and loiter time.
- What is the turn-around time to recharge, refuel, and reload batteries/ordnance?
- What speeds and altitudes is the particular UAV capable of, laden and unladen?

Guidance

Consider how the drone navigates and operates. How will jamming/spoofing affect it? This dictates threat profiles, CUAS options, and detection ability.

- Piloted, semi-autonomous (normal COTS function); variable degree of autonomy but self-stabilizes and can land or return to home if there is a loss of signal.
- Fully autonomous (programmed); no inputs are required and may not emit any radio signals.
- If fully autonomous, is it GPS dependent or does it use INS?
- Are the pilots competent fliers? Are they dependent on digital maps to navigate?
- Where do the control signals originate? Ground-level LOS, like a COTS drone? Is the pilot in an elevated position? Perhaps the drone is getting its signals from a remote repeater or an airborne relay.
- Can you jam or spoof the signals?

Sensor package

- Is it capable of night flight/attack? If so, does it have image intensification or infrared cameras, or both?
- Do you know how capable the camera package is for an ISR mission?
- Is it carrying SIGINT sensors to snoop on radio signals and traffic?
- Is the drone perhaps carrying a jammer to interfere with your communications?
- Does it have a laser designator for other weapons?

Weapons payload?

If the drone is armed, the type of warhead can potentially indicate what the targets may be and how serious the threat is.

- Consider the type of the munition or warhead; a grenade might mean hunting individuals or groups on foot down whereas an integral warhead may indicate a "suicide" drone.
- What is the lethality and accuracy of the munitions carried? Take into consideration the UAVs stability and precision along with the competency of the pilot when judging aim.
- How many shots is the aircraft carrying? Is there more than one to account for misses or so it can shift to a new target without returning for rearming?
- Attack mode: direct attack, terminal, or stand off?
  - **Direct attack:** drops unguided bombs or grenades usually vertically.
  - **Terminal:** "suicide" drones; flies directly into target and detonates on impact.
  - **Stand off:** launches munitions (rockets/missiles) which may or may not be guided.
- Does the aircraft have to be in a certain attitude or altitude envelope to deliver the weapon? Is there a "safe" over/under height/range the UAV can't deliver at?
- How will the payload weight and drag affect range and endurance?

Ch. 17 Attack of the Drones

UCAV: Armed Drones

The term "drone" has become synonymous with Unmanned Combat Aerial Vehicle, or UCAV, and small UCAVs have become common in modern warfare. Originally used for reconnaissance purposes in first-rate militaries, the small, modern consumer drone has become a staple of irregular warfare. Cartels have mounted automatic weapons on drones and ISIS used them to drop bombs on their enemies. No longer only a plaything or innovative camera platforms, drones will be used in any domestic conflict in the United States or elsewhere.

Drone warfare, expressly at the domestic level, is a perfect example of disruptive technology. Drones add a vertical attack element and remote surveillance capability that until now was beyond the ability of most participants in a civil conflict. Expectations of civil war or unrest merely being street battles and fights to secure high points (drone operator's vantage points) need to be adjusted.

To date, irregular forces have used drones for:

- Video has been used for propaganda purposes including showing successful attacks.
- Battle damage assessment (BDA) and casualty confirmation.
- General surveillance and reconnaissance.
- Studying attacks, defenses, and responses.
- Delivery of explosives.

Earlier, we explored how drones can be used for one's benefit. One must realize in a civil conflict your enemy will use them for *his* benefit. Warfare is not static and technology like UAS will be game changing. Armed drones will become more than the insurgent's eye in the sky but his precision guided munition too.

Due to small payloads, drones must use precision munitions or precise unguided delivery to be effective. This is a benefit as the smaller weapons can have more effect on target through greater accuracy. The increase in precision is a commander's dream but also makes ground warfare more impersonal. Small groups of soldiers or even an individual can be targeted by a drone when before such a target may have been an ineffective use of an attack plane.

Military forces have had the same aerial surveillance advantages since close air support was invented. Low flybys of helicopters and all manner of fixed-wing aircraft can suppress ground forces. Nothing is new about drones being used for suppressive effect, except that the cheap, easy to use technology has democratized airborne reconnaissance and even attack.

Unmanned aircraft offer a unique advantage to modern irregular forces that many guerilla and terrorist movements have not had; air power. Anti-tank mines, large IEDs, and rocket launchers have been in use against tracked and wheeled vehicles for decades, but vertical and precision attacks are something new. Only in the late proxy wars of the 21st century have insurgencies like as in Syria had access to guided anti-tank missiles like TOW and Javelin.

Air attack using modified mortar bombs or grenades and improvised warheads now can give this kind of capability to any force with UAS resources. Guided munitions were previously only attainable through foreign military assistance which may be denied or limited for reasons from political to financial. Not every group involved in a conflict will have the backing of the CIA. While the attack methods may vary from unsophisticated grenade drops from servo motors to ersatz anti-tank missiles created from RC jets, the potential for fast, precise strikes now exists on any UAS battlefield.

Weaponization

Drones can carry a surprising variety of weapons that are all up to the ingenuity of the user and their access to ordnance and explosives. A flamethrower was put on one UAV. The Internet was put into a panic a few years ago when a drone owner posted video of a quadcopter with a pistol mounted below firing away. The contraption appeared to be a homemade model and the pistol's recoil noticeably pushed the drone backwards with each shot. This prompted the FAA to investigate as putting weapons on drones is illegal.[50]

Latin American drug cartels are using these to deliver IEDs, often using a second drone to provide surveillance and guidance. One drone bomb was C4, and ball bearings pressed into a Tupperware plastic container.[51] Some of

[50] Remember everyone, this book is a thought exercise and not for use while the rule of law is functional.

these devices have been dropped like bombs while others have landed devices either as warnings or to emplace them for later detonation.

ISIS often dropped munitions out of a plastic tube when released remotely by a servo motor. 40mm grenades were popular with ISIS as they were light and could be lofted easily by consumer quadcopters. Larger drones can drop 60mm and 81mm mortar bombs. Homemade bombs often using plastic explosive have been seen in Latin American cartel wars and in the Middle East. Weapons don't need to be dropped; a more accurate strike, at the cost of the drone, can be delivered in a "kamikaze" attack involving terminal guidance to the target and detonation.

Payloads depend on speed and range required. Maximum payload for a large COTS quadcopter is about 4.5lbs (about 2kg). Optimal payloads are on average half a pound or less, up to 1.25lbs or half a kilo. About 1lb of C4 explosive is enough to destroy a vehicle. Custom multicopters or fixed-wing drones can carry larger warheads, though they do exceed the scope of this work.

Bare explosives can be studded with ball bearings or other metal to create shrapnel; however, this may take the weight limit over what small drones can carry. Thankfully, at least for now, it is nearly impossible to source explosives in the US without outright theft from military or commercial sources. Americans do not have the same access as insurgents in Iraq did. This may change in a civil war or if the

---

[51] "Jalisco cartel adopts new tactic: drones armed with C-4 explosive," Mexico News Daily, 8/18/2020.

military collapses. Domestic sources of explosives from construction/demolition companies or homebrewed plastic explosives are more possible in SHTF. Foreign actors may also supply explosives or munitions.

Targets

The issue with drones is not that they won't have enough targets but that there will not be enough airframes to attack targets. ISIS was able to use as many consumer drones as they could get delivered because they were well funded (until they weren't). Without both a reliable supply and the money to pay for drones, "suicide" UAVs being used as precision guided weapons is unlikely to be a ubiquitous part of domestic urban combat. This *may* be a concern if factions are being supported by foreign powers.

Even homebuilt drones will run out of parts eventually. A potential conflict with China only exacerbates potential supply problems as drones and the very components they are made of are manufactured over there or other Asian countries whose economies and supply chains would be disrupted by war. Tactical employment of terminally guided UAVs in battle requires a lot of drones. Thus, "kamikaze" drone attacks will have to be prioritized and use of reusable weapons-dropping platforms emphasized.

Tactical targets are things like fortifications, barricades, or concentrations of fighters. Strategic targets are those that weaken or demoralize your enemy without directly killing them. Strategic targets can be broken down into two groups; local and regional. Local targets are those that affect your daily life while regional ones are larger sites and facilities. Here are some examples:

- **Water:** local, your neighborhood well or city pumping station; regional, state aqueduct pumping plant.
- **Fuel:** local, a gas station; regional, a refinery.
- **Electricity:** local, a neighborhood substation; regional, a powerplant or long-distance transmission lines.
- **Transportation:** local, drone-delivered IEDs on the road; regional, drones bombing semi-trucks on the Interstate.
- **Persons:** local, a militia leader; regional, a political or government figure.

Terrorists or insurgents are going to go after strategic targets in order to get the most impact. This would include bombing oil refineries, assassinating politicians or popular figures, destroying critical electrical or communication notes, or pumping stations for water, gas, and oil. They may also use drones in attacks against sports stadiums, large concentrations of people, or aircraft.

In an insurgency, the main goal will be to harass your enemy and degrade his ability to fight. It may also be to force relocation or withdrawal due to inadequate resources. It would be easy for bad guys to detonate a drone bomb on or near power lines or a local substation. The same for an Internet hub (usually inside stout buildings). The only water source, like a municipal well, might also be attacked. Not all of these locations can be guarded around the clock.

Drones may not break the stalemate of trench warfare, but they can ensure that the killing continues unless used on a very broad scale in combination with other methods.

Organized, concentrated, and systematic attacks would be needed to kill enough of the enemy to render a position ineffective and with sUAVs dropping small munitions, this would be a tedious process. A large air or artillery strike could kill many of the enemy at once, but small grenade drops would be a suitable prelude to ground forces moving in.

Drones, when not used for armed reconnaissance or harassing missions, should be deployed to attack strong points. For instance, a drone may clear out a machine gun nest or clear the defenders from an entry point into a defensive line or position. An armed drone could be sent to recon for ambushes and strike any personnel lying in wait ahead of the advancing friendly unit. Missions that are especially hazardous for humans such as safely detonating an IED or counter-sniper work could be given to offensive UAS teams.

Drone combat

In addition to the above discussed surveillance and reconnaissance roles, drones may be used in the following manner to kill:

• Dual drone operations: Drone 1 overflies a target, performing reconnaissance. The same drone returns, or Drone 2 arrives, and delivers a hand grenade or explosive.

• Grenades or explosives may be dropped like an aerial bomb, or the drone can be terminally guided into the target before detonation. Drone attacks should be considered precision attacks.

- Drones may perform pre-attack recon from high altitude and attacks from lower altitudes, utilizing buildings, trees, or other visual obstructions to conceal their approach.
- Some models are capable of crashing through weak windows in a "kamikaze" attack.
- ISIS used drones to guide vehicular suicide bombers to their target and then remotely detonated the bomb at the most opportune moment.
- A second explosive may be detonated to kill those responding to the chaos of the first attack.
- Unarmed drones may act in a suppression role by mimicking the attack pattern of an armed drone.[52]
- Dropping smoke grenades in the open to provide concealment to attacking or retreating fighters.

Near future developments will include homemade loitering munitions or "suicide" drones. The most likely candidates for this are fixed-wing craft using electric or piston-engine propellers, though RC jet components could be used as well. Fixed-wing aircraft can have greater ranges, be capable of higher speeds, and can carry larger payloads than copter designs. These would essentially be lightweight guided missiles.

Bombing of structures

Aircraft bombing buildings or shelling them with artillery is something that small movements may want to imitate but can't achieve with UAS. This requires less precision than guiding a "suicide" drone into a doorway or window and

---

[52] There are countless stories of military aircraft out of munitions making low passes over enemy troops to suppress them. C-130 cargo aircraft have flown high orbits similarly to their armed AC-130 gunship counterparts to fool the enemy.

allows the delivery airframe to be reused for future missions.

Dropping of explosives on buildings—for example on the roof of a suburban home—is possible but probably ineffective for most UAVs. Data, however, is limited. Public information regarding the effectiveness of bare explosives detonated against civilian buildings is not easily accessible. Most of the demolitions data and video shows explosives inside homes, not falling on their roofs.

Small amounts of explosive can be quite destructive to smaller structures. An explosive charge ≤5lb (versus a traditional mortar or aerial bomb with a metal shell) should not penetrate standard residential and commercial roofs *prior to detonation*. Military weapons have a metal outer case to enable some penetration before detonation and fragmentation after. A block of explosive with the consistency of modeling clay falling from a drone *shouldn't* break through the roof, nor should grenades.

With the explosion occurring outside, at least half of the blast effects are going upwards. There will be no ground to focus more of the blast into walls, as if the explosive were detonated next to the house. With the amount of explosive, a drone can safely carry, a house shouldn't be totally destroyed. A wood roof in the area of the blast will be blown in and almost certainly the interior area below it.

Warheads detonated at window level outside will present a high-velocity flying glass hazard. For any detonation, residents in the home will face a danger of wood, metal, and masonry shrapnel. Note that any holes created by a preliminary blast may allow for subsequent explosives to be delivered to the interior, causing greater damage. Secondary explosives delivered after the first charge breaches the house and this should be *highly* anticipated after any such "bombing."

Shockwaves may enter the home and cause additional damage. The shockwave itself will also be dangerous. Hearing loss, either temporary or permanent, is highly probable. The blast may weaken structural components of the house causing partial collapse. Gas or electrical lines may be severed. Fire may occur.

Outdoors, unless a military weapon designed to produce shrapnel (grenade, mortar bomb) is exploded, blast effects and flying debris will be the main hazard vs structural collapse. Explosions at a close distance are still quite hazardous and a drone could approach to mere feet before command detonation. Another hazard would be the airborne emplacement of IEDs to be exploded at a later time.

Armed reconnaissance

First of all, anti-personnel UAS usage doesn't have to be lethal. Drones can perform suppression of enemy forces, in addition to direct attacks. By forcing troops to take cover or hide from its camera, this degrades their ability to carry out their mission, the textbook definition of suppression. This can be intentional if the target is conditioned to react to drones or unintentional if the drone's presence or behavior causes the target to act. An armed drone can provide traditional fire suppression if someone attaches a weapon to it.

An example of suppression is a criminal being pursued by officers "going to ground" when a helicopter shows up. Suspects often attempt to take cover under anything that will hide them. This was easier to do before law enforcement aircraft were equipped with thermal tracking gear. The author has even seen a helicopter locate a suspect hidden in elephant grass next to a golf course in daylight thanks to its FLIR camera.

While the helicopter is overhead, the suspect can't move. A combatant can't hide and fight, without giving himself away. Assuming there is no FLIR, being unable to continue to evade capture, the suspect is stuck while ground units search the area for his location. A flying drone can provide the same effect and more against a neighborhood defensive unit. In war, instead of search and capture the ground units would be moving in for a kill.

Armed reconnaissance by UAS is basically synonymous with an attack mission. An armed UAV is dispatched to find the enemy and attack him when found; a hunting mission. To differentiate between a pure attack mission and armed recon, the former already has the target objective in mind and the purpose is to inflict damage on the enemy. The latter may not know the location of the enemy and has a dual-role of information gathering with attack.

Reconnaissance in force, also *recon by fire*, involves intentionally making contact with the enemy and engaging him in combat. For reasons discussed elsewhere, UAS does not perform in this role well. The limited ability of many sUAVs to carry large payloads will limit how many targets they can attack, so an attack mission, once the weapons are empty, may transition to reconnaissance or providing targeting to other more capable platforms.

Supporting fires

Where UCAV employment is not possible or feasible, artillery is an option using the drone as a forward observer, allowing artillery strikes on targets out of view of ground troops. Aircraft spotting for artillery has been used since WWII but the proliferation of drones, potentially enabling an entire battlefield to be under constant, intense surveillance is new and game-changing.

UAS can conduct reconnaissance and targeting all by itself meaning a human doesn't even have to be physically proximate to the enemy to call down fire. There is little to no warning of an attack such as the screech of an incoming artillery shell or the distant report of cannon fire. Even if the drone is seen, it may be the only notice of a possible incoming barrage.

While an unarmed UAV may not be on an attack mission or flying in a targeting or forward observer role, targets of opportunity may appear during other missions. This flexibility makes a drone armed by proxy. A leader or UAS pilot should know, if any, long-range fires are available and how to coordinate with them. A forward artillery observer could be a member of the drone team or a pilot himself.

Anti-personnel

Drones stalking and hunting the enemy as individuals and small groups has proven to be viable, if not efficient on the scale of a nationwide war. Such missions are sure to be launched in smaller domestic conflicts. As gruesome as it is, some lessons can be learned from operations in Ukraine and other principals applied to anti-personnel use of UAS. While this is not functionally any different than a squad maneuvering into contact with an enemy element and engaging, the novel nature and attack vector is disturbing.

Drones can afford to be patient to search out targets. They can loiter, orbit, and change altitude to get a better look. Helicopters even in a slow hover don't have the same advantages. UAS's innate characteristics reward an operator's patience as he hunts, looking for the right angle or telltale that reveals a hidden soldier.

Looking up is difficult when wearing a helmet or other hat (cover). Helmeted or hat-wearing individuals may have less situational awareness than uncovered personnel. Attacking an unaware target is easier than attacking an alert target. Likewise, stationary targets are easier to locate and strike than mobile targets.

Flying in high ambient noise environments and downwind of the objective helps to mask rotor noise as heard by the target. Approaching at higher altitude and using the camera to search for targets, then only descending to commence an attack run will lessen the chance of early visual/sonic detection. Approaching over tree or vegetation cover denies a clear view of the sky and helps to obscure a UAV. Approaches flown out of the sun and departure runs *into* the sun use glare to hide in.

Prioritizing ideal defensive positions or obvious/suspected fortifications increases the chance of finding a target. Looking near low ground, broken ground, high points, or tree lines does the same. Signs of human activity such as tire tracks, disturbed soil, garbage, antennas, vehicles, or disturbed (trampled, cut, or broken) foliage also indicate enemy presence.

If an enemy individual is walking alone, he is probably near to more people from his side. Following him discreetly may lead the UAV back to a fighting position, shelter, etc. Tall buildings with excellent vantage points near enemy positions or in enemy territory may have an observer present.

Dropping munitions on a vehicle's hood will detonate the explosive at head and torso level. At ground-level detonations increases shrapnel and blast deflection plus hardened vehicles are less susceptible to ground-level explosion by design. Windshields will offer a lot less protection than any other part of the vehicle. Anti-personnel grenades can be dropped on/near armored vehicles to neutralize ground troops who are in the blind spot, or on top of, the vehicle—a sort of "scratch my back."

Vertical openings to the sky such as hatches, skylights, vents, or chimneys are vulnerable to attack. Horizontal openings to the ground are more difficult to strike, although an explosive detonated just outside the opening can send shrapnel and blast effects inside.

A Ukrainian drone pilot claimed to "train" Russian soldiers[53] to make it easier to drop more lethal thermobaric grenades more accurately and with greater survivability from lower altitudes. He tricks Russians to stay in their positions by dropping a fragmentation grenade outside the position. To avoid shrapnel, the soldiers stay in their foxhole, assuming they are doing the correct thing, only to be killed by a grenade better suited to confined spaces.

Note: Use of explosive and anti-personnel weapons, including less-lethal riot control items is *not* recommended against riots and similar urban unrest. Short of the direst circumstances in an active civil war or widespread, lawless combat, civilians *should not* be using armed UAVs against crowds or ordinary criminals.

Drop times and lead

Many online have attempted to estimate the time of drop for grenades based on attack footage from Ukraine. It appears that the altitude is overestimated based on a failure to account for the effect of drag of the munition, tailfins, and stabilizing mechanisms added. One such popular timing chart circulating online is as follows[54]:

53

www.reddit.com/r/CombatFootage/comments/11vmpbr/
ukrainian_drone_operator_describes_the_process_of/
[54] Distances rounded.

Time of fall under gravity, no air resistance (drag)

- 1 second (16 feet/5m)
- 2 seconds (65 feet/20m)
- 3 seconds (140 feet/45m)
- 4 seconds (260 feet/80m)
- 5 seconds (400 feet/120m)

These figures assume a fall speed of terminal velocity (32 ft/s (9.8 m/s)—1 g) and no drag. Unfortunately, this does not account for acceleration. A falling object does not instantly descend at terminal velocity nor do munitions fall in a vacuum. Speed builds up *until* it reaches terminal velocity and air resistance affects both acceleration and final speed.

To calculate the time it takes for a spherical object to fall from a specified altitude, the effects of gravity, air resistance, and terminal velocity must be factored in. The following equation is used to calculate the time of fall:

$t = (2h/g)^{(1/2)} \times [1+(V_t/V_0)^2 \times (e(-2gh/V_t^2)-1)]^{(1/2)}$.

Where: **h**=height

g=acceleration due to gravity

V_0=initial velocity

V_t=terminal velocity, calculated: $(2mg/(\rho ACd))^{0.5}$, where:

m=mass of the object

g=acceleration due to gravity (9.81 m/s^2);

ρ=density of air

A=cross-sectional area of the object

Cd=drag coefficient

For a M67 hand grenade, the drop time at sea level, accounting for acceleration and wind resistance would be approximately:

- 50m: 4.3 seconds
- 100m: 6 seconds
- 200m: 8.6 seconds
- 400m: 12.5 seconds

Without the correct coefficient of drag for the variable type and shape of the munitions dropped, only estimates based on the rough shape can be used. The wide variety of projectiles used makes it difficult to calculate the individual determinant factors regarding velocity and drag. Drop times are calculated using idealized coefficients of drag for a given weapon profile and weight.

The aim point against a moving target is chosen by estimating lead. A munition is released from a known altitude. Given the parameters of the weapon, including its mass, coefficient of drag, and cross-sectional area, the drop time from the release altitude can be calculated. Drop time is one factor in figuring where to aim and when to release.

The second and subjective factor is the travel speed of a walking/running human or a moving vehicle. Running and walking speed can be estimated using average figures or through speed estimation (which comes from experience). The time to travel the estimated distance at the estimated speed is used to calculate lead. Calculating the lead distance is trivial; correctly estimating the speed/distance is harder. Also, nobody can predict if the target will stop or change direction.

Ch. 18 Anti-armor/vehicle tactics

Tanks and armored personnel carriers (APCs)

The primary intentions of an attack on armor should be to disable the vehicle, kill the crew, and do so in a manner that causes any ammunition carried in the vehicle to "cook off" and explode. This will catastrophically damage the vehicle beyond repair, creates a spectacular explosion, and is good for friendly morale while damaging enemy morale.

While it is ideal to kill the crew and detonate any explosives, a mobility kill by destroying or disabling the engine or damaging the wheels/treads, is also a success. For wheeled vehicles, an explosion at or near the tires may be enough to disable the vehicle. This is more likely to be sufficient with unarmored civilian vehicles with their comparatively less heavy-duty tires. Run-flat tires may keep the vehicle moving for some distance but generally the effects of an explosion will not permit the vehicle to be driven very far.

The most expedient way of destroying an armored vehicle is by dropping a munition into an open and unoccupied hatch. Effects on video are rarely impressive but likely fatal to the crew. Evidence from Ukraine shows that quadcopters are accurate enough to drop small warheads (mortars, grenades) into hatches from above treetop height.

For tanks and APCs, the crew compartment will amplify the effects of any explosion or fire. Shrapnel will ricochet and blast effects will be magnified. Escape can be difficult and slow. A successful blast inside the compartment, even if it does not injure or kill all the crew, may render the vehicle non-mission capable and demoralize the survivors.

A low, slow approach is best for maximum accuracy but is also most hazardous for the drone as this will make it an excellent target for ground fire. The drop needs to be precise because a miss will likely result in the hatch being closed ("buttoning up") or the vehicle moving. A second munition should be carried, when possible, in the event of misses; a second, later pass will probably be an unlikely possibility.

Burning an occupied vehicle is also a successful attack. Firebombing requires less accuracy. A Molotov cocktail dropped on the top of an open armored vehicle creates an opportunity for the accelerant or flames to enter the cabin. Open hatches are the best, either occupied or unoccupied. Engine compartments are secondary targets. Flame being sucked in an air intake is bad for the engine.

The most vulnerable part of any armored vehicle is going to be the top (roof) and its wheels or tracks. UCAVs like "kamikaze" drones or loitering munitions are best used for top attacks due to the ability to carry a larger warhead that can punch through the armor. Satchel charges or shaped charge warheads can be dropped on the rear deck (engine compartment) and detonated to create a mobility kill. This may leave the crew alive in a manually functional compartment with working main weaponry.

Slat or cage armor is used to detonate shaped charges further away from the vehicle in order to deflect part of the explosive blast and reduce the penetrative power of the warhead. Overhead cages are not particularly common but may be increasingly seen as the drone threat increases. Some weapons may fail to detonate when hitting cages or their effects will be mitigated.

Misses may result in the crew "buttoning up" which protects them but reduces their visibility and effectiveness. External fuel tanks may be punctured or ignited (diesel is far more flame resistant than gasoline) by shrapnel damage that does not disable the vehicle. Vision blocks or camera systems may be disabled or damaged by blasts.

Note that for tanks in particular, and many APCs, there is a dead space above the tank where the main weaponry can't fire upwards. Pintle mounted machine guns are different matter, as are some newer remote gun mounts capable of high-elevation fire, but it still holds true. Vertical vision is poor in all vehicles. This is alleviated by opening hatches and the crew or commander looking outside, which makes them vulnerable.

Smoke grenades placed security *on* the vehicle can blind the crew. It is important that the grenade is dropped on the vehicle and in a location where it will not roll off. One such location may be the cowl beneath the windshield. Adhesives may need to be used. The goal is to force the driver to halt the vehicle and open the hatch in order to clear the grenade, which will create an opportunity for further attack. Smoke grenades on the ground may be ineffective because the vehicle can simply drive out of the smoke.

In attacking armored vehicles, low-cost "kamikaze" drones might be used. These would fly directly into the target and be fused to detonate on contact like a missile. While the explosive carried by a drone may not be as powerful or detonate with the carefully engineered fashion of an armor-piercing shell, the precision delivery may work better than simply dropping a small bomb. A terminally guided weapon would allow careful targeting on a soft point as well as more easily accounting for a moving vehicle's speed and maneuvers.

Vehicles can be destroyed or effectively disabled by:

- Killing the crew by dropping explosives or incendiaries through open hatches into the crew compartment.
- Disabling the engine by dropping explosives or incendiaries on the rear deck.
- Igniting external fuel tanks or rupturing them to spill fuel and create a logistic/range limitation.
- Blinding the crew or reducing visibility by destroying optical sensors, vision blocks, or shattering windshields.
- Creating mobility kills by blowing off/breaking treads and damaging wheels/tires.

Convoys and escorts

It is important to note that most vehicles will be faster than a quadcopter and most drones. This will allow vehicles with unimpeded paths to escape. Attacks made when vehicles are stationary or terrain that does not allow high speeds or rapid egress are the most successful. Some of these choke points are:

- Heavy tree cover.
- Soft, muddy, or boggy terrain.
- Narrow, curving, or mountainous roadways.
- Anywhere the roadway is partially or fully obstructed by debris or purposeful obstacles.
- Roads with ditches on one or both sides.

For a convoy, in area with little ability for lateral escape, such as a bridge or a narrow road, attacking the lead and rear vehicles first will help to freeze the convoy in place.

Armored vehicles (tanks) are often escorted by dismounted infantry troops. It would be negligent forget to attack the "leg" soldiers. Without troops to defend the armor from infantry assault, it becomes much easier for enemy troops without their own armor to employ anti-tank weapons like rocket launchers or even climb the tanks.

Targeting fuel tankers is not an instant army-stopper, but it is a viable tactic. It is likely that tankers are unarmored or are far less armored and much more vulnerable than the fighting vehicles. A mechanized unit cannot move without fuel, nor can an army fight without food an ammo. Plenty of attacks took advantage of any break where the crew was resting or resupplying as the vehicles were opened up and the crew outside.

Because weight and electrical supply is of minimal concern, vehicles are more likely to have anti-drone electronic protection than foot-mobile forces. These make take the form of multiple antennas in a cluster on top of the vehicle or a round, radar like dish. It is probable that if anti-UAV electronics are being used, probably only one vehicle in a convoy has it. These vehicles would need to be prioritized for attack or their systems disabled by ground forces to prevent jamming of attacking UAS.

Vehicles parked near any camouflaged position risk revealing the position. Keeping vehicles away from hidden shelters by at least 100 feet/30m decreases the chance of discovery. Proximity to military vehicles in the open is extremely hazardous as the vehicles are easier to spot and will clue in the enemy. Persons traveling back and forth could also be easily tracked to reveal the hidden position.

Armored cars and civilian vehicles

The US military uses tanks, cartels use homemade

armored vehicles known as *monstruosos*, and police use armored vehicles like the Lenco BearCat. The BearCat is a good example of an armored vehicle built on a heavy-duty pickup chassis. It in particular, in addition to its armor, has angled and sloped surfaces on the hood to deflect projectiles like Molotov cocktails. The bodies are typically constructed to avoid retention of thrown objects.

The Lenco BearCat provides standard ballistic protection of up to 7.62x51mm NATO and is upgradable to protect from .50 Browning (NIJ Level IV/B7 rating). The .50 caliber rating appears to apply to the sides of the vehicle ("vertical panels" per the manufacturer) and is spec'd to 10 shots or 1 20mm shot. While Lenco claims its one-piece wall armor is produced through a "secret and proprietary process" it is made from half-inch thick "Mil Spec" steel. Depending on the exact hardness of the steel, this would be consistent with NIJ Level IV protection.

Kevlar ballistic 'Skip Round' skirts which double as casualty litters can be placed along the running boards to stop shots or shrapnel from going beneath the vehicle. Optional window screens may be fitted to protect from thrown projectiles which will affect any air-dropped munitions. Vehicles may be fitted with a closed-air system to provide fresh air in a compromised environment, which may offer some protection from smoke.

They are built on a standard Ford heavy-duty pickup chassis. While visibility is done through armored glass and is only slightly more restricted than a standard vehicle of similar configuration, there are cameras in various positions around the vehicle up to 360°. Upward visibility is limited to the windshield and roof hatch. The roof hatch may be fitted with an optional armored cupola shield.

A similar vehicle is the MRAP (mine-resistant ambush protected) which were built as a response to IEDs demolishing Humvees. These vehicles place a high emphasis on protection from mine or buried IED detonations below the vehicle. V-shaped hulls channel the blast towards the sides of the vehicle. Many of these vehicles were sold as surplus through the US DOD Law Enforcement Support Office (LESO) "1033" program to law enforcement agencies.

In unarmored or lightly armored vehicles, attack the engine compartment. Where weight savings or economy is concerned, armor will prioritize the passenger compartment meaning that the engine is lightly protected if at all. For vehicles that do not have mine-resistant armored hulls, explosions under the vehicle can be devastating. However, dropping an explosive in front of a vehicle to detonate under the vehicle would be obvious and a driver could simply swerve away from the device.

Troops are vulnerable during any break where the men are resting or when deploying from the vehicle. Note that exposed riders on the running boards is common as well. One such opportunity may be a "downed man" drill where personnel deploy to recover a wounded person. Police armored vehicles often have their doors open to improve access and communication. Officers also tend to cluster around or behind their armored vehicles during briefings, standoffs, or during gunfights, creating a close cluster of soft targets.

Vehicle/armor attacks generally

- Vehicles are more likely to have anti-drone electronic protection than troops on foot.
- Disabling the vehicle itself could be considered a success by itself. Otherwise, a second attack might follow to neutralize the occupants, usually after they have dismounted.
- The top (roof) of armored vehicles is going to be the weakest and least-armored side.
- Shaped charges are best for defeating armor.
- Thermite can burn through light armor and destroy engines.
- Often tanks and other armored vehicles are seen with cargo racks filled with things like sleeping gear or rations. These cargo or fuel tank stores can be easily ignited.
- Dropping munitions on a vehicle's hood will detonate the explosive at head and torso level. At ground-level detonations increases shrapnel and blast deflection plus hardened vehicles are less susceptible to ground-level explosion. Windshields will offer a lot less protection than any other part of the vehicle.
- Armored vehicles must have their hatches closed at all times except when occupied and in such cases, there needs to be an air guard on watch.
- Anti-personnel grenades can be dropped on/near armored vehicles to neutralize ground troops who are in the blind spot, or on top of, the vehicle—a sort of "scratch my back."

EMCON

EMCON, or emissions control, usually refers to limiting radio transmissions to avoid interception and triangulation. It is a signature management technique. It also includes emitting any kind of electromagnetic energy, including light, and sound. EMCON is primarily used in military and defense applications to reduce the electromagnetic (EM) signature of equipment and prevent detection by hostile forces that may be monitoring for EM emissions.

Often patrolling military units will go radio silent and not transmit using their radios for any reason as any intercepted communications can alert the enemy of their presence or be triangulated. In UAS, radio signals are vital for the system to work (except for fully autonomous flight) as commands and video signals will need to be transmitted back and forth. Some simple mitigation measures can lower the probability of interception, but not eliminate it.

Using a low-power transmitter can significantly reduce RF emissions. The higher the power output, the stronger the radio waves and the further they can travel. At low power, the radio waves produced will be weaker, and they will not travel as far. Pilots should ensure that they use the lowest power output that is appropriate for their flight needs.

Choosing an uncommon frequency can help reduce the chance of detection if the adversary does not expect to detect a signal there. Using directional antennas can help focus the radio waves in a particular direction, reducing the overall RF emissions. Flying at a lower altitude reduces the distance radio waves can travel due to interference from obstructions and the radio horizon.

Launch and recovery

- Don't be predictable. Always launch and land drones out of sight from potential adversarial observers. Dense urban environments provide numerous protected launch points and concealed avenues of approach. Use battle or ordinary environmental noise to mask rotor noise.
- When possible, land and recover the drone in different locations away from your home/bivouac or immediate area of operations to prevent adversaries from easily locating you.
- Flightpaths for launch and recovery should utilize terrain masking to travel a distance away from the landing pad/operations area before ascending to altitude. Fly the drone between buildings, terrain, or trees. Ascend and descend well away from the operator.
- If possible, have the operator remain concealed a distance away from the landing pad and have someone else physically launch/recover the drone.
- Never fly a drone directly back to your area of operations or landing pad; fly in a different direction after reconning a target. Be sure to fly an indirect, deceptive course back.
- Alert your neighbors and friendly forces when you launch a drone, so they do not mistake it for an enemy craft. Monitor enemy communications for their reaction to the drone.

Extremely low altitude (ELA) flight

Medium to high altitude flight is a privilege of air superiority, including relative impunity from surface-to-air defenses. A realistically contested air environment is something foreign to Americans reaching back decades. Even in Ukraine and the Middle East sUAS have heretofore been able to operate with little fear of being shot down. The proliferation of UAS and CUAS has not reached a point where one necessitates the other as much as helicopters made SHORAD[55] and MANPAD[56] common within armies.

As UAS presence in battles increases, so will defenses. The escalating arms race will eventually negate the relative safety that altitude has to offer for drones. Now, UAVs are operated at high and medium altitudes to limit exposure to small-arms fire, increased range, and for superior observational perspective. This can't last forever. A high-flying drone has a clear line-of-sight to it from the ground, making it a sitting duck for any CUAS soldier with an EW capability. High altitude flight (for a drone) is for a world with limited CUAS capabilities.

Against an enemy with low CUAS capabilities, a high flying drone benefits from its small size being hard to spot and a reduced or non-existent sound signature high in the sky. Drones fly high in part to reduce the likelihood their distinctive sound is detected. This inherent stealth gives drones a high degree of protection simply by going unnoticed. To date, this is the main way battlefield UAVs have been successful.

In the ever evolving race between offense and defense, drone tactics must evolve if they can no longer fly with impunity. The loss of invulnerability of altitude will be traded for low-altitude cover and concealment. UAS operations must evolve to adopt tactics similar to how an infantryman uses terrain, structures, and vegetation to maneuver safely.

Extreme-low altitude flight is attractive for survivability, attack, and gaining intelligence. ELA flight includes terrain

---

[55] Short range air defense
[56] Man-portable surface to air missiles

masking and contour flying. Operation at just over head-height but below the rooftops of shorter buildings offers the maximum protection and concealment much the way a trench offers troops shelter from snipers and artillery.

Survivability is perhaps the most pressing case for ELA. To survive an electronic shootdown attempt, a drone will need to fly nap-of-the-Earth missions, through trees, and behind buildings. Not only will this be for concealment but to help protect against CUAS EW electronic emissions. Putting anything between a drone and a RF gun will help attenuate jamming signals that may disable the drone.

The problem is that low-level flight can cause interference with the control and telemetry signals between the aircraft and the operator, so it is not practical in many cases to have a pilot standing off from safety a great distance to control the drone. The operator has to be close or in an elevated position with a line-of-sight unless some sort of repeater is utilized.

Problems associated with ELA flight
- Natural and artificial obstructions causing loss of signal
- Inability to visually see the aircraft
- Multipathing
- GNSS (GPS) loss-of-signal

Mitigation
- Using specialized directional antennas optimized for the environment
- Repeaters on high terrain or buildings
- Airborne repeater drones, tethered or untethered
- Mesh networks
- Physical maneuvers and position to maintain LOS

The pilot needs to remain within a line-of-sight of the UAV; a building or terrain feature cannot come between the two or else the signal will be interrupted. A pilot *not* in an elevated position would need to follow the drone on foot and may be in rather close proximity to the front line/enemy in order to maintain good communications with the UAV. The exact distance will vary based on the geography, equipment, and situation.

Unconventional approaches may be used. For instance, a UAS team may let a drone hover while they climb several stories or to another elevated position that gives them a better vantage point and greater signal propagation. A pilot may stand in front of a building, using it for cover, as he commands the drone to pop-up over or peek around the sides of the building to obtain imagery.

In an urban environment, buildings can provide a physical, sensory (sight and sound), and electronic barrier between a UAV and the enemy. A drone might dash from building to building in short hops that deny enemy CUAS the opportunity to fix it and shoot it down. A savvy operator may make hit-and-run attacks with the drone approaching from a safe position and immediately returning behind it. Silent, invisible approaches at medium altitude can be replaced by darting out at from unexpected places and times in an aerial ambush.

Natural areas will often lack the background noise that may drown out the distinct hum of a drone, making it easier to hear a lurking UAV but cover and visual concealment are still effective. While a drone may be seen moving behind trees, the leaves and limbs will deflect some bullets and attenuate radio signals, complicating both electronic detection and countermeasures. Mountainous terrain also provides more opportunities to obtain a high place to operate the UAV from, granting it greater range and better use of hiding behind terrain in defilade.

Terrain masking

UAVs can utilize natural and artificial cover and concealment for protection when flying. Cover is usually a structure or a vertical ground feature that is sufficient to block radio waves, laser beams, and kinetic projectiles. Concealment is anything that will keep a drone visually hidden from an observer, such as vegetation. Utilizing cover/concealment to hide a UAV from visual or electronic detection is known as *masking*. Masking enhances survivability and maximizes surprise.

This is both to limit visual detection but also to protect the aircraft from kinetic fire and electromagnetic detection/attacks. Buildings and terrain block radio signals that might be picked up by detectors or at least obscures it the signals. If they are not terrain masked, UAVs' composite bodies are hard to spot on radar in addition to their size and flight characteristics.

A smart pilot will use terrain to his own advantage but flight at low altitudes will present challenges from obstructions like trees, wires, utility poles, antennas, buildings, and narrow defiles. The pilot must maintain radio contact with his UAV (RLOS) and to a lesser degree he or the observer visual contact.

Use of terrain to conceal or mask the flight of a UAV from the enemy must be balanced with maintaining a RLOS to the control station at all times. A pilot in an elevated position operating the drone through terrain below him or use of an elevated repeater helps obviate the signal obscuration problem. Obviously, an approach above terrain or structures relieves the need to consider elevated control locations but negates the advantages offered by extreme low-altitude flight.

Contour flying maximizes the use of terrain masking by flying very low behind buildings or landscape features, going around or between features whenever possible instead of over. Be aware that during contour flying the terrain may canalize the flightpath to a point where enemy observation or defenses are concentrated. Escape routes or the room to take evasive actions may be restricted as well.

Popup maneuvers involve approaching the target area at low altitude, possibly using contour flying, and climbing to an exposed altitude only immediately before engaging a target or conducting ISR. A popup maximizes the use of terrain masking for as long as possible until the UAV must be exposed to complete the mission. Generally, after a popup the drone remains exposed until its mission is complete, although it can hide again.

Peeking is when a UAV briefly exposes itself from behind cover or concealment to make an observation, designate a target, or fire a weapon. It then moves laterally or vertically behind protection to avoid enemy observation or CUAS, loitering until its next move. Contour flying can be used on the approach and egress. Peeking differs from a popup as peeking is a more persistent behavior that seeks to maximize the use of cover/concealment to extend the duration of its activity and thus its survivability.

Terrain/flying tips

- Loiter on reverse slopes or behind buildings whenever possible.
- Use visual ground clutter such as vegetation or cityscapes to obscure direct observation.
- Avoid routes that restrict flightpath where the only escape is up.
- If CUAS cannot be avoided entirely, attempt to fly at the extreme margins of its envelope.

Pop-ups and peeking: the periscope method

Treat drone observations like a submarine raising its periscope. Periscopes pop up for just a brief span of time and are pulled back down as soon as possible. This is because the scope itself and its signature on the waves, the "feather," can be spotted by ships or aircraft. See what you need to see and land; constant observation isn't always going to be necessary.

When a shootdown is likely, a drone can be rapidly launched on a zoom climb out of range, the camera quickly spun in a pattern to get video of the area, then rapidly descended to safety. Video can be reviewed for intelligence once the drone is down. This minimizes the time the drone is in danger or that it is observable to the enemy. Submarine captains use a similar technique when making periscope observations.

This periscope technique can be used to minimize the chances that an enemy might become aware of surveillance or reduce his ability to react. An enemy may know that a drone is flying behind a nearby terrain feature peeking out at him but is unable to do anything about it.

Use visual obstructions to hide the drone when making low-level observations. Pop up and "peep" over structures, trees, etc. Don't just hover out in the open where an adversary can see your drone and shoot it down. In this manner, drones can maneuver like a soldier taking advantage of cover.

Sneak-and-peak and hit-and-run tactics will enhance the survivability of drones while adding a new dimension to UAV warfare. No longer will the threat just be "up" but it will be looking over shoulders and peeping from behind cover as an enemy approaches. As long as the control signals and video can be transmitted, drones will move with the terrain and cityscape.

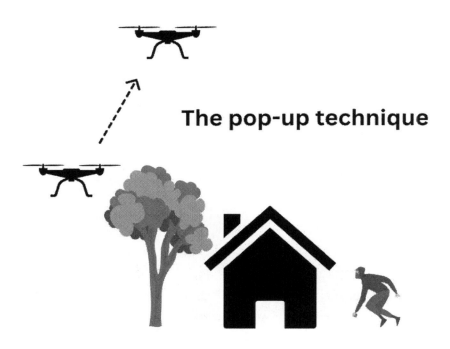

The pop-up technique

Open terrain

In open terrain, there will be little opportunity to hide a UAV behind cover or concealment and it can be seen flying a long way off. Altitude should be used instead. Fly the drone as far and high as feasible from the target so the drone appears as small as possible, hopefully going unnoticed. UAVs, above a certain altitude (dependent on the size of the drone), are practically invisible to the human eye and silent. Use the camera to zoom in.

If open ground must be crossed, but there is a backdrop of trees or structures, handrail the far perimeter of the open area so the drone is lost against the visual clutter and can duck behind easily it if necessary. Backdrops are considered from the point of view of the target or the observer whose notice the pilot wishes to evade. The backdrop could be near or far but works best if there is low contrast between the airframe and the color of the background.

If the observer is in an elevated position, consider flying the drone very low so it does not silhouette against the sky but must be distinguished from objects on the ground. Even remaining very low to the ground, but at a distance, so the low angle places the UAV below the top of distant high terrain may help. Ideally, the oblique background should vary in color and visual texture, such as a forest or broken ground, rather than a uniform ground surface.

Try and fly behind the line-of-sight of an adversary or to the rear of where their attention is likely focused if no other approach vector is possible. Attempt to do this in combination with another diversion.

Stealth

Drones may not be heard or seen by people on the ground, often going totally unnoticed at high flight altitudes.

Their stealth is an inherent capability due to their size. They may be operated at altitudes where the rotor noise is not heard, or it easily blends in with the ambient noise. The airframes themselves are also relatively small and can be visually overlooked if flying at a high enough altitude or the model is quite small. Visual detection range is typically 100 yards/meters, and the sound can be detected at 40 yards/meters.

Paint drones in a neutral gray color as many military aircraft are painted. This color blends in with many different sky conditions and will help lower observability against urban landscapes. Light sky blue is another color consideration. Disable or tape over any anti-collision or navigation lights for day or night flying.

Fly well above and away from pets or livestock to avoid spooking animals whose noises or behaviors may alert the target. Fly in high ambient noise environments to mask the rotor noise. Flying downwind of the objective will help carry sound away.

Approach over tree or vegetation cover so there is not a clear view of the sky. If possible, fly when the sky is overcast, or clouds are broken to reduce the contrast between a clear blue sky and the UAV airframe. Fly in/out of the sun or hover in an observer's line-of-sight and the sun to use the glare to your advantage.

The direct route is not always the best. Fly deceptive courses and approach from unexpected directions, such as entering an adversary's rear area from the flank and flying forward. Use terrain masking, cover, and concealment to limit potential observation or fly at or above 400 feet to "hide in the sky" as a very small object that is unlikely to be seen. Fly over unoccupied public spaces where the chances of being seen are lower. Roads are not only good to navigate by, but drivers' attention will be on the road, not looking up for drones.

Avoid flying at window level when possible in hostile or unknown territory. If ELA flight is unavoidable, maintain a respectable stand-off distance from structures. Do not hover or linger outside windows whenever possible.

Noise

UAVs make a distinctive noise that most people in the 2020s immediately associate with a drone. *Drone* itself is derived from the word for a male bee who got the name based on the buzzing sound that bees make. Sound signature needs to be taken into serious consideration as drones will be often heard before they are seen. A downwind approach will help reduce the noise signature at the cost of endurance (depending on the windspeed) while an upwind approach will increase the chances of early detection by ear.

A quadcopter can be easily heard within 100 feet (30m) and depending on the size of the drone and the background noise, up to 330 feet (100m) in a moderately loud environment. The most important variable besides distance is background noise. A quiet forest environment will allow a drone to be heard a long way off, while in a noisy city beyond 100 feet it may not be heard at all.

Be aware that the buzz of a multicopter is a very distinctive sound. Pilots should be familiar with the sound signature of their aircraft at various power levels, altitudes, power settings, and across different ambient environmental noises. Fly well above and away from pets or livestock to avoid spooking animals whose noises or behaviors may alert the target.

Motor noise is caused by the propellers or rotors interaction with the air. The actual electric motor itself should be silent. Some of the factors that affect prop/rotor noise are:

Size: Larger drones require larger motors and rotor/propeller blades and will produce more noise. Combustion and jet engines (not found on most sUAS) will produce the most noise.

Rotational speed: High RPM is characteristic of a smaller drone as smaller blades need to turn faster to generate the required thrust like how a hummingbird's wings are often practically invisible. The small size and high speed results in the distinctive high-pitched whirring sound. Larger blades produce more thrust and accordingly can spin more slowly and thus quietly.

Motor shaft/arm interference: The shaft or arms for the motors creates a "floor" where high pressure air can form due to the downdraft of the blades. This produces low-frequency pressure and its associated sound waves.

Prop/rotor characteristics: Factors variable to the individual prop/rotor design affect sound as well. Blade size is proportional to the air displaced. Angle and pitch of the blade, as well as the chord and other design factors, all affect the sound it makes. Some props/rotors may be custom designed to minimize their sonic signature.

The noise level will vary depending on the airframe and the background environmental noise but in very quiet areas large copters may be heard at hundreds of yard/meters away. Keep the UAV at least 100 feet to over 400 AGL to minimize the sound heard on the ground. Hard surfaces (buildings, streets, concrete, water) will reflect sound and soft surfaces like vegetation or will reduce it.

Flying downwind of the objective will help carry sound away. Fly in high ambient noise environments to mask the rotor noise. To reduce the noise signature on the ground, use other environmental noise to mask the motors' buzz, fly downwind of the target, keep the drone moving, and use camera zoom to avoid flying closer than necessary.

Reconnaissance flights

Consider that the point of origin and ingress/egress routes may reveal your location and the flightpath/behavior may disclose intentions. Increasing the flight distance, adding extraneous flightpath segments, launching/recovering from alternate locations, or overflying innocuous points may mask these things. For focused recon, be aware that the drone may betray your interest of that person, place, or group.

Flights should be planned intentionally to gather the information (to answer the "question") desired, such as checking a mall for looters rather than flying around randomly. Gratuitous flying should be avoided; UAS recon should be purposeful, add value, and beneficially augment human recon by removing someone from danger, providing new information, or acting as a force multiplier. For a zone recon, use the drone to fill in the blanks that other forms of recon or intelligence cannot.

To maintain surprise as a unit advances, do not overextend from the phase or front lines but remain slightly behind, looking "over the shoulder" of friendly forces. Drones scouting ahead of advancing troops should not give away the approach. Reconnaissance should be done far enough in advance of an attack that the enemy does not anticipate an imminent assault. Conversely, the mission should not be flown so early that the tactical picture has changed by the time the assault does begin.

Plan for a recon mission to transition to another type. For instance, a recon of the mall might turn into surveillance, so it would behoove the pilot to go to the mall first to maximize endurance should the drone need to loiter, before potentially proceeding on to objectives where less time will be spent.

If investigating a hasty SPOT report, such as gunshots, obtain as much information about the location and potential suspects so the flight can proceed directly to the likely incident scene or the escape routes, rather than waste time and battery life hunting for activity. Do not unnecessarily loiter about an objective. Get the information/imagery needed and move on. Record so you can review footage later.

Deceptions, diversions, and distractions

Dense urban environments provide numerous protected launch points and concealed avenues of approach. Sound will often be the only advance warning of a drone attack as the hum of aircraft will usually be noticed before it becomes visible. Battle or ordinary environmental noise may alternatively mask, incidentally or deliberately, rotor noise.

A canny operator will wait to launch the aircraft from a near-by ready launch point (RLP) to minimize flight time; the RLP may also be a concealed (to sound and sight) protected area where the drone could hover for a short time prior to the ambush. Then, perhaps in concert with a forward observer or more likely a second drone being used for surveillance, the pilot can initiate an ambush.

Drones can be used to spook or mislead the enemy about your intentions. Reconnaissance and surveillance may be used to indicate a false interest in an adversary's activities or position to distract him from the real intent. Repeat ISR missions may be used to annoy and harass him. Forces that have been discovered and reconnoitered may be forced to change positions or tactics to mitigate the damage from intelligence that UAS may have gathered.

Fake landings by following all landing procedures until very low to the ground and out of sight of potential observers, then fly away at low-level behind concealment before climbing again some distance away.

Fly past reconnaissance objectives in a straight line while observing them with the gimbal camera. Orbit another location or fake target of interest somewhere else before returning the same way to continue observations. Feign attacks by maneuvering over troops in the same manner as an attacking drone. Fly low enough to attract attention. The goal should be to spook the adversary into running for cover.

Induce alert fatigue so the enemy doesn't associate drones with an imminent attack; repeatedly conduct reconnaissance only to lull them into complacency. When the attack commences, hopefully they assume the drone is just doing its usual flyby. If possible, have multiple drones of different models, configurations, or paint schemes to deceive the enemy about how many you might have or into thinking two or more groups have UAVs.

Try and fly behind the line-of-sight of an adversary or to the rear of where their attention is likely focused. A drone can stealthily approach from behind terrain, buildings, trees, etc. and pause behind concealment if an observer turns to investigate. Drones should be considered stalking predators like a lion creeping through the grass to ambush a big game hunter focusing on an elephant.

Drones can be used not only as a diversion, but as an attention-getting distraction. A low flying drone could be used to focus the attention of an enemy during a critical moment when his eyes and concentration needs to be elsewhere.

One instance of this (whether intentional or unintentional) is an October 18, 2022, incident[57,58] where Sacramento County Sheriff's deputies killed a domestic violence suspect who was armed with a shotgun. The man, with a hostage, went outside where SWAT was waiting for him. A team waited around the corner and an armored vehicle sat in front of the home.

A drone hovered about fifteen feet above the ground in front of the door. The suspect is seen in the various videos stepping outside and looking up at the drone, keeping his attention focused on it. He is then shot in the head by a SWAT deputy, the armed suspect likely never processing the deputy's presence in the open. The hostage was not

---

[57] https://www.kcra.com/article/suspect-dead-after-shooting-involving-sacramento-county-sheriffs-office/41694400
[58] https://www.youtube.com/watch?v=qBZDCpTRBAo

harmed.

Defensive flying and evasive maneuvers

Extensive evasive maneuvers or long deceptive flightpaths may drain the battery and reduce the overall mission time or time on-station. Deceptive or evasive return paths should be considered in calculating endurance. A drone that went into its battery reserve may be forced to fly directly home to avoiding a crash landing, which may give away your location.

Upon hearing gunshots, observing someone firing, or seeing tracers, immediately maneuver the drone. Two-axis (vertical and horizonal) movement is preferred. Straight up will be expected by a cunning adversary, but movement in any direction will interfere with the shooter's point of aim.

Don't stop to think which the best way is to fly to safety, etc. Move immediately, disrupt the shooter's aim, and then fly smartly. Maneuver now, navigate later. You should already have thought about and planned safe egress routes and an evasion drill *before* shooting starts.

- Fly above rooftop and treetop height and remain out of effective rifle range (horizontal: 300-800 yards/meters and 900-2,400 feet AGL).
- Remain above 200-400 feet AGL to avoid small-arms fire and increase altitude to well-above 400 feet to 1,600 feet AGL if fired on with rifles.
- In any event where small-arms fire or directional CUAS is used, immediately engage in evasive maneuvers.
  - Maneuver erratically.
  - Increase altitude.
  - Increase distance from the threat.
  - Fly low behind cover and concealment if it is difficult to get out of range.

Note that low-level flights using terrain masking can increase the chance of a shootdown or collision with an obstruction. To avoid a shootdown, fly fast, frequently changing directions unpredictably, and never approaching from the same direction twice in a row. Do not deliberately fly a drone into the line of friendly fire; they may shoot your UAV down or cease fire to avoid hitting it, which may negatively impact their operations.

When flown high, fly as high as possible to maintain a low visual and noise signature. Only approach as low or as close as necessary to make clear visual observations. Use camera zoom to your advantage. When flying below rooftops, consider that enemy observers may be in windows above ground level.

When possible, given the mission parameters, maintain visual contact with the drone. This is important as you may need to take evasive action if a "killer" drone is launched to intercept yours. The onboard cameras may not give any warning of an airborne attack.

Other considerations

UAVs seen immediately prior to an attack, either a ground assault or indirect fire, give away the element of surprise. A pattern emerged of drones appearing above an area shortly before an attack which allowed Ukrainian forces to anticipate that enemies would attack shortly. The phrase "when the balloon goes up" relates to observation balloons being launched before Civil War battles, so the phenomenon is not new. Consider if deploying a drone in advance of an attack will give away your intentions.

Having a drone on station long before an attack begins or intermittently at unpredictable times and for varying durations may be one way to lure an enemy into complacency.

The presence of a drone indicates many things to an outside party, not all of which are good. UAS can be a deterrent because a group that has aerial observation capabilities is a group that is likely well-prepared and equipped. It may also turn a group into a target because the group may be considered well-off enough to have a drone, which means they may have stockpiled food, ammunition, etc. that's worth stealing along with the support equipment (electricity, computers, radios). Truthfully, most miscreants aren't smart enough to consider either fully.

A downed and captured drone can lead to intelligence exploitation of the wreckage. A registered drone used in conflict applications as the registration could become evidence for later prosecution or retaliation. Many COTS models carry flight data records which can include information about the flightpath, takeoff/recovery zones, and in some cases, video may be stored onboard.

Intelligence exploitation mitigation techniques include:

- Remove any registration or identification marks, including serial numbers ("sanitizing").
- Disable Remote ID (RID) broadcasts before flight and remove any modules.
- Using only remote video storage (transmitted back to the controller) instead of onboard storage media.

■ ■ ■

About the Author

Don Shift is a veteran of the Ventura County Sheriff's Office and an avid fan of post-apocalyptic literature and film. He is a student of disasters, history, current events, and holds several FEMA emergency management certifications. You can email him at donshift@protonmail.com or visit www.donshift.com.

Fiction works include the Ventura Sheriff EMP series, *Hard Favored Rage* and *Blood Dimmed Tide*, where deputies must survive after a devastating electromagnetic pulse destroys the electric grid. *Late For Doomsday* and *Limited Exchange (1 & 2)* are novels of surviving and evacuating after a nuclear attack.

All works explore the realities of emergency planning and personal survival in the face of low probability, high impact events that highlight the shortcomings of a technology and infrastructure dependent nation. Non-fiction titles include *Nuclear Survival in the Suburbs* and the *Suburban Defense*, *Suburban Warfare*, and *Rural Home Defense* guides.

This page has been intentionally left blank.

Made in the USA
Las Vegas, NV
22 November 2024

12387241R00225